Li Tianji's

The Skill of Xingyiquan

Available from tgl books
Jiang Rongqiao's Baguazhang
Li Tianji's The Skill of Xingyiquan
Yan Dehua's Bagua Applications
Di Guoyong on Xingyiquan: Volume I, Foundations
Di Guoyong on Xingyiquan: Volume II, Forms and Ideas
Di Guoyong on Xingyiquan: Volume III, Weapons
A Shadow on Fallen Blossoms
Falk's Dictionary of Chinese Martial Arts
Beijing Bittersweet
Shadowboxing in Shanghai

 www.thewushucentre.ca

Li Tianji's
The Skill of Xingyiquan
20th Anniversary Edition

形意拳术

李天骥，李德印 编者

A translation from the Chinese, with commentary,
by Andrea Mary Falk

Translation copyright © 2000 Andrea Mary Falk

20th Anniversary Edition ISBN 978-1-989468-20-3

20th Anniversary Edition copyright ©2021 Andrea Mary Falk

(First edition ISBN 978-0-9687517-1-8)

All rights reserved.

This book or any portion thereof may not be reproduced or used in any manner whatsoever without the express written permission of the publisher except for the use of brief quotations in a book review or scholarly work.

Published by tgl books, Québec, Canada.

Library and Archives Canada Cataloguing in Publication of first edition

LI, T'IEN-CHI, 1914-1996. LI TIANJI'S THE SKILL OF XINGYIQUAN. TEXT IN ENGLISH, WITH APPENDICES IN ENGLISH AND CHINESE. TRANSLATION OF: XINGYIQUANSHU. 1. HAND-TO-HAND FIGHTING, ORIENTAL. I. FALK, ANDREA, 1954- II. TITLE. III. TITLE: SKILL OF XINGYIQUAN.

GV1112.L52213 2000   796.815'5   C00-910846.7

Translated by Andrea Falk, 1995, Morin-Heights, Canada

tgl books is based in Canada. Its publications are available through www.thewushucentre.ca.

The techniques described in this book are performed by experienced martial artists. The author, translator, and publishers are not responsible for any injury that may occur while trying out these techniques. Please do not apply these techniques on anyone without their consent and cooperation.

共同努力，认真研究，将武术推向世界。

赠

霍安娣留念：

中国武术协会
李天骥
1988年10月14日
于杭州国际武术节

**Work together, study hard,
and bring wushu to the world.**

Given to Andrea Falk by master Li Tianji, October 1988,
at the Hangzhou International Wushu Festival

Table of Contents

Author's Preface ix

About the Author x

Translator's Preface xi

Editor's Preface to the 20th Anniversary Edition xii

Chapter One: Background Theory

    1.1   The Development of Xingyiquan 1

    1.2   The Characteristics of Xingyiquan 5

    1.3   The Value of Training Xingyiquan 7

    1.4   Training Requirements of Xingyiquan 10

Chapter Two: Basic Techniques

    2.1   Ready Stance, *santishi* 41

    2.2   The Five Elemental Phases

            Split, Chop 44

            Drive, Crush 48

            Drill 53

            Cannon, Pound 56

            Wring, Crosscut 60

    2.3   The Twelve Animals

            Dragon 63

            Tiger 68

            Monkey 73

            Horse 81

            Alligator 83

            Chicken 87

            Sparrow Hawk 95

            Swallow 98

            Snake 102

            Wedge-Tailed Hawk 106

            Eagle and Bear 108

Chapter Three: Solo Forms

    3.1   Five Elemental Phases Connect 113

| | 3.2 | Mixture Of Moves, *Zashichui* | ....121 |
| | 3.3 | Comprehensive Xingyi Form | ....141 |

Chapter Four: Partner Forms

	4.1	Five Elemental Phases Contend	189
	4.2	Three Hands Clash Stationary	194
		Moving	196
	4.3	Protect the Body, *Anshenpao*	199

Chapter Five: Stance Training for Health 215

	5.1	Dragon	218
	5.2	Tiger	221
	5.3	Ape	223
	5.4	Bear	224
	5.5	Regulating the Health	226

Appendix: Classic Texts 229

1. Poem of the Ultimate Principle 230
2. Poem of the Two Primordial Forms 230
3. Explanation of the Two Primordial Forms 231
4. Poem of the Six Combinations 232
5. The Meaning Taken from the Twelve Animals............233
6. Explanation of the Three Segments 234
7. Explanation of the 'Seven Flows' 236
8. Explanation of the Five Elemental Phases 237
9. Explanation of the Four Tips 241
10. Explanation of the Eight Requirements 243
11. Poem of the Eight Words 245
12. Poem of 'Number Nine ' 248
13. Poem of Fighting Methods 250
14. Explanation of 'Seven Quicks' 252
15. Poem of the Seven Stars 252
16. Guo Yunshen speaks on Xingyiquan 253

Pronunciation of Chinese pinyin transliteration 257

About the Translator

Author's Preface

The People's Sport Publishing House asked my father, Li Yulin 李玉琳, (1885-1965) back in 1958 to write a book called "Xingyiquan." A draft of the completed portion was included in the 1961 martial arts textbook of the National Sports Colleges and Schools. It was most unfortunate that he was unable to complete his work. Father's alternate name was Runru 润如. His whole life was dedicated to researching and teaching Xingyi, Taiji, Bagua, and other martial arts. He apprenticed with the famous masters Hao Enguang 郝恩光 and Sun Lutang 孙禄堂, and received coaching from masters Li Cunyi 李存义 and Zhang Zhaodong 张兆东. I started training at home as a child, and started to learn Shaolin boxing and Xingyi when I was eight. This book is the completion of the book started by my father. The original draft was lost during the ten years of turmoil. Only today have I finally completed the work of organizing and writing.

Xingyiquan is one of the main traditional martial arts in China. It has a longer history than Taiji and Bagua. This book is in accordance with the methods of the Xingyi most widely practised in the country, maintaining the traditional style as much as possible. In some areas of China, the flavour and methods may differ, but the basic requirements are all the same. The actual contents of the book are mostly the basic techniques and some model traditional forms. Some contents, such as the Comprehensive Xingyi form and the standing for health training, are the culmination of many years of teaching and experience. I have not included weapons training in this book. In terms of theoretical explanations, I tried to stick with the needs of teaching and training. I have included some classic texts though, for the reader's reference.

I received a great deal of help in writing this book from my friends in the martial arts field, Tang Hao 唐豪 and Xu Zhidong 徐哲东, among others, and for this I thank them most gratefully.

Since my abilities are limited there are many shortcomings to the book. For this I beg the indulgence of the reader.

Li Tianji

李天骥

December, 1980

About the Author

Li Tianji 李天驥 (1915-1996) was born in Hebei province. As a young boy, he trained martial arts with his father, Li Yulin 李玉琳 (1885-1965), a well known master. Li Tianji became known for his ability in Taiji, Xingyi, Wudang, and Shaolin boxing. He graduated from the Shandong Martial Arts Centre in 1931 and was kept on as a coach until 1939. He then moved around, mostly in the north-east of China, teaching Taiji until 1949. From 1950 to 1953 he coached in Harbin, Heilongjiang, and directed the Harbin Wushu Association. In 1954 he coached at the National Coaching Association, and from then on took on work in the Wushu Research Department and the Wushu Administrative Department at the National Sports Council. He was selected for the post of wushu vice secretary of the National Wushu Association in 1964. He was given the highest accreditation level as a wushu judge in 1979. When China opened up in 1980, he was able to travel to Japan, Singapore, and other countries to teach.

Li Tianji was on many committees that developed wushu teaching materials, wushu competition rules, compulsory forms, and the simplified Taiji form. He co-authored 'The Simplified Taiji Form,' 'Simplified Taiji Sword,' 'Six Section Tantui,' 'Taiji Boxing Exercise,' and 'Wudang Sword.'

In addition to his Xingyiquan of this book, the Baguazhang in the national Sports College textbooks, up until the 1986 edition, was essentially what he had developed from his father's Sun style Baguazhang, with a few adjustments. So, although Li Tianji did not teach me, I learned his Baguazhang at the Beijing Physical Culture Institute. We met quite often while I was a student there, from 1980 though 1983, and during the 1980s when I went back for international competitions. He was a gentleman and a scholar, and I am proud to have known him.

With Li Tianji, Nanchang, 1983.

Andrea Falk

霍安娣

February, 2021

Translator's Preface

I chose this book to translate for three reasons – the quality of the contents, the quality of the man who wrote it, and familiarity with the style. I have great respect for the main author, Li Tianji, as one of a great generation of traditional martial artists who lived into the modern era. I met with him many times throughout the eighties at wushu meets and he was always supportive of me and my attempts to learn the tradition. I am sorry I was not able to show him my translation. As for the book itself, as master Li explained in his preface, it describes the way Xingyi is done in much of China. It is almost exactly the way I learned it as a full time martial arts student at the Beijing Physical Culture Institute from 1980 to 1983, so I felt both qualified to translate it and glad to help spread it in the West.

Relevant Chinese terms are noted in characters, and the classic texts in the appendices are given in full. I used simplified Chinese characters because that was how the published book was written. I used the *pinyin* system of romanization because that is what is used in China.

I have made some comments throughout the book, but you don't have to pay any attention if you don't want to – the book stands on its own. My comments either explain things that might have been taken for granted in writing to a Chinese audience, or add my own experience from training in China and teaching in the West.

I was taught Xingyi by both Master Xia Bohua 夏柏华, my primary coach, and Master Men Huifeng 门惠丰, for which I will always be grateful. I owe thanks to my parents for their endless and repetitive proof reading. And many thanks to Sensei Mike Chin who always answered "C" when asked "which is better, A or B?" as I worked through the classic texts. Without his imagination and encouragement I would have translated them straight, which wouldn't have been as much fun (we also discovered a lot of similarities between Xingyi and Aikido, but that's another story…).

Any mistakes in the book are mine alone. I hope that you like this book as much as I, and apologize for the fact that a translation is never as good as the original.

Andrea Falk

霍安娣

July, 2000

Editor's Preface to the 20th anniversary edition

When I started tgl books in 2000, I did my best with the technology available at the time. Many things have changed over the years, particularly in the manner of entering the Chinese characters and the pinyin with tones. That was very difficult at the time, and made for the spread out nature of this book – a separate line for each was necessary. My computer programs and my ability at graphic reworking has improved. So I thought a fun project might be to redo the Li Tianji book to tighten it up a bit, making it thinner and less expensive to mail. I had to dig out some old printer's PDF files, as the original files were long gone, so it was a bit more of a project than first envisioned. In the end, the size savings was not much, but just finally having the technology to improve the overall look, increase the size of the images, and make the cover in colour made the new edition worthwhile.

Going through the book, I found that the translation was remarkably good, considering that I have had twenty years to develop my skills since then. There are some words that I have come to deal with differently now, but more by preference – not because they were wrong. Those I have let stand. In some places I have added another possible translation to a word, and in some places have made some minor adjustments. Overall, though, I have left the book as it originally came out.

At this 20th anniversary of the establishment of tgl books, I have finally completed the reworking of all the books to be available for print to order. To celebrate, I have made hard cover copies of all the translations – the Jiang Rongqiao, Yan Dehua, and Di Guoyong books, as well as this one.

In my earlier translation I did not properly credit Li Deyin with his work on the original book. His name was in the original as co-author, but I simplified things by just having Li Tianji's name. In spite of this, Li Deyin always supported my book and made it available to his students, and for this, I thank him.

Andrea Falk

霍安娣

February, 2021

CHAPTER ONE

BACKGROUND THEORY

1.1　THE DEVELOPMENT OF XINGYIQUAN

Xing-yi quan 形意拳 (form and intent boxing) is an ancient style which holds an important place in the history of Chinese martial arts. It has been known variously as *xin-yi quan* 心意拳 (heart and mind boxing), *xing-yi quan* 行意拳 (theory and practice boxing), *xin-yi liu-he quan* 心意六合拳 (heart and mind six harmonies boxing), and *liu-he quan* 六合拳 (six harmonies boxing), and is still called *xin-yi quan* 心意拳 (heart and mind boxing) in some areas of China. Some say the name Xingyiquan is used because of the high degree of unity demanded between internal and external – the intent manifesting the internal, and the body manifesting the external form. Others say it is because Xingyiquan is an animal imitative style that creates its shapes in the imagination.

According to historical records, Xingyi has a history of over three hundred years. It was created in Puzhou 蒲洲, Shanxi province 山西, during the period of the late Ming and early Qing dynasties[1]. Its creation is generally credited to Ji Longfeng 姬隆丰 although various records also give his name as Ji Longfeng 姬隆风, Ji Jike 姬际可, Ji Longfeng[2] 姬龙风, or two separate people, Ji Long 姬龙 and Ji Feng 姬风. One record[3] written in Henan in 1735, states,

---

[1] Translator's note: Ming 明 dynasty 1368-1644, Qing 清 dynasty 1644-1911 – so the period between dynasties is the mid 17th century.

[2] Translator's note: The characters for Long of these two Ji Longfeng's are different.

[3] *Quanlun zhiyixu* 拳论质疑序 (an inquiry into boxing)

"There are a lot of martial styles whose origins are unknown, but we do know that *liuhe* boxing comes from two men in Shanxi called Ji Long and Ji Feng who lived at the end of the Ming dynasty. They so excelled in spear techniques that many considered them spirits, and there was much speculation about who their teachers might have been. They thought that in their time of peace, when all weapons had been melted down or put away, they would have no idea how to fight if they met with an unexpected attack. This is why they developed spear techniques into hand techniques. This fighting theory came from one source but took on a myriad of different forms, and the style was called *liuhe*." This record also states; "The heart is united with intent, intent is united with energy, and energy is united with force, the shoulder is united with the hip, the elbow with the knee, and the hand with the foot. These are the six harmonies." A later record,[4] written at the end of the Qing dynasty, states; "This style came from two people, Ji Long and Ji Feng, from Puzhou in Shanxi province. They came from local families and trained in martial arts for many years, but there is no record of any prior generations."

Some materials on Xingyi claim that it was created in the Song[5] dynasty by Yue Fei 岳飞, while others say it was brought from India late in the fifth century by Da Mo 达摩.[6] A record[7] from 1750 states that Yue Fei excelled at spear techniques, used these in his fist technique, and taught a style called *yi quan* 意拳 (idea boxing) which was outstanding. The record continues "One surnamed Ji 姬, with the name Jike 际可, also called Longfeng 隆风, born at the end of the Ming or beginning of the Qing dynasty, from the Feng clan in Pudong, trained with famous masters in the southern mountains. He obtained Wu Mawang's boxing treatise and later learned from Cao Jiwu 曹继武." There are no historical records, however, of Yue Fei, Da Mo, or Cao Jiwu in relation to Xingyi, and many scholars of wushu history feel there is inadequate proof that they developed Xingyi boxing.

Also, according to a Shaolin monk, the Shaolin temple at Lingshan mountain has had a style called *xinyi quan* 心意拳 (heart and mind boxing) or *xinyi ba* 心意把 (heart and mind grappling) since very early on, and it is one of

---

[4] *Xinyiquan yuanweikao* 心意拳原委靠 (the whole story of *xinyi* boxing)

[5] Translator's note: Song 宋 dynasty 960 – 1279.

[6] Translator's note: Yue Fei was a famous general who lived 1103 to 1142. Da Mo was a monk who lived c.? to 535 and came to the Shaolin temple from India.

[7] *Liuhequanxu* 六合拳序 (a record of six harmony boxing)

the best styles of the temple. In 1963 I went to the temple to see the style *xinyi ba* practised by the old monk Wu Shanlin 吴山林. The character of his movement was very similar to the Xingyiquan practised now, which gives food for thought for Xingyi historians. It remains to be investigated to what extent the *xinyi ba* of the Shaolin temple is related to the Xingyiquan taught by Ji Longfeng.

Ancient records clearly state that, from the beginning, Xingyi placed equal emphasis on health and fighting, and that the style was quite straightforward. The basic techniques were six forward stances and six back stances. The forward stances were powerful and the back stances were soft. The moves emphasized the six harmonies, five elements, and alternation between force and softness. The basic requirements were the body of a dragon, the shoulders of a bear, the legs of a chicken, the hands of an eagle, the hugging arms of a tiger, and the sound of thunder.

By 1736, Xingyi was widespread in Henan, Shanxi, and Hebei provinces. Ma Xueli 马学礼 in Luoyang (Henan province), Dai Longbang 戴涟邦 in Qi county (Shanxi province), and his student Li Luoneng 李洛能 in Shenzhou (Hebei province) continued the tradition of Xingyi and taught many students. Xingyi developed a great deal over the next hundred years, with many skilled practitioners all around China. Xingyi proved to be a solid fighting style, and evolved many more techniques and a variety of branches. For example, in Shanxi the style is tight and crisp with clean and agile power; in Henan the style is fierce, tough, and solid; in Hebei the style is expansive, stable and solid.

Each locality has its own variations. There is considerable interaction between Shanxi and Hebei provinces, so their contents are quite similar. The basics in both provinces are the 'three bodies stance' [sāntǐshì 三体式], the techniques of the five elemental phases[8] – split, drive, drill, cannon, and wring [pī, zuān, bēng, pào, héng 劈、崩、钻、炮、横] and twelve animals – dragon, tiger, monkey, horse, alligator, chicken, sparrow hawk, swallow, snake, wedge-tailed hawk, eagle, and bear [lóng, hǔ, hóu, mǎ, tuó, jī, yào, yàn, shé, tài, yīng, xióng 龙、虎、猴、马、鼍、鸡、鹞、燕、蛇、鲐、鹰、熊]. Some areas in Shanxi use the six-harmony stance or *dantian* stance instead of *santishi* for the standing training, and have ten animals instead of twelve. The ten solo forms

---

[8] Translator's note: Metal [jīn 金], wood [mù 木], water [shuǐ 水], fire [huǒ 火], and earth [tǔ 土].

are: the Five Elemental Phases Connect [wǔxíng liánhuán 五行连环], Mixture Of Moves [záshì chuí 杂式捶], Four Grapples [sìbǎ quán 四把拳], Eight Postures [bāshí quán 八式拳], Twelve Punches [shíèr hóngchuí 十二洪捶], In And Out Of The Cave [chūrùdòng 出入洞], Five Phases Mutual Creation [wǔxíng xiāng shēng 五行相生], Dragon And Tiger Fight [lónghǔ dòu 龙虎斗], Eight Skills [bāzìgōng 八字功], and Upper Middle And Lower Eight Hands [shàng, zhōng, xià bāshǒu 上、中、下八手]. Sparring forms include: Five Elemental Phases Contend [wǔxíng xiāng kè 五行相克], Three Hands Clash [sānshǒu pào 三手炮], Five Flowers Clash [wǔhuā pào 五花炮], Protect The Body [ānshēn pào 安身炮], and nine links [jiǔtàohuán 九套环]. The twelve weapons forms include: Continuous Sabre [liánhuán dāo 连环刀], Three Harmonies Sabre [sānhé dāo 三合刀], Continuous Sword [liánhuán jiàn 连环剑], Continuous Spear [liánhuán qiāng 连环枪], Continuous Staff [liánhuán gùn 连环棍], Three Talents Sabre [sāncái dāo 三才刀], Three Talents Sword [sāncái jiàn 三才剑], Moving Step Sword [xíngbù jiàn 行步剑], Six Harmonies Sabre [liùhé dāo 六合刀], Six Harmonies Spear [liùhé qiāng 六合枪], Six Harmonies Long Spear [liùhé dà qiāng 六合大枪], and Wind Wings Trident [fēngchù dǎng 风翅谠].

Henan province has ten animal forms for its basics – dragon, tiger, chicken, eagle, snake, horse, cat, monkey, sparrow hawk, and swallow. Solo and sparring forms include the four-fists eight-techniques of head-fist, leading, eagle grabbing, and sticking hands, Dragon And Tiger Fight, Upper Middle And Lower Four Grapples, Ten Shapes Combine As One, Xinyi Sparring Form, and others.

In recent years many Xingyi masters have contributed much in the way of theory and technique. Among those who work to spread Xingyi are Guo Yunshen 郭云深, Li Cunyi 李存义 and Zhang Zhaodong 张兆东 of Hebei province – Che Yiji 车毅斋 and Song Shirong 宋世荣 of Shanxi province – and Mai Zhuangtu 买壮图 and Bao Xianyan 宝显延 of Henan province.

In 1911, Xingyi master Li Cunyi 李存义 created the Chinese wushu association in the city of Tianjin, where he trained many teachers and helped to unite the martial world. In 1914 a teacher from his association, Hao Enguang 郝恩光, was the first to introduce Xingyi boxing abroad, into Japan. In 1918 in Beijing Han Baoxia 韩暴侠 beat the previously undefeated Russian fighter, Kang Qin'er 康秦尔, which greatly increased the influence of Xingyi boxing.

Sun Lutang 孙禄堂, Shang Yunxiang 尚云祥, and other famous masters did a great deal of work to spread Xingyi in the area around Beijing and Tianjin. Sun Lutang created a style which combined the theories of Xingyi, Bagua and Taiji boxing, and his books[9] also had much impact.

After liberation in 1949, Chinese martial arts became even more widespread. They became popular among the masses. Xingyi spread further throughout the country, and became one of the styles in the national martial arts meets and competitions. In the national meet of 1980, both young and old athletes from nineteen teams (Beijing and Shanghai municipalities, Shanxi, Yunnan, Sichuan, Jiangsu, Anhui, Ningxia, Shaanxi, Henan, Jiangxi, and other provinces) performed Xingyi. The athletes carried on the traditional characteristics of Xingyi, and demonstrated creative new techniques.

For many years Xingyi standing postures have been used extensively in physical therapy. When used in conjunction with *qigong* and therapeutic exercises, good results are shown.

Xingyi has spread to Southeast Asia, Japan, North America, and other countries, which now have associations and publications. In this way, Xingyi contributes to the cultural exchange between the peoples of China and the world.

1.2 THE CHARACTERISTICS OF XINGYI QUAN

1.2.1 Plain and straightforward　　　　　朴实明快

The moves of Xingyi are plain. They mostly come and go in a straight line, one limb extending as the other flexes, with little extraneous movement. In action, Xingyi is fast and powerful, combining soft and hard with a natural beauty. As the techniques are mastered, power is evident in simple, unadorned moves – no extras can be added, as they would destroy the original flavour. This characteristic of straightforwardness also applies to fighting, which emphasizes a quick and direct attack to get to the opponent first. The goal of a hit is "one inch wins," or "once you start you're already there." These phrases describe the simple, fast, and powerful moves.

---

[9] 拳意达真 (A Study Of The Meaning Of Boxing) and 形意拳学 (The Study Of Xingyi Boxing), among others.

1.2.2 Tight and well-knit 严密紧凑

Xingyi emphasizes strength and speed. It moves quickly with small amplitude. The phrase "the elbows never leave the ribs, the hands never leave the heart" means that as the hands go in or out they stay close by the body, like a twisting rope, so the power is complete, compact, and never collapses. To say that the hands "rise like a steel rasp and drop like a hook pole" means that the power is short and tight, twisting as it strikes, and is tightly coordinated with the bodywork and footwork. To stride forward, the hip joint is rolled to close the groin, the knees are flexed and the foot turned in, the toes grip the ground. Likewise when turning around, the centre of the body (the lumbar area) leads the movement, which is fast and compact. This compactness clearly differs from the extended and large range moves of style of long fist.

1.2.3 Settled and stable (firm) 沉实稳健

The stance is solid and the footwork firm – "stride out like driving a plough, plant the foot like growing a root." The chest is wide and the abdomen solid, the energy is sunk to the *dantian*, and the energy and strength are united. Because of this, the upper body is open and natural, and the lower limbs are steeled and firm; movement is neither floating nor stiff, and gives a feeling of outward ease and inward solidity. Solemn and comfortable, the whole body holds internal strength throughout.

1.2.4 Coordinated and integrated 协调整齐

The whole body is united, the action regular, and the feet and hands are well coordinated. Classical texts say, "a strike must start in the body, and arrive together in the hand and foot," and "if the hand arrives before the foot, the strike will not succeed; if the hand and foot arrive together, the strike will go through the opponent like cutting grass." Xingyi requires the coordination of not just foot and hand – but rather of hand, eye, body, and steps – "if one branch moves, a hundred branches follow." When hitting, the three tips – fingertips, toes, and nose – align, and the three segments are synchronized – the tip segment starts, the middle segment follows and the root segment chases. On this foundation, intent moves energy and energy creates strength, so that the mind, breath, and strength are coordinated. The resulting synchronization of external and internal is such that once you move there is nothing that is not connected. In the past Xingyiquan was also called Liuhequan (six harmonies boxing) – a reference to the three internal and three external linkups. The former three are emotion with intent (also called spirit and mind, or heart and eye), intent with energy, energy with strength. The latter three are shoulders with hips, elbows with knees, hands with feet. These linkups show the high degree of coordination required in Xingyi.

1.3 THE VALUE OF TRAINING XINGYI QUAN

1.3.1 Xingyi is a physical activity that benefits both body and mind.

Xingyi is excellent for conditioning the body, with a decided training effect on muscular strength. Young, strong athletes can develop the muscles of the entire body. The phase of muscular training is to improve conditioning for future needs. To build a good foundation you have to solidify the body.

When the arms stretch out or draw in they keep close to the ribs, which creates antagonistic resistance. When the hands raise or lower they outwardly rotate and drill out, then inwardly rotate to spiral and turn, which twists the forearms, biceps, triceps, and deltoids. The power used to roll, twist, strike and spiral calls for contraction of all the muscles, and trains them effectively by using them against each other.

There are also strict guidelines for the stances and footwork. A straight advance, for example, requires a long step that is fast and lands solidly such that the body neither rises nor falls. This puts a great deal of stress on the legs. The twelve animal forms have many jumps, drops, and quick spins, which give the muscles and ligaments a complete workout. For example, *golden rooster shakes its tail* and *golden rooster reports the dawn* require steady stances, full power in the arms, lifting and pressing-down power in the palms, and quick explosive power through the muscles of the abdomen, upper back, and lower back. Over time, the muscles of the entire body develop great power.

The nervous system is also trained. This type of activity requires the coordination of the eyes, hands, feet and body, so that the whole body moves as a unit. The spirit must be attentive and body and mind united in order for intention to lead movement. In this way the cerebellum is activated to regulate the movement, which serves to coordinate the central nervous system and the functions of the brain. This kind of neural excitation by concentrated activity also serves to give an active rest to the brain, as parts of it are shut down. So the practice of Xingyi not only works up a sweat, it also serves to dissipate fatigue and replenish well being.

Xingyi also has an excellent effect on the internal organs and the cardiovascular system. It requires that the chest is relaxed and the abdomen solid and the breath pulled down to the *dantian*. Purposefully increasing the depth of breathing strengthens the diaphragm, so that long term practice improves respiratory function. Abdominal breathing causes the diaphragm to move down, which increases the movement of the organs in the abdominal cavity. This helps to improve the blood flow in the abdominal cavity, which aids digestion and other metabolic processes.

Many techniques in Xingyi are imitative, modeled on animals – each of which has unique characteristics. For example, to imitate convincingly the agility of a monkey, the fierceness of a tiger, the swiftness of a swallow, or the suppleness of a snake the athlete needs to develop speed, strength, agility and flexibility of the hands, eyes, body, and feet. This kind of activity can develop all qualities of the body and mind.

1.3.2 Xingyi has clear fighting characteristics

During the historical development of Xingyi, a rich variety of theory and experience in fighting strategy and technique has been accumulated. This variety becomes evident during training and develops an understanding of self defense, and trains fighting ability. Such awareness helps maintain students' interest.

In strategy, Xingyi emphasizes the following:

1) Fight to win.

Dare to fight as if you must win, bravely drive straight in – two Xingyi guidelines are "when you meet the opponent there will be one winner, face death without fear," and "if you can move in with one thought, you can stay in with one thought." Fighting builds the confidence to meet the enemy and win. Xingyi lore has many sayings to describe developing the spirit through fighting: "fight as you would walk along a road, see people as you would see grass," "when training, see a person in front of you, when fighting, act as if there is no one," "a brave person does not consider mistakes, one who considers mistakes finds it difficult to walk one inch," and "when anger fills the chest, what is difficult in pressing the enemy?"

2) Take the initiative.

Move in or out quickly, keep the initiative on your side. Xingyi sayings emphasize this: "the eyes are clear and the hands are fast, jump in and attack cleanly," "rise like the wind, land like an arrow, hit before the enemy expects it." On meeting the enemy to fight, make the first strike to take control, hit fast, and hit once. Attack before the enemy has prepared a defense to make him hit without thinking. Neither show your intentions nor telegraph your moves – avoid having your plans found out – "once you move it should be like the wind sweeping the ground." In tactics, keep the initiative in your own hands, hit close and fast – attack then dodge, dodge then attack, there is no need to move away. When hitting take the front door, go for the most advantageous places. "Put your foot in the centre, the place he defends – even an immortal would find it hard to counter that."

3) Keep your opponent off balance.

Xingyi calls the head, shoulder, elbow, hand, hip, knee and foot the "seven fists" – any one of them could strike, and you can use any one. If the opponent is far away, use the hands, if he is close, add the elbow. If he is far away, use the heel, if he is close, add the knee. Use the feet for seven-tenths of the attack, and the hands for three-tenths – unite the five phases and the four tips completely. When fighting, be absolutely empty or solid – like a tiger walks without making a sound, or a dragon moves without a trace – so that the opponent finds it hard to figure you out and defend against you. Classical texts say, "The fists hit three tips and no one sees their form; if they see the form then you can't succeed."

4) Adapt to circumstances.

Know yourself and know the other, see your chance and go for it – Xingyi emphasizes changing according to the opponent. When fighting an opponent, you can't stick to a plan, you must adapt according to what he does. The highest skill is to have no fighting strategy, no plans – only when there is no planning is there an effective plan. Against an opponent you have to see what he is doing, and combine defense with offense, using the techniques of watching, considering, and intercepting. When the opponent moves, use the opportunity which he shows you, quickly intercept, then when your intention arrives your hand arrives, when your hand arrives use your power, use the changes of hard and soft, empty and solid, rise and drop – "always move by using the chances you get." Xingyi fighting techniques show "six-sided" skills. These are: skill or ability [gōng 工, qiǎomiào 巧妙], flow or naturalness [shùn 顺, zìrán 自然], courage or decisiveness [yǒng 勇, guǒduàn 果断], speed [jí 疾, kuàisù 快速], relentlessness or mercilessness [hěn 狠, bù róngqíng 不容情], and true, or not letting the opponent's changes confuse you [zhēn 真].

Xingyi has a wide variety of attack and defense moves. Its solo shadow boxing and weapons forms have many hand techniques, footwork, leg techniques and weapons techniques, and all have attack and defense use. Some can be directly used in real situations, and others need to be figured out, which is another method of training for fighting strategy.

1.3.3 Therapeutic effects of Xingyiquan

Xingyi uses an upright posture and can be practised vigorously or gently, so people of all ages and physical conditions can do it. People with weak constitutions or chronic illnesses can select specific techniques and practise gently, or do just the standing training for its health-building effect. Recently some physiotherapy clinics, such as the clinic at Harbin Medical University, have had good results by combining Xingyi standing with other therapy for patients with conditions such as high blood pressure, bronchitis, and nervous disorders.

If you use Xingyi for therapy, select the simpler positions and moves, and make sure to keep your heart rate and breathing calm during practice. Keep the trunk upright and the body relaxed, and concentrate on what you are doing. This will put the nervous system in order, improve the functions of the internal organs, and improve emotional and physical condition. The combination of moving and standing practice used as therapy has the same effect as China's traditional breathing practices (*qigong*) and Taiji boxing. Some people with trouble moving their limbs have shown marked improvement with this type of practice under proper supervision.

1.4 TRAINING REQUIREMENTS OF XINGYIQUAN

1.4.1 Basic hand shapes, stances, hand techniques, and leg techniques.

This section introduces those techniques commonly seen and those used in this book. The names are consistent with the most common usage.

1) Hand shapes   shǒu xíng   手型

The shapes which the hands take, whether in movement or still.

1. Fist   quán   拳

The little finger, ring finger, middle finger, and index finger curl tightly, and the thumb presses on the middle segment of the middle and index fingers. The fist surface slants down slightly in a spiral so it is also called spiral fist [luósī quán 螺丝拳]. The main parts of the fist are the fist eye [quán yǎn 拳眼], fist heart [quán xīn 拳心], fist surface [quán miàn 拳面], fist back [quán bèi 拳背], and fist heel [quán lún 拳轮] (figure 1).

Fist position names:

Upright fist [lì quán 立拳]: When the fist eye is on top.

Face-up fist [yǎng quán 仰拳]: When the fist heart is on top.

Face-down, or prone fist [fǔ quán 俯拳]: When the fist back is on top.

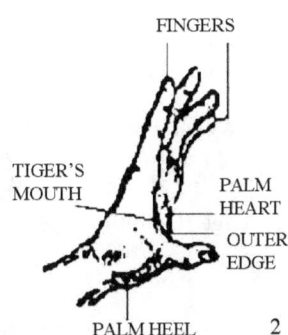

1

2. Palm   zhǎng   掌

The parts of the palm include: the fingers [zhǎng zhǐ 掌指], the palm heart [zhǎng xīn 掌心], the tiger mouth[10] [hǔ kǒu 虎口], the palm edge [zhǎng wài yuán 掌外缘], and the palm heel [zhǎng gēn 掌根] (see figure 2).

a)   Round palm (also called Xingyi palm)   yuán xíng zhǎng   圆形掌

All five fingers naturally separate, the thumb spreads out, the index finger pulls up, the tiger mouth pulls open, and the other three fingers slightly bend. The palm heart is concave as if holding a ball (figure 2).

2

b)   Unicorn horn palm (also called the character eight palm)

　　　lín jiǎo zhǎng, bāzì zhǎng   麟角掌, 八字掌

The thumb and index finger are straight and held open to form the Chinese character eight (八), while the other fingers curl (figure 3).

---

[10] Translator's note: The tiger mouth is the thumb web, the arc formed between the thumb and the index finger.

c) Sword palm jiàn zhǐ zhǎng   剑指掌

The index and middle fingers are held straight out together, and the ring and little fingers curl. The thumb is bent and spread open (figure 4).

3

4

The above palm shapes are also named according to how they are positioned:

Face-up [yǎng zhǎng 仰掌]: When the palm heart faces up.

Face-down, prone [fǔ zhǎng 俯掌]: When the palm heart faces down.

Upright [lì zhǎng 立掌]: When the palm heart faces the front and the fingers point up.

Upside down [dào lì zhǎng 倒立掌]: When the palm heart faces the front and the fingers point down.

Level [héng zhǎng 横掌]: When the palm heart faces the front and the fingers face one side.

Side [cē zhǎng 侧掌]: When the palm heart faces obliquely in.

Reverse [fǎn zhǎng 反掌]: When the palm heart faces obliquely out with the palm edge (the little finger side) up.

3. Hook   diāo gōu   刁勾

The wrist flexes and the little finger, ring finger, middle finger and index finger all flex. The thumb is straight and sticks to the second segment of the index and middle fingers; the fingertips do not join together (figure 5).

5

This hand shape is used in the partner sparring forms.

XINGYIQUAN: TECHNIQUES

2) Stances   bù xíng   步型

The position of the lower limbs when in a fixed stance.

a. Empty stance   xūbù   虚步

Open the legs back to front twenty to sixty centimetres apart. Flex both legs to sit, with the front unweighted and the back weighted. Roll the knees in slightly and sit most of the weight on the back leg. Keep the heels in line and the feet planted on the ground, the front foot pointed forward and the back foot turned out forty-five degrees. When the distance between the feet is about half a meter, this stance is also called the *santi* stance [sāntǐshì 三体式] or *xingyibu* [xíngyìbù 形意步]. This is the most commonly performed stance (figure 6).

b. Bow stance   gōngbù   弓步

Open the legs back to front, the front leg flexed with the toe forward, the knee in line with the toes. Extend the back leg naturally with the foot turned out forty-five degrees. Keep both feet solidly planted on the ground (figure 7).

c. Drop stance   pūbù   仆步

Squat fully on one leg with the buttocks close to the heel, and extend the other leg out to the side close to the ground. Keep both feet and heels solidly on the ground, with the toes turned slightly out (figure 8).

d. Horse stance mǎbù   马步

Open the legs and sit with the weight between them, the feet parallel and pointing forward about two or three foot lengths apart. Tuck in the knees slightly (figure 9).

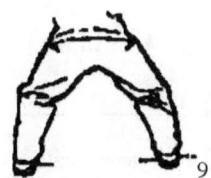

14   CHAPTER ONE: BACKGROUND

e. Half-horse stance   bàn mǎbù   半马步

Flex the forward leg and turn the foot in slightly. Sit on the back leg with the foot turned out at a right angle. Keep both feet solidly planted, about two to three foot lengths apart, and keep more weight on the back leg (figure 10).

f. One-leg stance, lifted stance, chicken pose stance

   dúlìbù, tíbù, jīxíng bù   独立步、提步、鸡形步

Flex one leg to half-sit and support the weight, and lift the other so that the instep sticks to the supporting leg. Tuck the lifted foot onto the ankle of the supporting leg,[11] the toes pointing forward and the foot parallel to the ground (figure 11).

g. Cross-sit stance, resting stance, scissors stance

   zuò pán bù, xiē bù, jiǎn zi gū bù   坐盘步、歇步、剪子股步

Cross the legs and sit or half squat. Turn the front foot out at a right angle, with the whole foot on the ground. Point the back foot forward and put the weight on the ball with the heel up. Tuck the knee of the back leg into the hollow of the knee of the front leg. When sitting all the way down, it is called a cross-sit stance (figure 12), and when sitting halfway down, it is called a half-sitting stance (figure 12b).

h. Cross stance, twisted scissors stance

   chā bù, jiǎo jiǎn bù   叉步、绞剪步

Cross the legs with the front leg flexed forward with the toes turned out and the foot fully planted. Flex the back leg slightly, with the toes pointed forward and the heel slightly

---

[11] Translator's note: The foot is usually tucked at the ankle except when performing the chicken form itself, then the foot is tucked about halfway between the ankle and knee of the supporting leg.

XINGYIQUAN: TECHNIQUES

off the ground. Put more weight on the front leg and turn the upper body around to the back in the direction of the front leg (figure 13).

i. T stance   dīng xūbù   丁虚步

Flex one leg to half-sit. Touch the ball of the foot of the unweighted leg lightly on the ground in front of or beside the supporting foot (figure 14).

j. Dragon riding stance   qíóng bù   骑龙步

Place the legs in almost the bow stance position, but slightly less far apart. Flex the back leg and raise the heel, and put the weight on the front leg or in between the legs (figure 15).

k. High raised stance, Raised knee stance

    gāo tí bù, tíxī dúlì bù   高提步、提膝独立步

Stand on one leg with the knee straight or slightly flexed. Lift the knee of the unweighted leg with the thigh parallel to the ground and the toes either dorsi- or plantar-flexed (figure 16).

3) Arm and Hand Techniques   shǒu fǎ 手法

The actions and techniques of the upper limbs.

a. Split, chop[12] (with fist or palm)   pī quán, pī zhǎng   劈拳、劈掌

Slide the fist up the chest, screwing up then extending forward. As the fist arrives in front of the mouth, open and inwardly rotate so that the palm heart strikes in a

---

[12] Translator's note: The action of the hands splits, or separates, with power applied in two directions. I also chose the translation 'split' over 'chop' because it requires more finesse to split a log than to chop a piece of wood. Skill lies in the twist of the wrist to split the log and prevent dulling the ax by a follow through into the wood. (I really did spend the winter in a cabin to translate this book, but never progressed past brutally chopping the wood and destroying the axe. Of course, that got me out of that chore…)

forward and down direction. Extend the shoulder and keep the elbow down and the arm bent, with the palm at shoulder height. Hit either with the heel of the fist or outer edge of the palm. Strike down from above, like splitting wood (figure 17).

b. Drive, crush, thrust[13]   bēng quán   崩拳

Punch directly forward from the waist, rotating the fist. The fist eye is up, between waist and shoulder height, with the arm slightly bent. Tilt the fist surface down to punch with the whole surface (figure 18).

c. Drill[14]   zuān quán   钻拳

Bring the fist up in front of the chest and punch forward between mouth and eye height. The fist is twisted so that its heart is angled in and surface angled up. Keep the elbow down and the forearm outwardly rotated (figure 19).

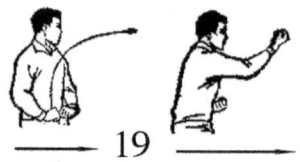

d. Cannon, pound[15]   pào quán   炮拳

(called upper block and punch: jià chōng quán 架冲拳 in other styles)

Twist one fist up in front of the chest then twist it out to block up, arriving beside the temple with the fist eye tilted down and the fist heart out. Bring the other fist past the ribs and twist to punch forward (or diagonally forward), with the fist eye up, between waist and shoulder height (figure 20).

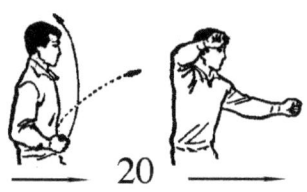

---

[13]Translator's note: I chose the word drive because that is the word I always end up using when trying to get students to punch properly – the punch drives from the rear leg, it is not snapped from the elbow. Thrust or crushing punch also works.

[14] Translator's note: There is no question on this translation, *zuan* turns while it advances, just like a drill.

[15] Translator's note: I chose the word cannon because in English it implies an oblique strike, which reminds the player to use the upper arm to deflect rather than block. Cannon is a bit stuffy when teaching – then, "pow" is still the best word to use. Pound also works.

XINGYIQUAN: TECHNIQUES

e. Wring, Crosscut[16]   héng quán   横拳

Bring one fist from the opposite side under the forearm of the other arm, twisting out angled to the front (like pulling out). Follow a curving line, ending with the fist heart on top between waist and shoulder height, and the elbow slightly bent (figure 21).

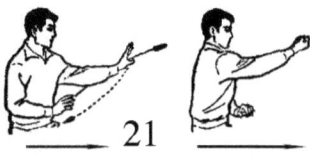

f. Slice up (with fist or palm)   liāo quán / zhǎng   撩拳、掌

Bring the fist (upright fist, lì quán 立拳) or the palm (side palm, cè zhǎng 侧掌) forward and up from below, for a forward slice (figure 22a). Bring the fist or palm back and up from below for a back slice (figure 22b). Swing with the fist eye down or the palm reversed for a reverse slice. The height is between the waist and shoulder.

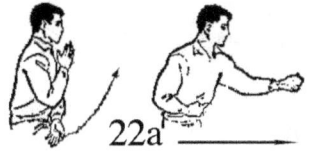   

g. Flick (with fist or palm), Scoop[17]   tiǎo quán / zhǎng   挑拳、掌

With an upright fist or side palm, scoop up to the front from below, to shoulder height (figure 23).[18]

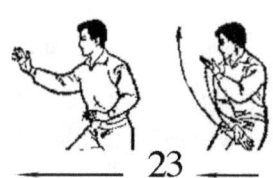

---

[16] Translator's note: Wring emphasizes the action of the two arms working together. Imagine wringing a towel between the hands, then keep the arms solid and drive forward from the legs. There is enough forward power, plus a distinctive twisting outward/inward force. Crosscut emphasizes the shearing power.

[17] Editor's note (2021): Scoop is a better translation. The technique does not flick with the wrist. The arm remains bent throughout, so the wrist is cocked. It is a much stronger technique than the word 'flick' suggests.

[18] Translator's note: The wrist snaps at the end, so the forearm acts sequentially after the upper arm. This differentiates the flick from the slice up. If the wrist does not flick, then this technique is called scoop, like scooping with a pitchfork.

CHAPTER ONE: BACKGROUND

h. Pound   zá quán   砸拳

Pound down from above, with the fist heart or back. It is also 'pound' if you smash the fist into the palm of the other hand (figure 24).

i. Hold, Hug   bào quán   抱拳

Bring both fists (or one fist and one palm) in from outside to an embracing position in front of the abdomen or by the waist. Keep the forearms tight to the waist and the fist heart facing up or in (figure 25).

j. Brace (with fist or palm)   chēng quán / zhǎng   撑拳、掌

Open the fists or palms to the sides or up and down, with the fist or palm heart facing out (figure 26).

k. Push   tuī zhǎng   推掌

Push straight forward with the upright or side upright palm, or push to the side with a side palm (figure 27).

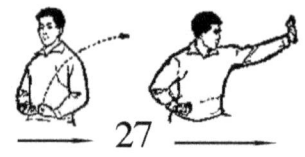

l. Shove   zhuàng zhǎng   撞掌

This is the same as a push, except that the arm is not fully extended.[19] Use a short burst of power (figure 28).

m. Lift, carry   tuō zhǎng   托掌

Lift out to the front with the palm heart forward and the fingers tilted down in an upside down palm [dào lì zhǎng 倒立掌]

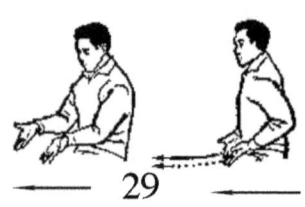

---

[19] Translator's note: The shove also tends to use the forearms as point of contact, while the push contacts at the tip. Editor's note (2021) A shove is also stronger than a push.

(figure 29). You could also lift up along the side with a face-up palm [yāng zhǎng 仰掌].

n. Stab (with fist or palm)   chā quán / zhǎng   插拳、掌

With the fist surface or the fingers of the palm pointing in the direction of the strike, stab down with force. Stabbing with the fist could also be called plant [zāiquán 栽拳] (figures 30a, 30b).

o. Wave away, swing   bāi zhǎng   摆掌

Swing one or both palms in an arc in front of the body towards one side (figure 31).

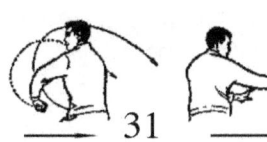

p. Block up, framing block   jià quán   架拳

Drill up in front of the body, then outwardly rotate by the head, to block above the head with the fist eye down (figure 32).

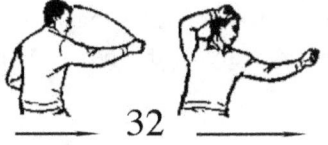

q. Press down (with fist or palm)   yā quán / zhǎng   压拳、掌

Outwardly rotate the forearm to press down. Apply force with the back of the fist or hand (figure 33).

r. Pull   lǔ zhǎng   捋掌

With an upright or side palm, pull down or back and down from above (figure 34).

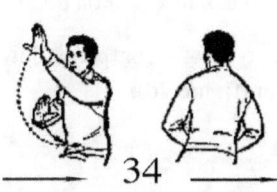

CHAPTER ONE: BACKGROUND

s. Hook   guà zhǎng   挂掌

As the opponent comes in, flow with his line of attack to sweep his hand diagonally up, down, or back (figure 35).

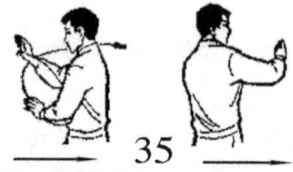

t. Thread   chuān zhǎng   穿掌

Thread the palm along the other arm, the ribs, or the outside of the thigh. Depending on the direction, this is called forward, backward, or sideways thread (figure 36)

u. Separate, Open (with fists or palms)   fēn quán / zhǎng   分拳、掌

Separate the fists or palms to the sides or to the front and back (figure 37).

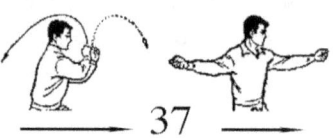

v. Cover   gài zhǎng   盖掌

Press down [àn 按] strongly with a straight arm from above the head (figure 38, right arm).

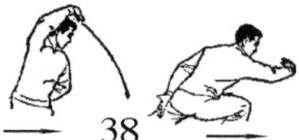

w. Push down   àn zhǎng   按掌

Press the palm heart down with force to the lower front or side (figure 39).

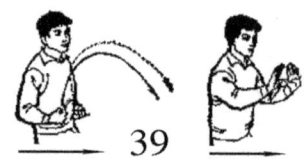

x. Tuck in   kòu quán   扣拳

Tuck the fist or palm down, twisting it over (figure 40).

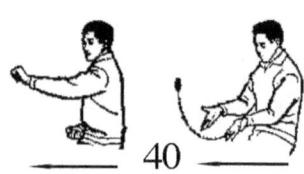

y. Uppercut   guàn quán   贯拳

Punch diagonally up from the lower side (figure 41).

41

z. Shake   dǒu quán   抖拳

Snap the body forcibly, causing the force to reach the front of the fist so that it shakes forward or sideways (figure 42).

42

aa. Slice   xiāo zhǎng   削掌

Slice diagonally up with the tiger's mouth in an upward slice, [shàng xiāo 上削] (figure 43) or diagonally down with the outer edge of the palm in downward slice [xià xiāo 下削].

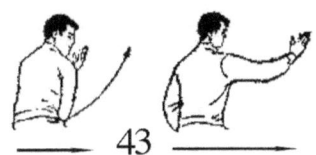
43

bb. Tuck   yē zhǎng   掖掌

Stab out to the back, sliding along the ribs (figure 44, left arm).

44

cc. Elbow strike   dǐng zhǒu   顶肘

Flex the arm to strike forcefully forward or to the side with the point of the elbow (figure 45).

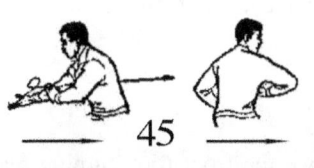
45

dd. Elbow cover   yǎn zhǒu   掩肘

Outwardly rotate the forearm and roll the elbow inward (figure 46).

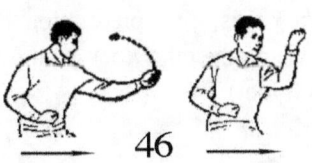
46

4) Footwork   bù fǎ   步法

The stepping of the lower limbs in action.

a.   Advance, enter   jìn bù   进步

Step the front foot a half-step forward, or the back foot forward (also called a forward step [shàng bù 上步], or both forward in turn (figure 47).

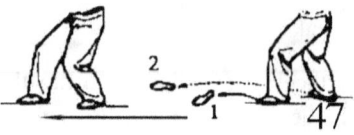

b.   Step back   tuì bù   退步

Step the back foot a half step back or the front foot back, or both feet back in turn (figure 48).

c.   Follow in   gēn bù   跟步

After one foot has advanced, bring the back foot a half step towards the front foot, to land behind it (figure 49, right foot).

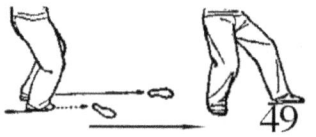

d.   Withdraw   chè bù   撤步

After one foot has retreated, bring the front foot back a half-step, to place close by the back foot (figure 50, left foot).

e.   Step forward   diàn bù   垫步

Move the front foot, turning out the toes, in preparation for placing the other foot (figure 51, left foot).

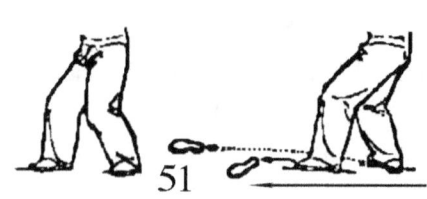

XINGYIQUAN: TECHNIQUES 23

f. Shin rubbing step, lift step mójìng bù, tí bù 磨胫步, 提步

Lift the back foot and bring it forward to stop at the ankle of the supporting leg, its arch sitting on the anklebone (figure 52, left foot).

g. Hook out bǎi bù 摆步

Advance the foot following a semi-circle, so that when it lands the toes are pointed out and the feet form the Chinese character eight 八 heel to toe (figure 53, right foot).

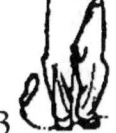

h. Hook in kòu bù 扣步

Advance the foot in a semi-circle, so that when it lands the toes are pointed in, so that the feet are 'pigeon-toed', forming the Chinese character eight 八 (figure 54, left foot).

i. Cross-over step gài bù 盖步

Lift a foot, step it across in front of the supporting leg, and land on the opposite side, legs crossed (figure 55).

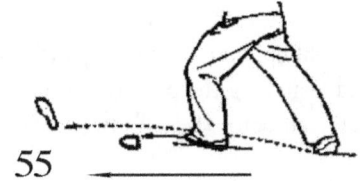

j. Back cross step dǎo chā bù 倒插步

Lift a foot, bring it behind the supporting leg, and land to the opposite side, legs crossed (figure 56, left foot).

24 CHAPTER ONE: BACKGROUND

k. Switchover step   huàn bù   换步

Switch the position of the feet, trading places, usually back to front, ending up in the same place (figure 57).

l. Aligned step shùn bù   顺步

A step or stance is 'aligned' when the same hand and foot move forward (figure 58).

m. Reverse step ào bù   拗步

A step or stance is 'reversed' when the opposite hand and foot move forward (figure 59).

n. Jump, switchover jump   tiào bù, huàn tiào bù   跳步, 换跳步

Push off with both legs to jump straight up, turning the body in the air and switching the position of the feet in the air before landing (figure 60).

o. Hop   zòng tiào bù   纵跳步

Lift one leg and push off with the other to bound forward, landing first on the foot which pushed off (figure 61).

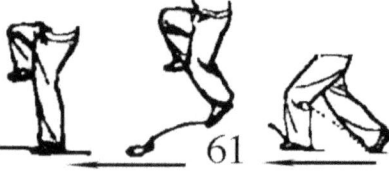

XINGYIQUAN: TECHNIQUES 25

p. Drive forward   zòng bù   纵步

Drive forward by hitting with the front leg, and pushing off forward with the back leg, but keep the back foot trailing close to the ground (the body does not rise). Just before the leading foot lands, quickly lift the foot that pushed off and settle it into the ankle of the other (figure 62).

q. Leap   yuè bù   跃步

Push off with the forward leg so that the body moves up and forward. Land on the other leg, and then land forward with the leg that pushed off (figure 63).

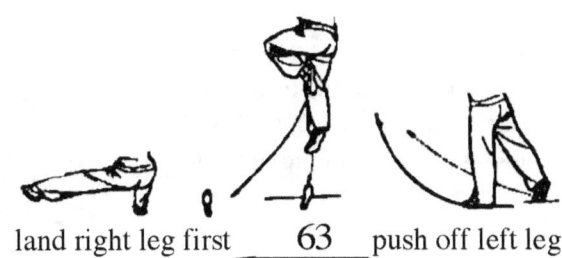

land right leg first   63   push off left leg

r. Parallel step bīng bù   并步

Bring one foot in beside the other. Bring heels together, feet parallel and pointing forward, or one turned out (figure 64).

s. Stamp   tā bù   踏步

Stamp the ground strongly with one foot and lift the other a bit (figure 65).

26   CHAPTER ONE: BACKGROUND

5) Kicks   tuǐ fǎ   腿法

The striking techniques of the lower limbs.

a.   Straight kick tī tuǐ   踢腿

Stand on one leg, lift the other straight with the ankle dorsi-flexed (pull the toes back), the force reaching the tip of the toes (figure 66).

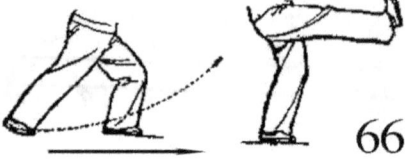

b.   Heel kick   dēng tuǐ   蹬腿

Stand on one leg, lift the other leg with the knee flexed, and then extend it to kick with the ankle dorsi-flexed, putting the force forward into the heel (figure 67).

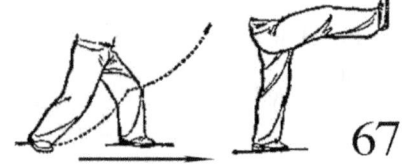

c.   Crushing kick   cǎi jiǎo   踩脚

Stand on one leg, lift the other leg with the knee flexed, dorsi-flex the ankle and outwardly rotate the leg, then kick down and forward with the heel (figure 68).

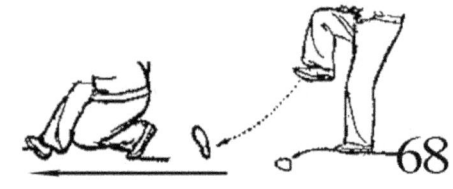

d.   Poke kick   diǎn jiǎo   点脚

Stand on one leg, lift the other leg with the knee flexed and the ankle plantar-flexed (point the toes), then extend it to kick with force reaching the tip of the toes (figure 69).

The forms use mostly these four kicks, but there are also many other kicks to train. Similar to many other styles, Xingyi kicks include straight swings [tī 踢], stretches [yā 压, hào 耗], swings [bǎi 摆], hooks [gōu 勾], snaps [tán 弹], sweeps [sǎo 扫], and entrapments [guà 挂]. To build a good foundation as a beginner, make sure to train both straight kicks and snap kicks to improve the flexibility of the legs, hips and back. Then when you train Xingyi you will be both agile and stable with enough elasticity. Many people think that Xingyi emphasizes hands over feet, so they do not have to practise leg skills, but this is not so.

1.4.2 Requirements for each part of the body

The Xingyi classics put all the requirements of the body position into eight essentials [bā yào 八要], also called the 'poem of the eight words' [bā zì jué 八字诀], which are:

one	carry or prop up [dǐng 顶] head, palm, and tongue.
two	concave or close [kòu 扣] shoulders, hands and feet, and teeth.
three	round [yuán 圆] upper back, chest, and tiger's mouth.
four	lively or alert [mǐn 敏] feelings, eyes, and hands.
five	hold or embrace [bào 抱] centre (*dantian*), intentions, and arms.
six	hang or settle [chuí 垂] energy, shoulders and elbows.
seven	flex [qū 屈] arms, legs, and wrists.
eight	hold erect or thrust out [tǐng 挺] neck, lumbar area and knees.

1) Hold the head up and the neck straight.

This requirement of Xingyi is similar to that of Taiji boxing, to maintain a lifting power, or to suspend the head. The Taiji boxing classic, the *Gongxinjie*, says, "When you can lift your spirit such that no part of you is sluggish, this is called suspending the head." Xingyi boxing classics emphasize, "Keep the head straight and the spirit will reach to the crown." In keeping the head up, you must neither leave the neck lax nor hold it tense.

In Xingyi classics, this is called "using the head to control the body." Keep the head straight and hold the neck vertical, as if to carry something on top of the head which you don't want to drop. When you rise or drop, or spin around, keep the upward force of the head throughout; don't let it sway around or tilt.

An "erect neck" means the neck is open and naturally upright, not held stiff so that the head cannot move at all.

While keeping the head up and the neck upright, pay attention to the following points. Keep your spirit natural and focused. Don't furrow your eyebrows to look tough or grind your teeth. Keep your mouth closed with the teeth closed and the tongue on the palate, which improves secretion of saliva. Breathe through your nose – don't open your mouth. Keep your chin in – don't let it stick out.

2) Extend the shoulders and drop the elbows

Extending [sōng 松] the shoulders is also called settling [chén 沉] or hanging [chuí 垂] the shoulders. When practising, extend and settle the shoulders into the action, keep them and the elbows set down. The hollow of the shoulder joint should pull in very slightly. This will keep the upper body open and create a force around the joints, so that all movement will be settled and solid. Extending the shoulders combines with relaxing the chest (containing the chest) so that the energy in pulled down and the lower limbs are steadier.

Never fully extend the arms to punch or strike, but keep the elbows tucked down. This differs from styles such as long fist. When bringing the arms in, keep the elbows tucked into the ribs, so that all the power in the body is pulled into the lower limbs and the body can work as a unit.

3) Keep the wrists cocked, the palms spread, and the fists tight.

When describing actions of the upper limb segments in Xingyi, the hands are called the tip segment, the elbow is called the central segment, and the shoulders are called the root segment.

Most basic palm techniques use a downward cocked wrist [tā wàn 塌腕] which places the palm heart facing forward and down and applies a two-vector force to the front and down.[20] The fingers are open, the index finger stretched up, the thumb opened with force, and the tiger mouth forms a semi-circle. The palm heart is concave, and no part of the hand is left slack. If you hold to these requirements whenever you train, you will greatly increase the strength of your fingers and wrists.

---

[20] Author's note: A few special cases such as the chicken, dragon and monkey forms, use slightly different palm techniques.

All fist techniques hold a tight fist to increase the strength of the arms. The thumb is flexed, with its final segment pressed on the middle segment of the index and middle fingers. When punching forward, keep the wrist straight so that the fist surface tilts forward slightly and the force reaches to the most forward part of the fist.

4)   Open the upper back and contain the chest.

An open upper back [bá bèi 拔背] is also called a taut upper back [jǐn bèi 紧背] or rounded upper back [yuán bèi 圆背]. This position is made up of two aspects. Firstly, as the head is raised up, the neck straightened, and the lumbar area pulled down, the upper back is stretched up and down [bá 拔]. Secondly, as the shoulders are settled and extended, the shoulder hollow pulled tight, the chest contained, and the hand extended forward, the latissimus dorsi are stretched out to the sides. In this way the muscles of the upper back have a certain tension up, down, left and right, which trains them to expand.

A contained or reserved chest [hán xiōng 含胸] is also called an expanded chest [shū xiōng 舒胸] or relaxed chest [sōng xiōng 松胸]. These all mean that the chest is held open, expanded, and natural, instead of being stuck out.

Containing the chest and opening the upper back are connected. If you open the upper back you will be able to contain the chest. But if you stick out your chest, your shoulders will be pulled back and you won't be able to open the upper back. The reserved chest and open upper back are completely natural positions and don't need to be overdone. Sticking out the chest and pulling in the abdomen or humping the upper back and caving in the chest are both wrong. Be careful not to roll the upper back too far forward, thinking to extend the shoulders more, because this causes "camel back". Also be careful not to overemphasize pulling the spine up and down and forget to stretch the back to the sides, because this may cause a puffed up chest or swollen abdomen.

In practice, this position of contained chest and open upper back is not absolute. Allow your upper body to expand and contract with the changes in the actions, which will help you do the moves correctly and also better train the upper body.

5)   Keep the lumbar area solid and the spine straight.

The moves of Xingyi are simple and straightforward, with few jumps. Most movement uses rotation so the body must move as a united, coordinated whole.

If the lower back (kidney area) is slack and weak then the entire movement will lose its centre, and any punch or kick will be powerless. So when training, keep the lumbar area solid and powerful so that it can act as the axis. A Xingyi classic says, "If you lean forward or backward then your postures have no power, if you lean to either side then the whole body is weak." It also says, "the body is like a bow, and the fist is like an arrow." These phrases perfectly express the position and use of the lower back area. If the trunk isn't held together and stretched then it can't act as a bow, and movement will be broken or weak. Keeping the lumbar area solid does not mean to hold it stiff, but to open it naturally, full of elasticity, so that it can act as the axis of all actions in the upper and lower limbs.

The requirements for the spine and lumbar area can't be separated. If you keep your lumbar area powerful and the head up then you will naturally hold the spine straight. When practising, the spine will extend, contract, and turn to give more power to the arms, legs, and waist. Be careful not to twist or sway the spine.

6) Tuck in the buttocks, lift the anus.

In Xingyi, the buttocks are consciously held in, and not allowed to stick out. This is also called "lift up the anus and roll in the hip," and "hold the anus in." To tuck in the buttocks, contract the anal sphincter muscle slightly to lift up, as if trying not to defecate, but do not tighten it so much that it pulls forward. This will keep the buttocks from sticking out, and hold the lumbar area, spine, and tailbone in line. It will also help you keep the chest contained and the upper back stretched, and sink the breath to the *dantian*. This is why the Xingyi classic says; "Once you lift the buttocks, your energy will reach to all four tips."

7) Keep the hips relaxed and well-knit, the knees tucked in and lively, and the feet flat and stable.

To advance or retreat, the legs are stable but agile. The footwork is mostly straight-line advance and retreat, and is based on a strong stance. Training emphasizes "fast hands and light feet – moving like a cat. Concentrate, show spirit, strike simultaneously with the hands and feet, and you will win for sure." This is why Xingyi requires that the moves are agile, the feet land solidly, and the hips, knees and feet be closely coordinated, with no slackness between them. When advancing or retreating, the hips lead the knees and the knees lead the feet. The hips are the root segment, the knees are the central segment, and the feet are the tip segment. When standing in a posture, the hips should be relaxed,

XINGYIQUAN: TECHNIQUES 31

but at the same time have a force pulling them in.[21] This combines with tucking the buttocks in, so keeps the upper body straight. The knees should stay flexed, with a force tucking them in slightly to prevent them swinging out. This helps keep the whole leg solid and stable. The legs should be flexed appropriately. If they are too straight they will be stiff, but if they are too bent they won't have any power. When moving, holding the hips relaxed but contracted will prevent the body from tilting and keep the whole body moving forward or backward as a unit; having the knees lively and natural will help the front foot lift and land with full range, and the back foot push off strongly. In this way stepping will be both agile and long range while remaining steady, with the power which comes from elasticity.

All of the above positions impact upon each other. In order to master these requirements the beginner must build a solid foundation by practising standing and the many basics.

Examples of common mistakes made by beginners:

a) Tilting the head and tensing the neck. Tenseness will cause the head to tilt and the neck to stiffen up. Another mistake is to let the head sway by leaving the neck loose.

b) Leaning the body. Any tilting of the body, forward or back, or side to side, or letting the buttocks stick out, will cause the body to lose balance.

c) Shrugging the shoulders, straightening the arms. It is a mistake to shrug the shoulders or allow one to lift up higher than the other. It is also wrong to extend the arm so much into the punch that it straightens.

d) Holding the breath, puffing out the chest. It is wrong to pull the shoulders back and stick out the chest. This may cause you to tighten up, hold your breath, or use force.

e) "Camel back", arched lower back. If the spine is bent you won't be able to expand and support yourself.

---

[21] Translator's note: Roll the hips means to roll the hip joints (greater trochanter) outward from the back in their sockets as if trying to pull them out from behind. This creates a closing in force around to the thighs and pushes your force into the feet, which triangulates back to your lumbar area. This holds the upper body steady without muscular tension.

f) Sticking out the buttocks, pulling in the abdomen. It is wrong to let the buttocks stick out or tilt to either side. It is also wrong to pull the abdomen in, because this causes breathing problems, tenses up the chest, and takes power away from the legs.

g) Sticking up the fingers, over-cocking the wrist. When punching, if the wrist is flipped up the force will be dissipated. Common errors for the drill fist are bending the wrist so that the fist is pulled back, or not fully twisting the fist. Common errors of palm techniques are keeping the fingers all together, leaving the tiger mouth loose, or sticking out the palm.

h) Trying to look fierce by furrowing the eyebrows, bulging the eyes, tensing up in spirit, or gritting the teeth. Mistakes in the opposite directions are tilting the head to look sidelong at the target, and not paying enough attention to what you are doing.

i) Sticking the hips out, leaving the groin area loose. If the hips are tilted forward the back leg will be stiff, the upper body will lean back, and the centre of gravity will rise. If the groin is left loose, the knees will slacken outwards and the legs will be weakened.

j) Leaving the knees loose, lifting the feet. If the knees are too bent they will lose all strength. If the feet aren't gripping the ground, the back foot will often flip up (the heel or outer edge of the foot will lift off the ground).

1.4.3 Stages and points to pay attention to in training

Xingyi training is generally divided into a foundation stage, an improvement stage, and a consolidation stage. The degree of skill differs for each stage, so the emphasis of training also differs. These skills have previously been organized into the three training stages by Guo Yunshen 郭云深 as obvious power [míng jìn 明劲], hidden power [àn jìn 暗劲] and transformed power [huà jìn 化劲].

1) The foundation stage: "obvious power" míng jìn   明劲

The beginner's main objectives should be to master the requirements of the basic positions, study the basic moves, and combine the three forms and three methods (hand forms, stances, body shape, hand techniques, footwork, and body technique) to make them all upright and round. Just as in learning calligraphy, you should work hard at writing each stroke carefully, getting the horizontal strokes level and the vertical strokes straight. At the same time you should train to improve strength, speed, flexibility and other basic body conditioning which will give you a better foundation. "You train to build a foundation, strengthen the body, harden the bones like iron, and become tough like a mountain." Guo Yunshen called this stage "obvious power," and in training emphasized "never change the rules."

Training needs during this learning stage can be summed up in five points:

correct	zhèng què	正确	positions must be right
clean	zhěng qí	整齐	movement must be orderly
smooth	hé shùn	和顺	advancing and retreating must flow
stable	wěn dìng	稳定	balance must be under control
solid	chōng shí	充实	strength must be full

a. Correct Positions:

When learning Xingyi you should first practise standing in each stance (such as *santishi* or another posture). "Standing" training helps you to feel and master the positions of each body segment and to develop correct postures. After attaining a good foundation with standing, then you can learn the standing posture of split (without the stride forward).

Once you can stand properly in split, you can train moving split, while maintaining the same rules as the standing posture. You must clearly stop at each position, then move. Practise every single posture of each form in this way. Make sure you follow requirements at all times such that the whole body is as it should be. Allow no carelessness. You should take special care to hold the body upright and straight, to expand to the eight directions, to coordinate the upper and lower body, to line up the hands, feet, and nose, and to keep the whole body under control.

b. Clean Movement:

The emphasis is on moving the hands and feet together so that the hands and feet arrive at the same time. Xingyi theory states, "the mind and breath strike together, the four limbs move together." If you can get your hands and feet to work together then all the moves will be correct, the upper and lower body will hit together, and your whole body will be coordinated. When training "obvious power," in order to hit with the hands and feet together there can be a clear sound as the foot hits the ground which comes at the same time that the upper limbs strike. When hitting the ground, the foot should stick close to the surface, and slide forward (or backward), stamping down. The foot should not lift up and whack at the ground. Once you have built a good foundation, you can gradually shift to "subtle power" and make little or no sound with the feet, which is the next step in the coordination of the whole body.

c. Smooth Footwork:

Techniques are always done in movement, so it isn't enough for the hands and feet to move cleanly, you also need to have smooth footwork before all body segments can work together. When you can advance and retreat, dodge and turn, while keeping the line of movement, direction, and timing of each part of the body, and the angles and position of the set postures exactly as they need be, only then can you avoid the errors of losing your centre, tightening up, breathing tensely, and losing balance. For example, when doing cannon punch, if you hit and step at the same time, but turn the front foot in or out too much, then the waist and hip will be twisted, and your whole body will tense up and destabilize. If the rear hand blocks too high or too much to the side, then the shoulder could lift, causing the body to tilt. If the hands and feet aren't smooth this will cause problems with breathing. Classical texts make exactly this point, "If it isn't smooth outside then it isn't together inside." From the very beginning you must try to be coordinated and smooth, keep the "three points" working together and the "four tips" closely connected, coordinate the upper and lower body segments, distinguish stance weighting and off weighting, and hold the body straight. Only then can you become naturally smooth.

d. Stable Balance:

Xingyi moves quickly with force, and differentiates distinctly between action and stillness -"initiate action like an avalanche, set into the ground like a tree putting in roots." During practice, you must pay particular attention to keeping your balance. Your ability to keep stable will improve as you get used to the techniques and as your body becomes conditioned. In the beginning stage you must develop strength of the lower limbs and flexibility of the lower back and legs, and repeatedly solidify the basic moves and basic requirements. You must especially train "standing" to get the upper body extended and the lower body solid, to give you a stable foundation, and to allow your energy to reach from the crown of the head to the tip of the toes. When practising the five basic techniques, keep the positions at the same level – do not rise and drop at random. Whether advancing or retreating, rising or dropping, stay light, agile, stable, and strong. When practising the twelve animals, whether you extend or contract, move horizontally or vertically, rise, land, or turn, you must "move like the wind and stand like a nail." As you land, flex the knees, roll the hips, and grip the ground with your toes to prevent your upper body from swaying.[22]

e. Solid Strength:

When learning, the fist must be tight, the stances stable, the feet solid, the strikes fast and strong, and the power full. All the muscles are trained by contracting against each other. When advancing, the front foot should stick close to the ground so that the force goes straight forward, and the back foot should drive with full force into the ground such that "the feet tread the centre door and don't land empty." Breathe out to gain power to drive the back foot. Whenever the front fist punches with an outward rotation to shake outward, the rear fist rotates forcibly inwards with a tucking in force; if the left fist drills upwards then the right fist pulls downwards – the hands balance each other. The forearms rotate inward and outward, like wringing a rope, so that as one rises and drills the other lowers and rolls, both twisting and rolling back and forward as a unit. When the arms pull in they must stick tight to the body; "the elbows never leave the ribs, the hands never leave the heart, follow the body tightly like going in and out of a hole." This will make the body hit as one unit.

Being solid does not mean being tense. You must not tense the chest, pull in the abdomen, hold the breath or use brute force. You should keep the spirit calm, the chest open, the abdomen solid, and the breath natural so that the muscles can contract or relax as need be. The segment using power will be hard but still soft, fast as lightning, and the other segments will be naturally open, relaxed and steady. The chest especially must keep empty and calm.

2) Improvement stage – "hidden power"   ànjìn   暗劲

The requirements of this stage are:

linked (flowing)	lián guàn	连贯
round (smooth)	yuán huó	圆活
supple (pliable yet tough)	róu rèn	柔韧
complete (integrated)	wán zhěng	完整

---

[22] Translator's note: Hold the ground with the meaty ball of the toes, don't curl the toes under.

Guo Yunshen called this stage that of "hidden power." He said: "The spirit and energy are expanded and not broken, movement is rounded and not blocked," and "train in order to lengthen the ligaments, combine the channels, and lengthen without weakness." When training, work on linking the basic positions and basic moves together so that you can move comfortably. This makes the movement smooth, integrated, expansive and precise.

To be "linked together" means that every single position has total coordination between the seven body segments – head, shoulders, elbows, hands, knees, hips, and feet. To be "smooth and integrated" means to achieve the six unities of the internal and external, and the seven sequential movements of the upper and lower body. That is, that the head leads the body, the waist (lower back) leads the hips, the hips lead the knees, the knees lead the feet, the shoulders lead the elbows, the elbows lead the hands, and the hands lead the fingers. In this way the entire body moves as a unit.

Training during this stage emphasizes flexibility and agility. Practice can be either fast or slow, changing naturally. At this point, when the postures stop, power should continue, and when the power changes, intent should continue. In this way the rhythm is quick and clear, and has a sharp yet continuous feel. Power should be both hard and soft, combining both without losing either. Do not hold the fists too tight. Punch as if pulling on a spring, this will make techniques solid yet elastic. Perform split as if chopping an object in front of you. The hands should be springy whatever the technique – whether they are both striking to the front, one twisting to the left as the other twists right, one driving up as the other presses down, or one striking forward as the other pulls back. This elastic quality differs from the quality sought in the previous stage of training, which was obvious and hard power. In the previous stage you sought to be clear, quick, hard and fierce; now you should seek to be subtle, solid, and agile. The sound the landing foot makes should also change from loud to soft, from clear to quiet (with a slight sound). Training in this way it appears as if the strength lessens, but actually the power of the body is increased through coordination. The power instead of being obviously shown is hidden inside. This improves reaction time, agility, and other qualities.

3) Consolidation stage: "transformed power"　huà jìn　化劲

In this, the highest stage, built on the foundation of the two preceding stages, the intent and movement are united to a high degree to combine the shape with the spirit. Guo Yunshen called this stage that of "transformed power." We can call it the "natural stage" when the shape and idea unite, and movement becomes relaxed and easy. When training at this stage don't be held back by outward form – "the body moves as lightly as a feather," and "the heart is empty and the body is relaxed." What the mind thinks the body does – the hands shoot out as soon as you think. Training of the "intent" is emphasized over that of the "form." There can be no brute force in the body. At any time during the light and soft movement the body can perform an explosive movement by uniting all body segments with the breath to concentrate on one point. The explosive power spoken of by past martial arts masters – which combines intent, breath and strength, is exactly this kind of movement. Move then change, change then explode, quickly concentrate – do as you please. This is a highly coordinated and agile type of power.

The emphasis at the consolidation stage of training is on four qualities:

light (relaxed)	qīng sōng	轻松
quick (agile)	líng qiǎo	灵巧
empty (still)	xū jìng	虚静
united (form and shape as one)	xíng yì hé yī	形意合一

Although the characteristics of movement and the method of using power are dissimilar to the previous stages, the basic requirements for the hands, eyes, body, techniques, and stepping are identical. In addition to these basics even more emphasis is placed on the "six internal and external unities" and the "unity of form and thought," as these are expressed in the changes between movement and stillness, hard and soft, and empty and solid.

The above three stages are a progressive process which will take the practitioner from the basics to familiarity and then to skill. The foundation of each stage is identical. Each practitioner must train hard at the beginning to build a solid foundation, work hard to understand, and perform each requirement at all times during practice.

1.4.4 Things to watch out for while learning

1) Advance progressively and improve gradually

Just because the moves are simple, do not expect to learn a lot quickly without understanding. You must learn things in the proper order and build a good foundation to improve gradually and progressively. If you learn one technique poorly, don't go on to the next. Only when you have built a good foundation of the basics should you go on to forms and weapons. If you try to learn a lot quickly then your postures and moves will probably remain incorrect for a very long time while your skill will probably remain at half its potential, and your body's functions will not improve much. People often feel that *santishi* and the five basic techniques are simple and boring and so don't bother to train these basics. They go on instead to forms, to learn a lot of different things. Because they have neglected basics they never become skilled.

2) Practise regularly and persistently

Since Xingyi practice has no place or time limitations, it can be practised by anyone. It can be practised inside or out in any place where there is a bit of flat surface with air circulation. But you must have a clear goal, persevere, and train every day according to a plan. You must not "go fishing for three days and dry the nets for two." People who train for many years and have a certain grasp of basics, but keep taking breaks, never get the full benefit of training. If training is broken up, and the amount of training varies irregularly from a lot to a little, then the muscles, joints and internal organs don't adjust to the training load. This can cause injuries. To bring about physical conditioning and improve skill level the prerequisite for Xingyi training, as for any physical training, is consistency.

3) Adjust training to suit the individual

Some teachers feel that, as a 'hard' style,[23] Xingyi is only suited to strong young athletes. This is incorrect. Many famous Xingyi players only mastered it in middle age. For example, Li Luoneng 李洛能 from Hebei started Xingyi at thirty-seven. After ten years he was highly skilled and got the nickname "Li the magic fist." His student, Li Jingji 李镜斋, became an apprentice at sixty-three, and trained until he was over seventy. Experience has shown that not only strong young men can practise Xingyi, but so can the elderly, weak, and women. You need only organize training to suit individual capabilities.

The contents and methods of training and the progressions and requirements need not be the same for everyone. Older or weaker people can practise less of the 'obvious power' and do the moves a bit slower. Those with

---

[23] Translator's note: One way of categorizing Chinese martial arts is into 'hard' such as Shaolin, Southern, Longfist or other quick styles which emphasize physical prowess, and 'soft' such as Taiji, Bagua and other styles which emphasize *qi* over strength. In this categorization, Xingyi falls into 'soft,' but its training methods, especially at first, are the hardest of the 'soft' styles.

chronic illness can start with standing practice and split standing, and gradually add movement as they become stronger. Training intensity should be adjusted to accommodate people of different fitness levels.

A teacher should establish a training plan according to the specific fitness of each student, so that the student can achieve the goals set out. One example of a training routine is to do two repetitions of each of five lines of techniques with a five to seven minute rest between each. Do not sit down during the rests. This workout will take one-half to one hour. After a period of training the density and intensity can be increased. For example, do three repetitions of each form or decrease the rest period between forms. You can also simultaneously increase the range of movement of the positions (lower stances, longer steps) to increase the training load. Under normal circumstances you must progressively increase the training load according to a set plan. If you feel temporary changes or physical maladjustment, adjust the plan to fit the situation. The player should be in good spirits after each training session.

While training you must be sure to warm up and cool down properly, and wear light and comfortable clothing and shoes.

4) Breathe naturally

Four of the worst mistakes in Xingyi are to stick out the chest, suck in the stomach, hold the breath, and tense up. When training, be sure to relax the chest, keep the abdomen solid and breathe naturally. Never hold the breath. In order to do this, the body techniques must be expansive and the footwork and hand techniques must be coordinated and smooth. If the external actions are smooth then so will be the internal. The player just needs to remember to keep movement in accordance with the requirements and in line with his or her body's abilities. Breathe out when the movement calls for breathing out and breathe in when the movement calls for breathing in. In this way air and energy can reach to all parts of the body without blockage and internal workings can synchronize with external movement.

Some players make the sound heng [hēng 哼] when striking down or doing an explosive move, in order to show that the power was complete, the breath helped the power, and the breath and force were one. This is not at odds with breathing naturally, because it is an exhalation, which comes from the movement, not something added on for effect. Classical texts of Xingyi also used the term "thunder sound [léi shēng 雷声]." Actually, when training, even without paying attention you always inhale when gathering in force and exhale when expending force; inhale when turning and exhale when setting in position;

inhale when bringing a hand in and exhale when punching or striking out. This helps concentrate your force and keep the moves tied together. It unites breath with force. It is entirely in accordance with your body's natural physiological needs and those of the moves. Beginners, however, should not be forced to try to make a sound when hitting because this might throw off their coordination. You also should not consciously control your breathing and force it to coordinate exactly with the moves. When learning you should try to breathe naturally and keep movement smooth.

CHAPTER TWO

BASIC TECHNIQUES

2.1 Ready Stance[24] ("three bodies posture")

sāntǐshì 　　　　三体式

Standing in *santishi* is the most important basic practice because it sets the body into the posture of Xingyi. All other Xingyi techniques come out of this posture. There are many variations in styles of Xingyi, but all have the same guidelines for *santishi*. There is a saying that the ten thousand techniques all come out of the *santishi*.

  The specifics are as follows: Stand with the body straight, arms hanging naturally, head held up, heels together with the feet at a ninety degree angle to each other. Look straight ahead (figure 1).

Main points: Concentrate. Hold the head up naturally. Keep your face natural with the mouth closed and the tip of the tongue on the palate. Do not puff up the chest or hunch the back. Keep the entire body relaxed.

  Without moving the right foot, pivot the left foot on the heel forty-five degrees right (to the centre line), while turning the body partially to the right; keep the arms hanging by the sides and keep looking forward (figure 2).

Main points: Turn the body at the same time as the left foot turns. Don't swing the body or drop a shoulder.

  Slowly bend the legs and sit into a half-squat with the weight a bit more on the right leg. Lift the left forearm up in front of the body to place the left hand in front of your chest (a bit to the left) with the palm down and the

---

[24] Translator's note: I call this *santishi* throughout the book, rather than translating it, as it occurs so often and has no adequate translation. Just the stance, with different arm position, I call *santi* stance, and the whole posture I call *santishi*.

fingers forward. Lift the right forearm up so that the right hand is on top of the left (the right index finger on top of the left middle finger). The elbows are flexed. Keep looking straight ahead (figure 3).

Main points: Do not lean forward or back. Keep the shoulders settled down and the elbows tucked in by the ribs. Keep the body steady with the head up, the hip joint rolled,[25] the knees flexed and the lumbar area flat.

Without changing the direction your body faces, place the left foot forward, the heel in line with the right heel, about two foot lengths apart, the legs bent with the weight a bit more on the right leg. Extend the left hand forward at chest height with the elbow slightly flexed (palm down, fingers open, and palm concave). Bring the right hand down in front of the abdomen, the proximal end of the thumb against the navel, and the wrist cocked. Look at the index finger of the left hand (figure 4).

Main points: Keep the upper body upright, leaning neither forward nor backward, but turned at forty-five degrees to the line of vision. Hold the head up with the neck straight. Keep the face natural, the teeth lightly clenched, and the jaw pulled in.

Keep the shoulders settled down, with the shoulder bowl pulled back. Keep the elbow of the left arm (front hand) down and flexed – the left hand index finger must be pulled up [tiǎo jìn 挑劲], and the thumb opened out to the side, so that the tiger's mouth forms a semi-circle with the concave palm. The right forearm should stick to the right side of your abdomen, with the fingers open and the wrist cocked.

---

[25] Translator's note: Close the front of the hip joint slightly by opening within the hip joint as if trying to roll the knees in, but without letting the knees move. The opening roll of the hip joint pulls the knees naturally into a strong position – do not pull them in beyond this.

The chest is contained, not tense, the ribs open, the chest calm and empty, the abdomen naturally full [settled energy – chén qì 沉气]. The lumbar area flat, the buttocks tucked in, and the anal sphincter pulled in.

The hip joints are pulled in; the knees pulled slightly in – the forward knee bent so that it does not pass the heel, and the buttocks in line with the back foot. The toes grip the ground. The weight is mostly on the right leg, The front leg is thus more empty than solid, and takes little of the weight.

Breathe naturally. Concentrate. Keep the strength steady.

The above guidelines must be strictly adhered to. None can be ignored. *Santishi* will help develop internal strength and regulate your breathing. Even more important is that it manifests the basic requirements and characteristics of Xingyi. The beginning student can use it to master the training requirements and set up a good base for further learning. Even those with some background should continue to stand in *santishi*, to further master the requirements of Xingyi and solidify their basics.

The *santishi* described above is 'sideways single weighted.' In addition to this there are 'sideways double weighted' (the weight falls evenly on both legs), and 'straight single weighted' (the upper body faces straight ahead) among other methods.[26] In spite of the differences in angle and weighting, the requirements for the body segments are the same.

Other branches of Xingyiquan also have other ways of sitting into the ready stance described above, such as:

1) Stand straight up; bend the knees; screw out the right hand (keeping the left at the waist); step out with the left foot, then strike out [pī 劈] the left hand into the *santi* stance.

2) Stand straight; lift [tuō 托] the hands out to the side then lower them in fists in front of your abdomen while bending the knees; then screw out the right fist, step out with the left foot and strike [pī 劈] out the left hand into *santishi*.

---

[26] Translator's note: A full empty stance trains leg strength, a stance with a weight ratio of seventy:thirty combines agility with stability, and a sixty:forty stance gives a more forward attacking attitude.

2.2 THE FIVE ELEMENTAL PHASES[27]   wǔ xíng   五行

The five most basic techniques of Xingyi are split [pī 劈], drive [bēng 崩], drill [zuān 钻], cannon [pào 炮], and wring [héng 横]. These moves are simple and clean, and are practised to both sides. These techniques used to be named after the five elemental phases – metal [jīn 金], wood [mù 木], water [shuǐ 水], fire [huǒ 火], and earth [tǔ 土] – and so altogether were called the five elements boxing [wǔ xíng quán 五行拳]. Other techniques are based on these five, so the beginning student must focus training on them to build a good foundation.

1. SPLIT, CHOP   pī quán   劈拳

Split practice involves alternating right and left split and right and left steps. Classic texts refer to it as "the head of the five elements, like an ax, with the intent of chopping". Split, along with drive, drill, cannon and wring, together make up the five-element form, that is, the foundation form of Xingyi. Split is the most basic skill.[28]

1.1   Ready stance   yù bèi shì   预备式

The ready stance is *santishi* (figure 1-5).

Get into *santishi* in the same way as described above (see figures 1, 2, 3, 4).

1.2   Split, left entry

   pī quán zuǒ qǐ shì   劈拳左起式

Starting from *santishi*, lower the left hand while forming a fist, make a fist with the right hand, and

---

[27] Translator's note: The five forces of nature, dynamics of matter, natural properties, principles, fundamental processes. There is no good quick translation for *xing*. "Element" is often used, but this brings to mind the Western element chart, so I prefer not to use it. Please note that this *xing* 行 is a different character than the *xing* 形 of *xingyi*.

[28] Author's note: The following description of the split technique is the 'moving stance method' [huóbù 活步] which uses the half-step in. Beginners should train the 'fixed step method' – keep the same requirements as described below, but do not bring the back foot in. This stance will be larger, like the *santishi*. To develop good basics, first train the fixed step split, then the moving step. Also, in some areas of China the move is done entirely with closed fists, but the other details are similar.

turn the fists over (fist hearts face up) at either side of your navel, the forearms tight against the sides. Look ahead (figure 1-6).

Step the left foot forward about a foot-length, with the foot hooked out about forty-five degrees and the knee flexed, then shift the weight to the left leg – extend the right leg without moving the right foot, so that the leg is straight without locking. Outwardly rotate the left forearm and bring the left fist up past the chest then drill out to the front from under the jaw, following an arcing line (fist heart obliquely up and slightly out, the little finger on top and the elbow dropped down). The extended left arm maintains a bend, and the fist is at nose height. The right fist does not move. Look at the left hand (figure 1-7).

Main points: The angle of the body does not change. Clench the fists tightly. Do not tense the chest or hold the breath. Lower the left hand in a circular path, pulling it back and down, not just straight back. Keep the shoulders down. Keep the arms in tight to the ribs. Turn the fists over simultaneously at the waist.

The left fist must extend at the same time as you step forward. The angle of the body does not change when drilling and stepping forward – do not bring the back shoulder forward to bring the shoulders even. Bring the left fist up close by the chest then drill out strongly in front of the mouth. Keep the lumbar area flat and the head up.

1.3   Split, right landing   pī quán yòu luò shì   劈拳右落式

Step the right foot strongly forward (do not lift it too high) with the knee slightly flexed, then step the left foot in, weight still on the left leg. Outwardly rotate the right forearm and bring the fist past the chest then drill out in front of the mouth, inwardly rotating the arm with open palm, and split to the front (palm forward and down, elbow slightly flexed). Turn the left fist over to the inside – open the palm and lower it in front of the abdomen, the thumb tightly on the navel (the same as the left *santishi*, but in a slightly shorter stance). Look at your right index finger (figure 1-8).

Main points: The right split is coordinated with the right foot landing. Do not lift the body when stepping – keep steady. All requirements are the same as the *santishi* except that the stance is slightly shorter.

1.4   Split, right entry   pī quán yòu qǐshì   劈拳右起式

Lower the right hand and form a fist (close it while lowering). Form a fist with the left hand at the same time, and turn the fist hearts to face up at either side of your navel with the forearms tightly held in to the sides. Look forward (figure 1-9).

Step the right foot forward with the foot hooked out about forty-five degrees and knee slightly flexed. Without moving the left foot, push the left leg back so that it is straight without locking, and shift the weight to the right leg. Bring the right fist up the chest then drill out from under the jaw (fist heart angled up) then turn it over and out (little finger side turns up while the elbow keeps down). The right arm is not quite fully extended and the right fist is at nose height. Do not move the left hand. Look at the right fist (figure 1-10).

1.5   Split, left landing   pī quán zuǒ luò shì   劈拳左落式

The move is the same as that described for figure 1-8, but transposes right and left (figure 1-11).

You may continue to practise going forward by going on to the right landing stance – stepping the right foot forward and performing split with the right hand. In this way the left and right can be practised over and over.

FIVE ELEMENTAL PHASES   47

1.6   Split turn   pī quán huí shēn   劈拳回身

Finish in a left split before turning. To turn, lower the left hand and form a fist. Change the right hand to a fist as well. Turn the two fists up at either side of the abdomen. Next turn the left foot in by pivoting on the heel to turn the body around one-eighty degrees to the right. Turn the right foot on the toes to keep it pointing straight ahead. The heel is off the ground in a right empty stance. Look ahead (figure 1-12).

Main points: When turning, make sure that the body doesn't bob up and down or sway around. Coordinate the turning of the left foot with the lowering of the hand and the turning of the body. Keep a level gaze – do not look down. Keep the lumbar area flat and the head up.

1.7   Split, right entry   pī quán yòu qǐ shì   劈拳右起式

Step the right foot forward, turning the foot out with the knee slightly flexed. Without moving the left foot, push back with the left leg – straighten it without locking the knee. The weight shifts to the right leg. Bring the right fist up your chest then drill out to the front from under the jaw (fist heart almost up, the little finger turned over on top, elbow down). The right arm is not fully extended and its fist is at nose height. The left fist does not move. Look at the right fist (see figure 1-10, but going in the opposite direction).

Continue left and right until you get back to the starting position in a *left split*, then turn again as described in move 1.6 *split turn*. Perform all the moves as described above.

1.8   Split, closing stance   pī quán shōu shì   劈拳收式

When you get back to the starting position, perform split turn and step the right foot forward to drill the right hand. Then step the left foot forward and split with the left hand. Bring the right foot in a half-step into split left landing (figures 1-13, 1-14, 1-15).

Bring the left foot in beside the right and bring the left arm back to the chest. Slowly lower the arms to the sides of your body and stand up (your body still oblique to the front). Bring the breath down to the *dantian* and relax the shoulders. Look straight ahead (figure 1-16).

2.   DRIVE   bēng quán   崩拳

Drive is a method whereby the fists drive out alternately, directly to the front. The punch must be fast and powerful. It uses the power of the whole body coordinated exactly with the footwork. The footwork consists entirely of the right foot driving powerfully into the ground to charge the left foot forward, then stepping a half-step in. When the left foot lands the weight is still on the right leg (in some areas of China they alternate the forward foot, so the front foot steps forward and the back leg advances, then the other foot steps in). The knees remain flexed and the body keeps down. Drive is a powerful technique, ancient records say "the driving punch is like an arrow – it shoots into its target."

2.1   Ready stance   yù bèi shì   预备式

The same as *santishi* (figure 2-1).

FIVE ELEMENTAL PHASES   49

2.2   Right drive   yòu bēng quán   右崩拳

Starting from *santishi*, keep the angle of the body the same while forming fists in a spiral shape. The left fist eye is on top, the elbow slightly bent. Turn the right fist over (bring the fist heart up) and keep the right elbow and forearm sticking tightly to the right side. Look at the left fist (figure 2-2).

Stride the left foot out to the front, then follow in with the right foot, the weight staying on the right leg, heels in line about twenty to thirty centimetres apart. When stepping the left foot forward, drive the right fist out towards the left arm (fist eye on top, fist surface slightly inclined to the front), and bring the left fist in to the left side under the left ribs (fist eye on top). The right fist is extended in front and the left leg is in front. Look at the right fist (figure 2-3).

Main points: After forming a fist with the left hand, the elbow still points down and the shoulder is held down. The head stays straight. Although the fist is held tightly, the chest should not be tensed up, nor should the breath be held – breathe naturally.

When stepping the left foot forward, do not lift it too high. When landing it, land on the heel, but do not stamp the ground. Push hard with the right leg – take a long step but do not allow the body to rise. When punching with the right hand, extend the right shoulder forward and pull the left hip in, keeping the upper body obliquely facing the left, with the right elbow down. Keep the body steady, the head up, and the lumbar area flat. Coordinate the right punch with the landing of the left foot.

2.3   Left drive   zuǒ bēng quán   左崩拳

Continue to drive the left foot forward and bring the right foot in (the same footwork as the right drive). Drive the left fist out past the right arm (fist heart facing right) and pull the right fist into to the right side (fist heart up). The left fist and left leg are now forward. Look at the left fist (figure 2-4).

50 CHAPTER TWO: BASIC TECHNIQUES

Main points: The body faces diagonally to the right during the left drive. Do not extend the left shoulder forward too much. Keep the hips pulled in. The other body segments have the same requirements as the right drive.

2-4

2.4 Right drive   yòu bēng quán   右崩拳

Repeat move 2.2, *right drive* (figure 2-5).

2.5 Left drive   zuǒ bēng quán   左崩拳

Repeat move 2.3, *left drive* (figure 2-6).

The *right drive* and *left drive* can be repeated to the front as many times as desired, according to the space available. Complete a *right drive* to prepare for the *drive turn*.

2.6 Drive turn   bēng quán huí shēn   崩拳回身

Complete a *right drive* (figure 2-7).

Bring the right hand in to the right side (fist heart up) but do not move the left hand. Turn the left foot in (about ninety degrees). Turn on the toes of the right foot to keep it pointing forward as the body turns. Look forward (figure 2-8).

FIVE ELEMENTAL PHASES 51

Bring the right fist up across the chest then drill out from the mouth with the arm slightly bent (fist heart obliquely up and slightly out, little finger twisted up). Raise the right knee with the toes hooked up to the right. Bend the weight-bearing left leg. Look at the right fist (figure 2-9).

Kick out strongly with the right foot, landing with the foot transverse to the line of action. Step the left foot a half-step in, heel off the ground. The left knee is tucked in behind the right knee in a cross-sit stance. As the left foot lands, bring the left fist up the chest then along the right arm, open it and split down (palm facing the lower front). Lower the right fist in front of the abdomen and open it (thumb against the navel, palm forward). Look at the left index finger (figure 2-10).

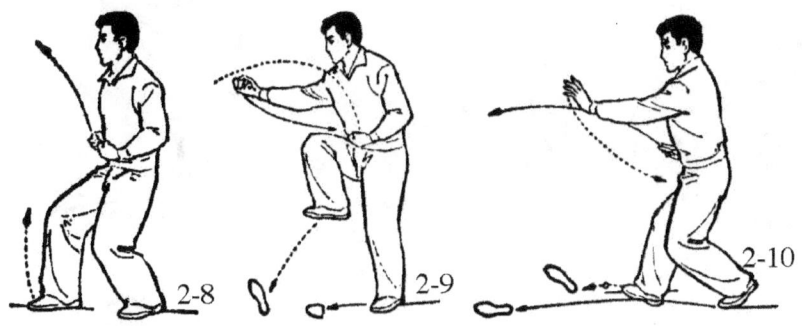

Main points: Coordinate the turning of the left foot, the pulling in of the right hand, and the turning of the body. Do not stop for too long after this action. Do not lower the head or lean when turning.

Coordinate the upward drill of the right hand with the lifting of the right knee.

Drive the right foot out to stamp down hard. Cross the legs tightly together. Coordinate the left split with the right foot landing.

2.7 Right drive yòu bēng quán   右崩拳

Form fists. Step the right foot forward then push off to drive the left foot forward, then bring the right foot in, the feet about twenty to thirty centimetres apart. Drive the right fist straight out and pull the left fist in to the left side. This is the same as the previous right drive (figure 2-11).

Continue to alternate right and left drive until arriving back at the original starting place. The number of repetitions is limited only by the ability of the practitioner. Once back to the start (in a right drive) perform drive turn again, then the drive closing stance.

2.8   Drive closing stance   bēng quán shōu shì   崩拳收式

Turn the body to the right. Lift the right leg, and perform a split the same as the drive turn as described in move 2.6 and *right drive* as in move 2.7 (figures 2-12, 2-13, 2-14, 2-15).

On completion of the *right drive,* take a step back with the right foot without moving the body, then drop the left foot back behind the right, crossing the legs – the left foot in line and the right foot across the line of action, the left heel slightly off the ground in a half-sitting stance. While stepping the left foot back, the left fist hits forward and the right fist pulls in to the right side (fist heart up). Look at the left fist (figures 2-16, 2-17).

Flex the left elbow and lower it past the chest, lowering the hands by the sides. bring the right foot beside the left (still turned forty-five degrees out). Stand up slowly, keeping the body turned obliquely to the right. Keep the shoulders down. Look straight ahead (figure 2-18).

FIVE ELEMENTAL PHASES   53

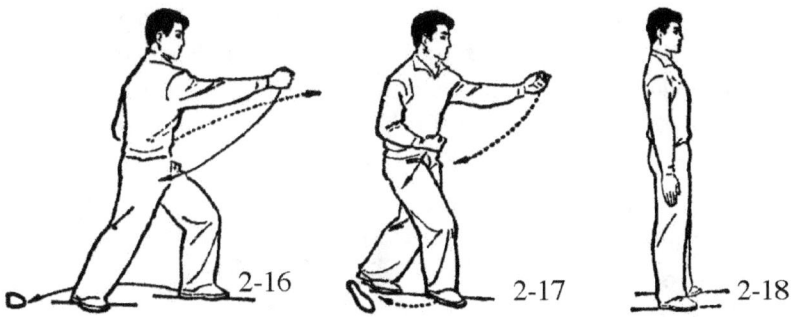

Main points: When stepping the right foot back, do not move the fists or turn the right shoulder. When stepping the left foot back, first stamp the ground with the heel, then lift the heel slightly – keep the knees tightly together in the cross-sit stance (the left knee in back of the right). Coordinate the left stamp with the left punch.

3.   DRILL   zuān quán   钻拳

The footwork of the drill is the same as that of the split. The hand technique involves alternately drilling the fists out. Drill is a fierce technique – the classics say, "drill is like an electric shock."

3.1   Ready stance   yù bèi shì   预备式

The same as *santishi* (figure 3-1)

3.2   Right drill   yòu zuān quán   右钻拳

Starting from *santishi*, form a fist with the left hand and lower it into the abdomen, turning it over (fist heart up). Bring it up by the chest and drill out from the mouth (forearm outwardly rotated, fist twisted out). Form a fist with the right hand, turning the fist heart up, and hold it tightly by the right side. While drilling with the left hand, step the left foot forward, the foot hooked out and the knee flexed. Look at the little finger of the left hand (figure 3-2).

54   CHAPTER TWO: BASIC TECHNIQUES

Take a large step forward with the right foot, then a half-step in with the left, sitting on the left leg. Bring the right hand up past the chest and drill out in front of the mouth, to nose height. Outwardly rotate the left fist (turn the wrist in) and pull in back to the abdomen (fist heart down, thumb against the navel). Look at the little finger of the right fist (figure 3-3).

Main points: Coordinate the left step with the left drill, and the right step with the right drill, such that the hands arrive as the feet stop. Take large steps, land on the heel, and do not lift the feet too high. The power of the drill is concentrated on the front of the fist so the front of the fist must be lined up with the toes and the nose. The fist, toes and nose form a triangle. The drilling fist is twisted out, but the pressing-down fist is twisted in. Keep the elbows down, the shoulders down, and the stance steady.

3.3   Left drill   zuǒ zuān quán   左钻拳

Step the right foot forward with the foot hooked out. Take a large step forward with the left foot, then step the right foot in with the weight still on the right leg. Turn the left fist over and bring it up the chest to drill out from the mouth along the right fist (fist heart up at nose height). Inwardly rotate the right fist (tuck in the wrist: kòu 扣) and bring it back to the abdomen (fist heart down, thumb against the navel). Look at the little finger of the left fist (figures 3-4, 3-5).

FIVE ELEMENTAL PHASES 55

Main points: Coordinate the right step with the right drill, and the left step with the left drill, so that the hands arrive with the feet. Take a large step, landing on the heel, but do not lift the feet too high. The power of the drill is concentrated on the front of the fist. The front of the fist must be lined up with the toes and the nose, so that the fist, toes and nose form a triangle. The drilling fist is twisted out, the pressing-down fist is twisted in. Keep the elbows down, the shoulders down, and the stance steady.

This alternation of left drill and right drill can be continued as many times as desired.

3.4   Drill turn   zuān quán huí shēn   钻拳回身

After drilling with the left fist (the left fist and foot are in front as in figure 3.5), hook the left foot in – pivot on the heel to turn the body around to the right one-eighty degrees (the same as the split turn). The arms stay in the same position relative to the body while turning and the right foot shifts on the ball to keep it straight. Next step the right foot forward, hooked out, and bring the right fist up past the chest to drill out above the left fist (fist heart up). Inwardly rotate the left fist (wrist tucked in) and bring it in to the abdomen (fist heart down, thumb against the navel). Look at the little finger of the right fist (figures 3-6, 3-7).

Main points: When turning, look at the left hand and turn the arms with the body. Keep the power solid. Turn the right foot once the body has turned ninety degrees. Keep the head up and the lumbar area flat.

Do not stop in this position – step immediately into the left drill. Continue back to the starting place. The number of repetitions depends on the practitioner and the space available.

CHAPTER TWO: BASIC TECHNIQUES

3.5 Drill closing stance   zuān quán shōu shì   钻拳收式

On returning to the starting place, perform another turn, then stop in the left drill stance. Lower the left arm past the chest to bring the hands to the sides. Bring the left foot in to the right and stand up. Keep the upper body still turned slightly to the right, drop the shoulders. Breathe steadily. Look ahead (figure 3-8).

4. CANNON   pào quán   炮拳

Cannon punch footwork follows a wavelike line, advancing diagonally to the right and left. The footwork introduces lift as well as the step forward, advance, and step in. Hand techniques use fists – one blocking and one punching – and alternates right and left. Body technique is in the reverse stance diagonal to the line of attack. The technique is exciting and lively.

4.1 Ready stance   yù bèi shì   预备式

The same as *santishi* (figure 4-1).

4.2 Right cannon punch   yòu pào quán   右炮拳

Advance the left foot a half-step directly forward, twisting the left palm outward (palm diagonally facing the upper right, fingers forward). Extend the right palm forward until it faces the left palm, then push with the left foot and advance strongly with the right – the body must not rise – flex the knee in a half-squat, then bring the left foot a step in to stick by the right ankle. As the right foot advances, form fists and pull them in tight to the sides of the abdomen (fist hearts up). Look straight ahead (figures 4-2, 4-3).

Step the left foot to the forward left, then half-step in with the right foot, weight on the right leg. At the same time bring the left fist up past the chest and face then drill up to the front (fist heart first in then turning to face out) to stop by the left temple (the fist heart forward). Punch (drive) the right fist from the waist to the direction to which the left foot has advanced (fist eye up, elbow slightly bent, fist at heart height). Look at the right fist (figure 4-4).

Main points: The left foot and right hand drive forward together. The right foot lands as the hands pull back.

The right fist strikes as the left foot lands. As the left hand comes up, it must move with the body turn – it first follows the chest then drills up past nose height, and finally turns up – it must not block straight up. The block must not be too high, the shoulders must remain level and settled.

4.3   Left cannon punch   zuǒ pào quán   左炮拳

Step the left foot a half-step forward, flexing the knee to half-squat. Step the right foot in to stick by the left ankle. At the same time, lower the left fist and bring the fists in together to either side of the abdomen (fist hearts up). Look to the forward right (figure 4-5).

Step the right foot diagonally to the forward right, then step the left foot in – keep the weight back on the left leg. Drill the right fist up past the chest and face then turn out

58   CHAPTER TWO: BASIC TECHNIQUES

beside the right temple (fist heart forward). Drive the left fist out from the abdomen in the direction that the right foot has stepped, (fist eye up, elbow slightly flexed, fist at heart height). Look at the left fist (figure 4-6).

Main points: The right foot and left hand drive forward together, the left foot lands as the hands pull back.

The left fist strikes as the right foot lands. As the right hand comes up, it must move with the body turn – it first follows the chest then drills up past nose height, then turns up. It must not block directly up horizontally. The block must not be too high and the shoulders must remain level and settled.

4.4   Right cannon punch   yòu pào quán   右炮拳

Step the right foot a half-step forward, flexing the knee in a half-squat, then lift the left foot to hang by the right ankle. Lower the right fist and bring it in with the left to either side of the abdomen (fist hearts up). Look to the forward left (figure 4-7).

Advance the left foot and punch with the right fist (figure 4-8).

Continue to alternate right cannon and left cannon punches as many times as space permits. Finish in a left cannon punch to prepare for the turn.

4.5   Cannon punch turn   pào quán huí shēn   炮拳回身

On arriving at left cannon (figure 4-9), stop for a second, then pivot on the ball of the left foot, turning back around to the left. Bring the right foot around with the body and place it beside the left foot. then lift the left foot to stick by the right ankle. Lower the right fist to the front, bringing it in together with the left fist to either side of the abdomen (fist hearts up). Look to the forward left (figure 4-10).

FIVE ELEMENTAL PHASES 59

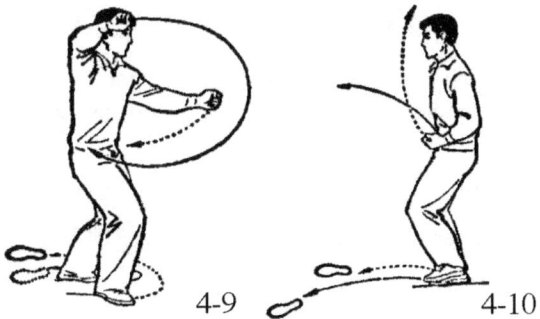

Stop slightly, then drive the left foot out to the forward left. Punching with the right fist in the right cannon stance (figure 4-11).

Step the left foot forward and advance the right foot to punch with the left fist, in the left cannon stance (figures 4-12, 4-13).

Carry on repeating left cannon and right cannon punches until you arrive back at the starting place. The number of repetitions depends on the stamina of the player.

4.6   Cannon punch closing stance   pào quán shōu shì   炮拳收式

Once arriving back at the starting point in a left cannon punch, perform another turn (see description of movement 4.5 for cannon punch turn) into a right cannon punch. Stop slightly, then lower the hands down in front of the chest to the sides. Bring the left foot in beside the right to stand up. Look forward (figure 4-14).

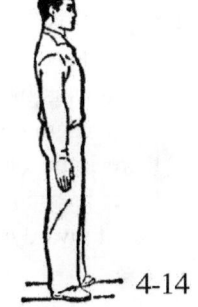

5. WRING   héng quán   横拳

Wring also uses a wave-like curved line to advance obliquely, similar to the cannon punch but it does not use the lift step after the advance or the turn. When the wringing punch drives out it applies strength both to hit forward and to press out to the side. The wring technique is soft but not lax.

5.1   Ready stance   yù bèi shì   预备式

The same as *santishi* (figure 5-1).

5-1

5.2   Right wring   yòu héng quán   右横拳

Form fists with both hands, then advance the left foot out diagonally to the forward left. Step in a half-step with the right foot, keeping the weight on the right leg. At the same time bring the right fist in front of the chest twisting then striking out to the front from under the left elbow (fist heart turning to face up at mouth height). Keep the right elbow slightly bent. As the body turns left, pull the left fist back under the right elbow (fist heart down). Look at the right fist (figure 5-2).

5-2

Main points: When striking forward with the right fist, the fist heart turns over – upward and outward. The left arm twists inward and downward. The force of the arms is like wringing a rope, there is no relaxation at all. The right fist has strength both in the forward punch in the rightward sideways power, but there is no obvious movement to the right. The arms close together, the knees press in, the head is erect, and the arms are settled. The right shoulder goes forward into the movement and the body is stable.

FIVE ELEMENTAL PHASES   61

5.3   Left wring   zuǒ héng quán   左横拳

Step the left foot a half-step forward. Bring the right foot past beside the left (without stopping) and stride out to the forward right. Then step the left foot up towards the right heel, keeping the weight on the left leg. At the same time, with twisting force, bring the left fist under the right elbow and punch forward (turn the fist heart up at mouth height, the elbow bent and the arm forming an arc). As the body turns right, bring the right fist back in under the left elbow (fist heart down). Look at the left fist (figure 5-3).

5-3

Main points: Don't turn the left foot out when stepping forward. When striding the right foot forward take a big step, but follow a curving line which passes by the left foot. When striding forward don't let the body rise, but keep it steady. Other requirements are the same as the right wring.

5.4   Right wring   yòu héng quán   右横拳

Step the right foot a half-step to the front, then stride out to the left front with the left, passing by the right foot. Then bring the right foot a half-step up, keeping the weight on the right leg. At the same time, twist the right fist and bring it in front of the chest then punch forward from under the left elbow (fist heart turning to face up at mouth height). At the same time, pull the left fist back under the right elbow. The action of all other parts of the body is the same as the *right wring* described above in 5.2 (figure 5-4).

5-4

Alternate left wring and right wring as many times as you want, according to the conditions under which you are training. Finish in a left wring to prepare for the turn.

5.5   Wring turn   héng quán huí shēn   横拳回身

After a left wring (right foot and left fist in front), stop for an instant, then turn around to the left by pivoting on the ball of the left foot and stepping the right foot beside the left, with the foot hooked in (figure 5-5).

62   CHAPTER TWO: BASIC TECHNIQUES

    Then step the left foot – pass by the right and stride out to the left front – and bring the right foot in with the weight on the right leg. At the same time as the body turns, punch the right fist out past the chest and under the left elbow, and bring the left fist in under the right elbow (fist heart down). Look at the right fist (figure 5-6).

Main points: Keep the body firm when turning around to the left. Twist the arms – the right twisting outward and the left twisting inward – with opposing forces. Don't take too big a step with the right foot on its first inward-turned step. Keep the body stable and agile, and move quickly.

    Continue as above, back in the opposite direction along the path you that came (figure 5-7).

Practise back and forth as many times as your stamina allows.

5.6   Wring closing stance   héng quán shōu shì   横拳收式

When you get back to your starting place, wait until you are punching with the left fist (left fist and right leg forward), then do a wring turn (figure 5-8) and a right wring (figure 5-9).

    Stop for an instant, then lower the fists in front of the chest until they hang by the side. At the same time, bring the left foot in beside the right and stand up. Look straight ahead (figure 5-10).

2.3 THE TWELVE ANIMALS

The twelve animal models were developed by taking the strong points of each animal's movement. The forms are short and lively and have a well rounded training effect. They help the player both to master the requirements of Xingyi and to improve conditioning. As the twelve animal forms were developed over time they became more enriched and varied. Xingyi initiated the original ideas from imitation, but the key is that the idea is taken. Imitation serves the techniques, and the techniques combine with imitation, but the forms are done with the human body, and the techniques are to be applied to fighting. Don't try to look like the animals – that is getting things backwards.

1. DRAGON   lóng xíng   龙形

The dragon is traditionally a mythical animal that soars in the heavens and swims in the oceans, capable of innumerable transformations. The first animal form, dragon develops the ability of the body to rise and drop, of the hands to extend and contract, and of the legs to jump and switch. It is the most active of the animal forms. It requires that you jump like "a dragon rising to heaven" and land like "a dragon rolling the waves." Someone has described the beautiful rising and falling, extending and flexing of the dragon form: "before one wave has receded the next is born, like a dragon moving through the water, suddenly leaping into the air with a clear and brave cry which startles everyone."

The dragon form rises and drops, following a straight line back and forth. When jumping the feet leap high, and when landing the legs drop into a tight cross-sit stance with the body tight to the ground. The body must be agile and

64 CHAPTER TWO: BASIC TECHNIQUES

compact, with all twists, turns, and jumps kept light. The hands drill as they rise and flip over as they lower; twist and roll without slackness.

1.1   Ready stance   yùbèi shì   预备式

The same as *santishi* (figure 1-1).

1-1

1.2   Dragon drops (right)   lóngxíng yòu luòshì   龙形右落式

Form fists with both hands (the left hand closes as it lowers). Lower the left fist in front of the body then lift it past the abdomen, chest, and chin and finally extend it out to drill (fist heart in at nose height). Extend the right fist out and up along inside the left arm until the fists are close together. Quickly turn the fists (rotate in) and open the palms to press down about twenty to thirty centimetres above the ground. The left palm ends up by the left hip, the arm flexed. While pressing down, turn the body left and the left foot out (pivot on the toes) and push with the right foot (the back foot) so that the heel leaves the ground. Lean forward and drop into a cross-sit stance.[29] The palms face down. Look at the right hand (figure 1-2).

1-2

Main points: Sit and press down quickly and as one movement. Sit on the back heel. Keep the lower back and head in line.

---

[29] Translator's note: Note that this is not the dragon riding stance, but a dragon specific cross-sit stance. The dragon cross-sit stance is elongated – the front foot is more stretched forward than the usual cross-sit.

TWELVE ANIMALS   65

1.3   Dragon rises and drops (left)   lóngxíng zuǒ qǐluòshì   龙形左起落式

Close both hands to fists (the right hand closes as it comes in). Pull the right hand in front of the body, across the abdomen and chest, then, passing close by the jaw, stretch it up and forward in a drill (fist heart in at nose height). Jump up at the same time, with a hard push off the ground with both legs. Switch the leg position in the air so that the right is crossed in front and the left behind. Stretch the left fist up along the inside of the right arm until the fists are close together. Quickly turn the hands and open into palms to drop down in front of the body about twenty to thirty centimetres off the ground (right palm at the right hip, both arms curved). When the palms press down, the body quickly turns right and squats into a cross-sit stance (right foot turned out and left heel off the ground). The palms face down and the body leans forward. Look at the left hand (figures 1-3a and 1-3).

1-3a   1-3

Main points: Stretch the arms up as you jump up, and pull down as you land. The legs should quickly cross over while still in the air.

1.4   Dragon rises and drops (right) lóngxíng yòu qǐluòshì   龙形右起落式

This move is the same as move 1.3, just transpose left and right (figure 1-4).

1-4

1.5   Rise, hop, double split

    qǐshēn tiàobù shuāng pīzhǎng   起身跳步双劈掌

Form fists with both hands (the right hand closes as it rises). Pull the right hand in to in front of the body, past the abdomen and chest, then up and out passing close by the jaw to drill out at nose height (fist heart in). The left fist stays by the waist. Step the left foot forward; stand up; then lift the right knee with the foot dorsi-flexed. Drive from the left foot (hop on one leg) and stamp with the right foot (the foot turned sideways) as you land, to form a half-squatting resting stance with the right leg in front and the left behind. While driving forward, reach the left fist out along the right arm. Once the hands cross, quickly flip them and press down–the left hand will be at shoulder height and the right in front of the abdomen. Look at the index finger of the left hand (figures 1-5, 1-6).

1-5 1-6

Main points: The right fist reaches forward in a drill when the left foot drives forward in a hop. The right foot stamps forward, applying force with the heel as the left hand grabs and applies pressure down.

1.6 Advance right drive jìnbù yòu bēngquán 进步右崩拳

Form fists. Step the right foot forward then stride with the left, pushing a half-step more with right to bring it in. Drive the right fist straight forward. Look at the right fist (figure 1-7).

1-7

1.7 Dragon turns around huíshēn shì 回身式

Bring the right fist back to the waist (fist heart up). Turn the left foot in (to face around in the direction you just came) and pivot on the ball of the right foot to turn the body one-eighty degrees to the right. Stretch the right fist out in the new direction past the jaw, passing it first by the chest. Lift the right knee with the foot dorsi-flexed, keeping the left leg slightly flexed. Look at the right fist (figures 1-8, 1-9).

TWELVE ANIMALS   67

1.8   Dragon lands (left)   lóngxíng zuǒ luòshì   龙形左落式

Land the right foot turned sideways then quickly squat. Pivot the left foot to align with the direction of the stance, the heel raised. Stretch the left fist along the right arm, and as it approaches the right fist, quickly open the hands palms down. Apply pressure down (palms down – left hand in front of the body twenty to forty centimetres off the ground and right hand by the hip). Keep the arms curved. When the palms press down, turn the body right and fully squat in a cross-sit stance. Look at the left hand (figure 1-10).

1.9   Dragon rises and drops (right)

      lóngxíng yòu qǐluòshì   龙形右起落式

Form fists and bring the left fist in to the body. Circle the fist in, then up along the chest and out from under the jaw to drill out at nose height. Jump up as you do this, pushing hard off the ground and switching the leg position in the air (left in front, right behind). Bring the right fist along the left arm – as it approaches the left fist turn both over and pressure down with the palms (both palms down). Pull the left hand back to the hip and the right down in front of the body about twenty to forty centimetres off the ground. Turn the body left and drop into a full dragon

cross-sit stance. Look at the right hand (figures 1-11, 1-12).

1.10   Rise, hop, double split

    qǐshēn tiàobù shuāng pīzhǎng   起身跳步双劈掌

This move is the same as move 1.5, except it is done in the opposite direction.

1.11   Advance right drive   jìnbù yòu bēngquán   进步右崩拳

This move is the same as move 1.6, in the opposite direction.

1.12   Dragon turns around   huíshēn shì   回身式

This move is the same as move 1.7, in the opposite direction.

1.13   Dragon drops (left)   lóngxíng zuǒ luòshì   龙形左落式

This move is the same as move 1.8, in the opposite direction.

1.14   Dragon rises and drops (right)   lóngxíng yòu qǐluòshì   龙形右起落式

This move is the same as move 1.9, in the opposite direction.

Continue on doing the dragon – do as many lines of repetition as your conditioning allows.

1.15   Dragon closing   shōushì   收式

On arrival at the starting point in left dragon drops, stand up, align the left foot with the direction of movement and turn out the right foot. Thread the left hand out under the right and bring the right back to the abdomen. This gets you back into *santishi*. Look at the left hand. Bring in the left foot and hand to finish. Stand up.

2.   TIGER   hǔ xíng   虎形

The actions of the tiger form imitate the fierce nature of the tiger and its ability to traverse mountains, leap gorges and pounce on its prey. The main action drives strongly forward with the legs while the body keeps steady. This is quite different from the dragon and monkey forms, which involve leaping and stretching the body. The tiger footwork is the same as that of cannon punch – it drives quickly and covers a good distance, lands steadily with no extra movement, and never lifts the feet very high. Each step drives diagonally forward, so that the whole form describes a wave pattern.

TWELVE ANIMALS 69

The arms of the tiger form work together. They 'pounce' with a forward and down force which comes from the power of the body. The elbows stick close to the ribs. The fists stick to the chest as they drill up, then rotate out and quickly turn into a pounce which combines the force of splitting with pressure down. The move resembles split but has much more power exerted down. This is specifically called a 'tiger pounce' [pū 扑] in martial arts terminology. This form trains the arms, chest and upper back, in order to develop the same strength and skill as when a tiger pounces on and grips its prey.

2.1   Ready stance   yùbèi shì   预备式

The same as *santishi* (figure 2-1).

2.2   Tiger form (left)   hǔxíng zuǒ shì   虎形左式

Step a half-step forward with the left foot. Reach forward with both hands, fingers reaching forward (palms facing each other). Look at the front hand (figure 2-2).

Stride the right foot forward then pull the left foot in so that it sits off the ground, dorsi-flexed, just at the right ankle. With the legs slightly bent, this forms a right one-legged stance. Bring the hands in to the waist, grabbing into fists (fist hearts face up). Look straight ahead (figure 2-3).

Stride the left foot out diagonally to the forward left, following with the right to end up in a left empty stance (like *santishi* – left foot in front and right foot about twenty to forty centimetres behind with more weight on it). Bring the fists up the chest (fist hearts in) then forcefully reach out from the mouth – inwardly turn and pounce with the palms to sternum height. The palms face forward (tiger mouths facing each other) with a downward pressure. Look at the left index finger (figure 2-4).

CHAPTER TWO: BASIC TECHNIQUES

Main points: The left foot steps forward as the right hand stretches out. When the left foot lands, don't hesitate but immediately and quickly drive forward, keeping the body steady.

The right foot steps forward exactly at the same time as the hands pull in – there must be no time lag. The elbows must pull in tight to the ribs – don't leave them sticking out. The left foot sticks tightly to the right ankle – don't touch it down. Keep the body steady, the lumbar area flat and the head straight.

The hands pounce as the left foot advances. Before the pounce, the fists spiral up as far as the mouth, stay close to the chest, then finally strike out quickly. This forms a circular motion; the hands must not push directly out. Keep the shoulders settled down, the elbows set in, the lumbar area flat, the neck upright, and the knees slightly rolled in.

2.3   Tiger form (right)   hǔxíng yòu shì   虎形右式

Step the left foot forward then pull the right foot in by the left ankle, keeping the legs tight together. Keep both legs bent with the right foot held off the ground by dorsi-flexure, to form a left one-legged stance. Open the hands and bring them in to the waist, fist hearts up, forearms stuck close to the waist. Look to the forward right (figure 2-5).

Stride the right foot forward to the right and follow in with the left foot a half-step so that the left foot ends up with the weight more on it (a right empty stance with the feet twenty to forty centimetres apart). Bring the fists up the chest (fist eyes in). As the fists arrive at the mouth, forcefully turn over the palms and pounce out to sternum height in front of the body (palms face forward and tiger mouths face each other). Look at the index finger of the left hand (figure 2-6).

TWELVE ANIMALS   71

2-5   2-6

Main points: There can be no time lag between the body segments when the left foot first steps forward and the hands pull back. When the hands pull in, the forearms must cling to the ribs, with no space between them and the body. The right foot must stick to the left ankle – don't touch down with the ball of the foot. The body must stay stable with the lumbar area flat and the head held up.

The right foot hits at the same time as the hands pounce. Before the hands pounce they must slide up the chest in a drill, and pounce out only after arriving at the mouth. In this way they follow a circle – they don't push straight out. Once the hands have pounced, check that the shoulders are settled, elbows set down, lumbar area flat, neck upright, and knees have an inward force.

2.4   Tiger form (left)   hǔxíng zuǒ shì   虎形左式

Step the right foot a half-step forward. Bring the left foot in to stick to the right ankle, foot off the ground and dorsi-flexed. Keep in a half squat, in a one-legged stance. Bring in the hands, forming fists by the waist (fist hearts up) with the forearms stuck to the sides. Look to the forward left (figure 2-7).

The rest is the same as the first *tiger form* (left) described above in move 2.2 (figure 2-8).

2-7   2-8

2.5 Tiger form (right)   hǔxíng yòu shì   虎形右式

The moves and main points are the same as the first *right tiger form* explained above in move 2.3 (figures 2-9, 2-10).

2.6 Tiger turns around   huíshēn shì   回身式

Once you have finished the right tiger form, pivot on the ball of the left foot to turn around one-eighty degrees to the left. Bring the hands in to the waist, forming fists (fist hearts up). As you turn, step the right foot around with the foot hooked in beside the left (about twenty to thirty centimetres). Then lift the left foot (ankle dorsi-flexed) beside the right ankle, holding the legs tightly together. Look to the left front (figure 2-11).

Main points: Turn quickly and step the right foot fairly close to the left. Lift the left foot as soon as the right foot lands. Keep the body steady – make sure you don't bob up and down. Keep the lumbar area flat, the head straight, and the forearms stuck to the sides of the waist.

2.7 Tiger form (left)   hǔxíng zuǒ shì   虎形左式

The actions and main points are the same as for *tiger form* (left) *(*move 2.4), but travel in the opposite direction (figure 2-12).

2.8   Tiger form (right)   hǔxíng yòu shì   虎形右式

The actions and main points are the same as the *tiger form* (right) described above (move 2.3), but going in the other direction. (See figures 2-5, 2-6).

The number of repetitions you do depends on your stamina and the amount of space you have. Finish the last tiger form with the right foot forward (a *right tiger form*) in order for tiger turns around to connect smoothly to the closing stance.

2.9   Tiger closing stance   shōushì   收式

On arriving at your starting place, do another *tiger turns around* so that you are in the *left tiger form* (facing the same way as the ready stance). Then bring the left foot in beside the right, lower the hands by the body, and stand up.

3. MONKEY   hóu xíng   猴形

The monkey form is one of the more active, agile forms of the twelve animals. The moves develop lightness and agility through dodging and jumping actions similar to monkeys. These moves include turning to either side, advancing and retreating, jumping distances and closing in tight. Quite a high degree of activity is involved. You have to train with speed and force while maintaining stability. You want to be agile and highly mobile, but at the same time make sure to finish and connect the moves. Make sure that you don't float lightly without power, sway, or lean.

In training this form you cross over your path. Some styles of Xingyi have the monkey go to four angles, some go to six. The moves are repeated to left and right in different directions and at different angles. To make it a bit easier, the description starts out with you facing east with your back to the west, and the moves are divided into six sections which travel in set directions (see the route chart). This is just to make it easier to learn. Once you are comfortable with the moves you can go in any direction you want.

CHAPTER TWO: BASIC TECHNIQUES

ROUTE OF THE MONKEY FORM

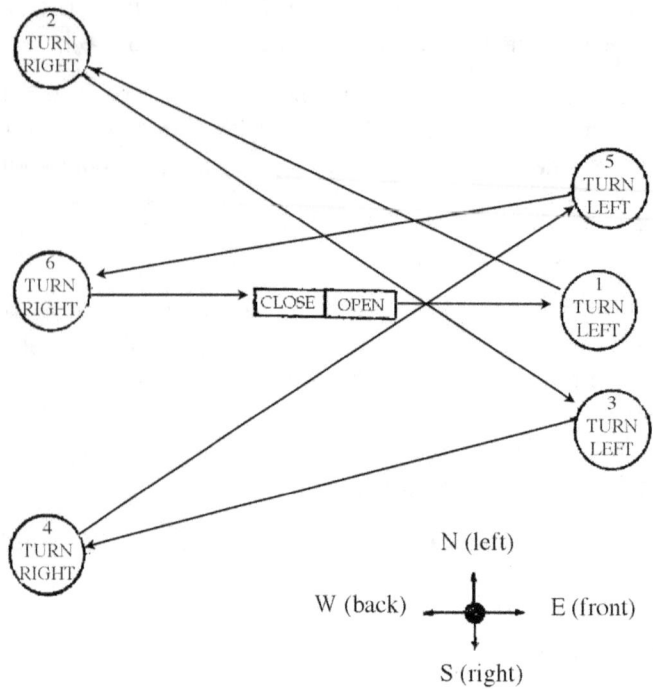

Monkey Form, Section One

3.1   Ready stance   yùbèi shì   预备式

The same as *santishi* (figure 3-1).

3-1

3.2   Left turn, monkey scratches its mark

zuǒ zhuǎnshēn yuánhóu guàyìn shì   右转身猿猴挂印式

Turn quickly to the right. Bring the left hand down and in in front of the chest (palm turning up). As the hand comes in, quickly turn the body left and bring the left foot in to stop slightly inside the right foot. Stride the left foot out to the front (hooked out). Rotate the left hand inward, flipping it to turn out. Push outward horizontally at shoulder height (little finger on top, palm centre to the outside). Look at the left hand (figure 3-2).

Shift to the left leg. Continue the turn to the left, and hook in the right foot towards the left, forming a character eight stance 八 (figure 3-3). Then take a big step back with the left foot in the same direction that the right foot points (south-east). Stretch the right palm out along the back of the left palm at eye height, and bring the left hand back to the abdomen (both palms down). Weight is on the right leg and eyes are on the right hand (figure 3-4).

Main points: When you bring the left hand in then turn it over and push out, the left foot comes in and hooks out at the same time. The eyes follow the turn of the body.

When turning in the right foot, turn the waist strongly left. The left foot steps back as the right hand stretches forward.

3.3 Monkey grabs the leash in its mouth

yuánhóu diāoshéng shì   猿猴叼绳式

Step the right foot quickly a half-step back. Touch the ball of the foot down with the knee bent and the weight on the left leg to form a right empty stance.[30] Bring in the right hand to protect the groin, and

---

[30] Translator's note: The author uses 'empty stance' here in the more common sense of a back weighted stance, which he described in the basics chapter as the 'T stance'. This move may be done with the supporting thigh parallel to the ground to give a more springy and athletic feel and to protect the body more.

place the left hand in front of the right shoulder at shoulder height (palm down).³¹ Look forward (figure 3-5).

Main points: When the right foot steps back, the body shrinks forcibly back with the back flat and the neck straight.

3.4   Monkey scrambles up a pole   yuánhóu págān shì   猿猴爬竿式

Step the right foot forward while stretching the right hand out under the left, to eye height. Pull the left hand back to the abdomen (both palms face down). Look at the right hand (figure 3-6).

Step further forward with the left foot, then hop forward, springing off the left foot as soon as you put the foot down. Lift the right leg³² as you jump and stretch the left hand forward and up, sliding it along the top of the right arm to eye height. Pull the right hand back to the abdomen (both palms face down). Look at the left hand (figure 3-7).

Stride the right foot forcibly forward; approach a half-step with the left foot as well. Stretch the right hand forward, sliding it along the top of the left arm to eye height, and bring the left hand back to the abdomen (both palms face down).³³ Look at the right hand (figure 3-8).

---

³¹ Translator's note: The hands and wrists are soft in *grab the leash* and *scramble up a pole*, with the fingers more rounded than in other animal forms. This makes the hands more like monkey paws and relaxes the arms for a quick, light action.

³² Translator's note: Lift the knee as high as possible to lift the foot (dorsi-flexed) as if to climb up your opponent.

³³ Translator's note: The final stance also may be done with the supporting thigh parallel to the ground. In this case, both hands are in front of the knees, at knee height. This makes it more monkey-like and differentiates it from *santishi*.

Main points: This whole move must be connected. Follow through each move with no hesitation. The hands must shoot out quickly. The jump must be for a good distance without losing stability. Extend the left hand at the exact moment that you push off with the left foot. Land under control. Look at each forward hand as the hands trade places in striking. Taking the opening move to face east, this jumping move will be to the north-west corner.

Monkey Form, Section Two

3.5   Right turn, monkey scratches its mark

yòu zhuǎnshēn yuánhóu guàyìn shì   右转身猿猴挂印式

Turn quickly to the left. Drop the right hand in front of the chest (turning the palm down). Step the right foot back beside the left and stop slightly. Then turn quickly to the right – stride the right foot quickly to the forward right with the foot hooked out. Inwardly rotate the right hand, turning it out to push away horizontally at shoulder height (little finger on top and palm centre out). Look at the right hand (figure 3-9).

Shift onto the right leg. Continue to turn right, turning the left foot and bringing it in by the right, to form a character eight shape 八. Then step the right foot again – follow the direction in which the left heel points (north-west) and take a big step back. Stretch the left hand out along the top of the right to eye height, and bring the right back to the abdomen (both palms down). The weight is on the left leg. Look at the left hand (figures 3-10, 3-11).

Main points: When the right hand comes in then turns to sweep out, it must move at the same time as the right foot comes in then hooks out.

The body and eyes must follow the turning movement. When hooking in the foot turn the waist forcibly to the right.

78   CHAPTER TWO: BASIC TECHNIQUES

3.6   Monkey grabs the leash in its mouth

yuánhóu diāoshéng shì   猿猴叼绳式

Pull the left foot back quickly a half-step. Touch the ball of the foot down with the knee bent and the weight on the right leg to form a left empty stance. Drop the left hand down in front of the groin. Place the right hand just in front of the left shoulder at shoulder height (palm down). Look forward (figure 3-12).

Main points: Contract the body as you pull the left foot back. Keep the lumbar area flat and the neck upright.

3-12

3.7   Monkey scrambles up a pole   yuánhóu págān shì   猿猴爬竿式

Step the left foot a half-step forward. Stretch the left hand out under the right to eye height, and pull the right hand back to the abdomen (both palms down). Look at the left hand (figure 3-13).

Step the right foot forward again, and as it lands spring off immediately to hop forward, lifting the left leg. As you hop, stretch the right hand out and up along the top of the left hand to eye height and pull the left hand back to the abdomen (both palms face down). Look at the right hand (figure 3-14).

Advance strongly with the left foot. Pull the right foot in a half-step. Stretch the left hand out over the right to eye height and pull the right back to the abdomen (both palms face down). Look at the left hand (figure 3-15).

3-13   3-14   3-15

Main points: This whole move is continuous with no hesitation. The hop forward and the hand extensions are fast. Jump for distance but keep control. Jump off the right foot and extend the right hand simultaneously. You must land under control. Follow the whole sequence of palm changeovers with the eyes. The hop moves towards the south-east.

Monkey Form, Section Three

3.8 Left turn, monkey scratches its mark

zuǒ zhuǎnshēn yuánhóu guàyìn shì   左转身猿猴挂印式

Turn sharply to the right, dropping the left hand down and bringing it in to the chest (turn the palm to face up). Bring the left foot in to the right, pause and turn left, striding the left foot quickly forward with the foot hooked out. Turn the left hand out and push outward horizontally at shoulder height (little finger on top and palm out). Look at the left hand. This move is the same as the left turn *monkey scratches its mark* in the first section (move 3.2), but to a different corner (figure 3-16).

The rest of the move is the same as *left turn monkey scratches its mark* in the first section (move 3.2), except that the turn around and step back must be bigger, in order to get into the north-east corner and turn to face south-west (figures 3-17, 3-18).

3.9 Monkey grabs the leash in its mouth

yuánhóu diāoshéng shì   猿猴叼绳式

This move is exactly the same as *monkey grabs the leash in its mouth* in the first section (move 3.3), except that it is done facing the south-west corner.

CHAPTER TWO: BASIC TECHNIQUES

3.10   Monkey scrambles up a pole   yuánhóu págān shì   猿猴爬竿式

This move is exactly the same as *monkey scrambles up a pole* in the first section (move 3.4), except that it hops towards the south-west corner (figure 3-19).

The actions of the fourth, fifth and sixth sections are the same as those of the first, second and third. The fourth section is done towards the north-east. The jump in the fifth section takes you west back to the starting position (see the route chart). Since the moves are all the same they will not be described again. Just remember that when the right hand is forward you will turn to the right, and when the left hand is forward you will turn to the left.

3.11   Monkey closing stance   shōushì   收式

When you have done the fifth section and end up with the right hand in front (at about the same place you started), turn again to the right to do the sixth section as far as *monkey grabs the leash in its mouth*. At this point the right hand is on top and the left foot is forward (figure 3-20).

Extend the left hand out from the chest and drop the right hand to the abdomen, placing the left foot forward into *santishi* (figure 3-21).

Stop here. Bring in the left foot, lower the hands beside the body, and stand up.

TWELVE ANIMALS   81

4. HORSE   mǎ xíng   马形

In Xingyi theory, the talent of the horse lies in the speed of its hooves, so the contents of the horse form emphasize the horse striking forward with its hooves as it gallops. In the horse form the arms twist and rotate as they strike forward in a charging action. The footwork demands a forceful drive off the back leg, a solid stand when set, and total coordination between the legs and arms. This is how to show the strength of the horse. The horse form moves in a straight line, and is of medium athletic intensity.

4.1   Ready stance   yùbèi shì   预备式

The same as *santishi* (figure 4-1).

4.2   Horse form (right)   mǎxíng yòu shì   马形右式

Step the left foot forward while forming fists (turn the left fist over so that the centre faces up). Shift a bit to the left leg (figure 4-2).

Take a long stride forward with the right foot then move the left a half-step in. Keep the weight back on the left leg. While doing this, turn the right fist over (fist centre faces up) and extend it out under the left arm to shoulder height. When the fists approach each other, turn them over (fist centres face down) to bring the left beside the right elbow. The arms form arcs. Look at the right fist (figure 4-3).

Main points: When the right fist strikes forward it must forcefully push forward – with charging power [chōng jìn 冲劲]. The left hand pulls forcibly back to increase the force of the forward strike. When the left leg steps in, be careful not to come in too close to the front foot. The knees should have a closing-in power, the lumbar area should be flat, the head erect, and the shoulders settled.

4.3   Horse form (left)   mǎxíng zuǒ shì   马形左式

Step the right foot forward, shifting weight to the front. Turn over the right fist (fist heart faces up) and pull the left fist back to the abdomen. Then drive the left foot strongly forward, following in quickly with the right, keeping the weight on the right leg. Turn over the left fist (fist heart faces up) and extend it out to the front, sliding under the right fist, to shoulder height. As the fists pass each other, rotate them both inwardly (fist hearts face down). Bring the right fist to the left elbow, keeping both arms slightly bent. Look at the left fist (figures 4-4, 4-5).

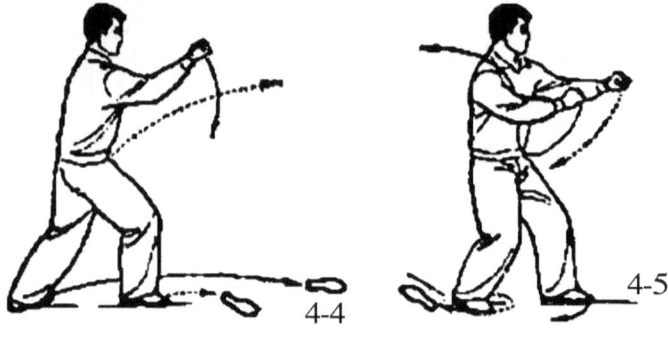

4.4   Horse turns around   huíshēn shì   回身式

Turn around to the right a full one-eighty degrees. Turn the left toes in by pivoting on the left heel, and pivot around on the ball of the right foot. Then step the right foot forward with the foot hooked out. Bring the right fist down to the abdomen, then drill up past the chest and out from under the jaw striking to eye height (fist heart diagonally inward). Bring the left fist back to the abdomen (fist heart down). Look at the right fist (figure 4-6).

TWELVE ANIMALS 83

4.5   Horse form (left)   mǎxíng zuǒ shì   马形左式

This is the same as the *horse form* (left) already described in move 4.3, except in the opposite direction (figure 4-7).

4.6   Horse form (right)   mǎxíng yòu shì   马形右式

This is the same as the *horse form* (right) already described in move 4.2, just heading in the opposite direction (figures 4-8, 4-9).

4.7   Horse Closing Stance   shōushì   收式

When you arrive back at the starting point, finish with the left horse form (left foot forward). Turn around (see description of move 4.4 and figure 4-6, *horse turn around*). After turning do another *left horse form* (see figures 4-4, 4-5), then stop. Bring the hands down to the left leg and stand up.

5.   ALLIGATOR   tuó xíng   鼍形

The alligator is an aquatic animal that has a similar form to a crocodile or lizard. It is over three meters long and its skin is like a suit of armour. In ancient times it was classified with soft-shelled turtles and dragons. It swims with agility and stability. This form exemplifies the total coordination of body technique, footwork, handwork, eyes and spirit. The hands, feet, shoulders and hips must

84   CHAPTER TWO: BASIC TECHNIQUES

have no stiffness at all. The whole body must be lively and full of spring. The turning of the waist or lower back area is especially emphasized to make it the leading centre of the whole body's movement.

When first learning, start slowly – later add speed. Only when you have learned the proper action slowly can you gradually turn right and left without stopping, getting the trunk to lead the limbs in a sideways shaking force. Your goal is a strong shaking motion, light and agile as if swimming. The footwork of the alligator form travels in an 'S' shape.[34]

5.1   Ready stance   yùbèi shì   预备式

The same as *santishi* (figure 5-1).

5.2   Alligator form (left)   tuóxíng zuǒ shì   鼍形左式

Turn right then left, bringing the left hand down, in, then turn it up with rolling force [guǒ jìn 裹劲] in front of the mouth to form a face down palm.[35] Drive the arm sideways to the left with the hand at mouth height and the arm curved (palm down). The left foot comes in with the left arm, then steps out to the forward left. The right foot follows the left, the ball of the foot touches down beside the left foot. Turn the right palm over to face up close to the abdomen. Look at the left hand (figure 5-2).

---

[34] Translator's note: Find some old 'Nature' tv shows – one shows the alligator sliding up from the water to grab a wildebeest. Once the prey is in the alligator's jaws, it whips its whole body back and forth to snap the spine of its prey. The force of this technique is the snap of the body, imagine your arms are the jaws so that you are not tempted to move them separately.

[35] Translator's note: The alligator form may be done with both hands in the unicorn horn palm throughout.

Main points: The left foot and hand move together. When the left hand braces out to the left the outside edge of the palm must have force. The wrist must be kept cocked, and the head straight.

5-2

5.3   Alligator form (right)   tuóxíng yòu shì   鼍形右式

Take a big step to the right front with the right foot, follow in the left, touch the ball of the foot down beside the right. Bring the right hand across the abdomen, up, and right, turning over to form a horizontal palm in front of the mouth. Brace out horizontally at mouth height, with the right arm held curved (palm down). Turn the left palm over and lower it in front of the abdomen (palm up). Look at the right hand (figure 5-3).

5-3

Main points: The right foot lands as the right hand braces out – there can be no time lag between the two. The bracing action needs force put into the outside edge of the hand, the back held flat and the head held straight. The left and right moves are continuous so that the arms swing back and forth without a break.

5.4   Alligator form (left)   tuóxíng zuǒ shì   鼍形左式

This is the same as the first *alligator form* (left) described in move 5.2 (figure 5-4).

5.5   Alligator form (right)   tuóxíng yòu shì   鼍形右式

This is the same as the first *alligator form* (right) described in move 5.3 (figure 5-5).

86 CHAPTER TWO: BASIC TECHNIQUES

5.6   Alligator turns around   huíshēn shì   回身式

After completing a right alligator form, bring the left foot in as if to place it down, but instead quickly turn around to the left and land it to the rear left, sweeping the left arm, palm down, around from the abdomen – up and leftward as you turn. The right hand also braces horizontally out to the right, coming down, in, then up across the chest to mouth height (palm down). As the right hand turns and sweeps around, the left turns over and lowers to the abdomen (palm up). The right foot follows the turn by stepping out to the right, and the left foot comes in to touch down beside it. Look at the right hand (figure 5-6).

Main points: The turn is quick – the left foot must come into the right as soon as it touches down behind. The arms swing continuously, moved by the turning of the body. The turning must be lively, not stiff.

5.7   Alligator form (left)   tuóxíng zuǒ shì   鼍形左式

This is the same as the first *alligator form* (left) described in move 5.2, but in the opposite direction (figure 5-7).

5.8   Alligator form (right)   tuóxíng yòu shì   鼍形右式

This is the same as the first *alligator form* (right) described in move 5.3, but in the opposite direction (figure 5-8).

5.9   Alligator closing form   shōushì   收式

On arriving back at the starting point do another *alligator turns around* to the left (as described in move 5.6) and another *left alligator form*. Then step the right foot back and bring the left hand down in front of the body. Lower both hands to the side. Bring the left foot in by the right and stand up.

6.   CHICKEN   **jī xíng**   鸡形

The chicken form combines actions which imitate the strong points of the chicken. This form has a rich content and a tight structure. It shows the chicken's stability standing on one leg, agility pecking rice, strength shaking the tail, and bravery of attack. It trains agility and coordination through its body work, footwork and handwork – all emphasize advance, retreat and turns. The *golden rooster stands on one leg*, for example, must be fast but stable, calling for solid leg strength. The *golden rooster shakes its tail*, as another example, requires the strength of the entire body to snap strongly yet with elasticity as if shaking off an opponent. The other moves train each body part and many types of skills through the variety of extensions and contractions, rotations, balances, and jumps.[36]

    The training load is quite large, and it gives an overall training effect. In hand techniques alone, there are outward braces, upward strikes, press downs, splits, threading palms, and stabbing palms, etc. The line of movement in the footwork is a straight line.

---

[36] Translator's note: Don't underestimate the chicken just because it is one of the more mundane animals in the list. I spent way too much time playing with them in China, and found them to have an extraordinarily fast, powerful, and accurate attack.

88 CHAPTER TWO: BASIC TECHNIQUES

6.1 Ready stance yùbèi shì 预备式

The same as *santishi*, but with just a bit more of a forward lean (figure 6-1).

6.2 Golden rooster stands on one leg jīnjī dúlì 金鸡独立

Thread the right hand forward from under the left to sternum height. Bring the left hand back to the left side of the waist (palm down). Lower the body and step the left foot forward with the knee bent, bending the right knee and raising the heel. Lean forward slightly. Look at the right hand (figure 6-2).

Stride the right foot forward with the knee quite bent. Bring in the left leg to place the foot (dorsi-flexed) beside the right ankle in a chicken stance.[37] Thread the left hand forward from under the right hand to sternum height and bring the right hand back beside the waist (palm down). Look at the left hand (figure 6-3).

Main points: Don't lean forward too much when stepping forward. Take a long step but keep it steady. When standing on one leg keep the lumbar area flat and the head up. Keep your concentration.

---

[37] Translator's note: The chicken stance throughout this form may be performed with the foot at the shin, halfway between the ankle and knee.

TWELVE ANIMALS   89

6.3   Golden rooster stands on one leg   jīnjī dúlì   金鸡独立

The only difference between this *golden rooster stands on one leg* and the preceding one (move 6.2) is that the preceding one started out by stepping the left leg forward from a *santi* stance, while in this one the left foot steps out from a raised foot position. The rest is the same (figures 6-4, 6-5).

6-4   6-5

6.4   Golden rooster stands on one leg   jīnjī dúlì   金鸡独立

Take a forceful step with the left foot. Follow with a right forward step with the knee well bent. Bring in the left foot as before to place it (dorsi-flexed) by the right ankle in a chicken stance. Look at the left hand (figure 6-6).

6-6

Main points: While driving forward with the legs the body must keep at the same height. Keep the legs tight together to keep well balanced. Step quickly and keep the spacing between steps tight. Keep the lumbar area flat and the shoulders relaxed.

6.5   Golden rooster pecks a grain of rice   jīnjī shímǐ   金鸡食米

Step the left foot forward. Bring in the right foot to just behind the left heel, squatting down a bit. Form a fist with the right hand (fist eye on top) and punch out from under the left hand. Slap the left hand onto the right wrist. Look at the right fist (figure 6-7).

90 CHAPTER TWO: BASIC TECHNIQUES

Main points: The front foot hits at exactly the same time as the punch. The step and punch must be fast. Keep the lumbar area flat and the head straight. The punching arm is not fully extended.

6-7

6.6 Golden rooster shakes its tail   jīnjī dǒulíng   金鸡抖翎

Turn ninety degrees to the right. Step the right foot back and push into the left a bit so that the feet are parallel, in a half-horse stance biased towards the right. Strike forcibly down with the left arm to brace to the lower left, the hand stopping by the left knee (palm down), keeping the arm bent. Brace up with the right arm, the right fist stopping beside the right temple (fist heart out). Look at the left hand (figure 6-8).

Snap the body quickly ninety degrees further to the right, pushing hard from the left leg and keeping the bracing force in the arms. The left arm braces further to end at the left hip. The right arm does not move relative to the body. Look to the lower front (figure 6-9).

6-8   6-9

Main points: The arms brace out in opposite directions at exactly the same time as the left leg pushes back. The turn is done by snapping the lower back area (waist and hips) strongly. This keeps the whole body movement together. Keep the lumbar area flat, the neck upright, and the hips rolled in. The whole move must be done quickly. The right turn comes from the backward drive of the left leg, so make sure the heel doesn't come off the ground.

6.7 Golden rooster blocks up   jīnjī shàng jià   金鸡上架

Step the left foot forward. Keep the knee bent. Bring the right leg in to place the right foot dorsi-flexed beside the left ankle – form a left chicken stance. Open the right fist and slide it down past the chest, moving close to the body, stabbing to the left side (palm out). Thread the left hand up across the chest to the right shoulder (palm in and fingers up). Look forward right (figure 6-10).

Main points: As the hands cross, the arms must stick close to the body and the arms must work together. The little finger sides of the hands are rolled in and the wrists and fingers held straight. The body must remain stable and not rock. The head should be upright and the lumbar area flat. The legs should stick together – the right foot must not touch down.

6.8 Golden rooster heralds the dawn   jīnjī bàoxiǎo   金鸡报晓

Step the right foot forward with the knee bent. Follow in a half-step with the left, keeping the weight on the left leg. Separate the arms up and down, so that the right lifts up to eye height (fingers up), and the left drops down to by the hip (palm down). Do not straighten the arms fully. Look at the right hand's index finger (figure 6-11).

Main points: The hands strike at exactly the same moment as the right foot lands. The upward striking arm especially must have force. Keep the shoulders settled, the head up and the lumbar area flat.

6.9 Advance split (left)   jìnbù zuǒ pīzhǎng   进步左劈掌

Do not move the left foot or hand, but step the right foot forward, hooking the foot out about forty-five degrees. Turn the right palm over to press down with the back of the hand (figure 6-12).

Step the left foot forward then step the right foot in a half-step – keep the weight on the right leg. Slide the left hand along inside the right arm and split to shoulder height, while bringing the right hand back to the abdomen (palm down and forward). Look at the left index finger (figure 6-13).

92 CHAPTER TWO: BASIC TECHNIQUES

Main points: Step the right foot as you press down with the right hand. Advance the left foot at the same time as you do the left split. Keep the left knee bent, the lumbar area flat, and the shoulders extended and relaxed.

6.10   Advance split (right)   jìnbù yòu pīzhǎng   进步右劈掌

Form fists. Lower the left fist then lift it past the chest to extend out from under the jaw (fist heart up). Step the left foot forward with the foot hooked out. Slide the right fist along the inside of the left arm to extend it out to the front. As the fists approach each other turn them quickly and open the palms, splitting the right to shoulder height and pulling the left back to the abdomen (both palms face diagonally forward and down). Step the right foot forward with the strike and bring the left a half-step in. Keep the weight back on the left leg. Look at the right hand (figure 6-14).

Main points: Pay attention to the same things as the preceding *advance split* (move 6.9), just transpose left and right.

6.11   Golden rooster stands on one leg

   jīnjī dúlì   金鸡独立

Form fists. Lower the right fist then bring it up past the chest to extend out from under the jaw, (fist heart up). Slide the left fist out along the inside of the right arm to extend forward. When the fists come together, open the hands and inwardly rotate the left to waist height and pull the right to the abdomen (palms face diagonally forward and down). Bring the right foot in quickly to take the place of the left – lift the left foot as soon as the right foot lands. Both knees are well bent, the left foot dorsi-flexed sticking on the right ankle in a one-legged stance. Look at the left hand (figure 6-15).

Main points: The right hand first comes back then extends. The left hand strikes as the right foot lands. You must be steady on the supporting leg. The right foot must stamp with force when it lands. The lumbar area should be flat, the head up, the shoulders extended and relaxed, and the body steady.

6.12   Golden rooster pecks a grain of rice   jīnjī shímǐ   金鸡食米

This move is the same as the first *golden rooster pecks a grain of rice* (move 6.5), but in the opposite direction (figure 6-16).

6.13   Golden rooster shakes its tail   jīnjī dǒulíng   金鸡抖翎

This move is the same as the first *golden rooster shakes its tail* (move 6.6) but in the opposite direction (figures 6-17, 6-18).

94   CHAPTER TWO: BASIC TECHNIQUES

6.14   Golden rooster blocks up   jīnjī shàng jià   金鸡上架

This move is the same as the first *golden rooster blocks up* (move 6.7) but in the opposite direction (figure 6-19).

6-19

6.15   Golden rooster heralds the dawn   jīnjī bàoxiǎo   金鸡报晓

This move is the same as the first *golden rooster heralds the dawn* (move 6.8) but in the opposite direction (figure 6-20).

6-20

6.16   Advance split (left)   jìnbù zuǒ pīzhǎng   进步左劈掌

This move is the same as the first *advance split* (move 6.9) but in the opposite direction (figures 6-21, 6-22).

6-21   6-22

Keep repeating the full sequence of moves as you see fit.

6.17   Chicken closing form   shōushì   收式

When you return to your starting point, finish with a *left split* in the same direction that you had done the ready stance. Bend the left arm and lower the hand down the chest, placing both hands to the side. Bring in the left foot beside the right and stand up.

7.   SPARROW HAWK   yào xíng   鹞形

The sparrow hawk is a bird of prey. The form of the sparrow hawk imitates the actions of the bird as it folds its wings in midflight, enters the woods, pierces the sky and flips over.[38] The form emphasizes body and hand technique, and is more complicated than the tiger, alligator, and snake forms. The move *sparrow hawk flips over*, for example, calls for swinging the arms in coordination with the body technique and spirit – it shows a tough coordinated attitude. This form is demanding for the shoulders, waist, hip and eye. The footwork of the form follows a straight line.

7.1   Ready stance   yùbèi shì   预备式

The same as *santishi* (figure 7-1).

7.2   Sparrow hawk folds its wings   yàozi shù shēn shì   鹞子束身式

Form fists. Rotate the right fist over (centre faces up) and extend it along under the left arm, forward and up to eye height. As the right fist extends, rotate the left (centre faces up) and bring it back to the abdomen (fist heart diagonally inward). As the hands form fists, step the left foot forward. As the right fist extends, step the right foot forward and bring the left foot in (dorsi-flexed) to stick beside the right ankle. Look at the right fist (figure 7-2).

7-1   7-2

---

[38] Translator's note: Find David Attenborough's 'The Birds' – the episode on flying. There is a slow motion sequence of a sparrow hawk flying through a compact English woods. It folds its wings in flight to squeeze through branching trunks, and even twists its body to go through feet first.

Main points: The right fist strikes at exactly the same time as the right foot lands. Keep the body steady, the shoulders settled, and the lumbar area flat.

7.3 Sparrow hawk enters the woods   yàozi rù lín shì   鹞子入林式

Step the left foot straight forward without moving the right. Keep the weight on the right leg. Punch the left fist straight forward to chest height (fist eye up). Externally rotate the right forearm and block up and out, fist by the right temple (fist centre forward and fist eye down). This is similar to a left cannon punch, but the stance is aligned – the same arm and leg forward. Look at the left fist (figure 7-3).

Main points: The left foot steps forward at exactly the same time as the left fist punches and the right arm blocks. Don't extend the left arm too much, the elbow should be above the knee. Roll in the knees slightly and keep the shoulders set down.

7.4 Sparrow hawk pierces the sky

yàozi zuān tiān shì   鹞子钻天式

Externally rotate the right forearm further and bring it down (turn the fist centre up). Rotate the left fist externally then hook it in. Extend the right fist above the left wrist and forward to eyebrow height (fist heart in). Bring the left fist back under the right elbow (fist heart down) with the elbow tight to the left side of the chest. Turn the left foot out and step a bit forward, then step the right foot forward as the right fist extends up. Look at the right fist (figure 7-4).

Main points: When lowering the right fist, roll the forearm and elbow as if wrapping around something[39] [guǒ jìn 裹劲]. Extend the fist forward only

---

[39] Translator's note: The action of the right arm first pressures out with the forearm, then rolls back and in to bring the fist past the ribs, and finally drills straight forward (a bit flatter than the *drill* technique). The action of the left arm also pressures out with the forearm, then presses down to give the right fist a clear path.

after the fist has rotated to turn the centre up. Hit with the right fist exactly at the same time as you land the right foot. Keep the shoulders settled and the head straight.

7.5   Sparrow hawk flips over   yàozi fān shēn shì   鹞子翻身式

Turn left, turning the right foot in. Bend the right elbow and follow the body around to the left. The left fist goes along with the turn, staying at the right elbow. It rotates out and comes across the chest to extend to in front of the left shoulder. While it does this, lower the right fist to come under the left elbow. Turn the left fist over (turn the fist heart in). Then turn around to the right and bring both fists from in front of the face to the rear right. When the right fist arrives at the rear right, bend the elbow to bring the fist in beside the waist (fist eye up). Lower the left fist past the right shoulder and across the abdomen, turn it and extend it out to the left side at waist height (fist eye up). Turn left and pivot the right foot to form an empty stance. Look at the left fist (figure 7-5).

Main points: The body rotates from right to left, then from left to right, then again to the left. Don't stop between any of the turns. Follow the rotation of the arms back and forth with your eyes. After watching the right arm as it turns to the right rear, turn the head quickly to the left. Squat a bit to lower the body when doing the final turn to the left, but don't lean forward too much. Make sure you turn from the centre of the body to maintain balance and coordination.

7.6   Sparrow hawk folds its wings   yàozi shù shēn shì   鹞子束身式

This move is the same as the first *sparrow hawk folds its wings* (move 7.2) except that the first starts out from *santishi*, and this repetition starts out with the hands already in fists (figure 7-6).

7.7 Sparrow hawk enters the woods   yàozi rù lín shì   鹞子入林式

This move is the same as the first *sparrow hawk enters the woods* (move 7.3) but in the opposite direction (figure 7-7).

7.8 Sparrow hawk pierces the sky   yàozi zuān tiān shì   鹞子钻天式

This move is the same as the first *sparrow hawk pierces the sky* (move 7.4) but in the opposite direction (see figure 7-4).

7.9 Sparrow hawk flips over   yàozi fān shēn shì 鹞子翻身式

This move is the same as the first *sparrow hawk flips over* (move 7.5) but in the opposite direction (see figure 7-5).

Practise the whole form back and forth.

7.10 Sparrow hawk closing form shōu shì   收式

When you end up back where you started in *sparrow hawk pierces the sky*, turn around with the *sparrow hawk flips over* and stop. Bring in the left foot and hand and stand up.

8. SWALLOW   yàn xíng   燕形

This form emphasizes the agility of a swallow as its swoops down over the water. The moves rise and fall, jump forward, stand on one leg and turn – particularly training the waist, legs, shoulders, and hip joints. The *swallow skims the water* seems simple but demands quite a lot of coordination between the upper and lower body. It has to be quick, forceful and lively. Its jump has to be for a good distance while the landing has to be steady. Finally, the spirit has to stay with the to and fro rotation of the body in order to successfully unite form with spirit. The footwork of the swallow form follows a straight line back and forth.

Traditionally this form always ends up in the *left split* before turning, but if you want to balance training you can add a *right split* after the left and do *swallow turns around* to the other side. In this way you can do a line with a left-sided *swallow skims the water* and come back with a right-sided *swallow skims the water* – this way gives a more balanced training effect.

8.1   Ready stance   yùbèi shì   预备式

The same as *santishi* (figure 8-1).

8.2   Swallow skims the water   yànzi chāo shuǐ shì   燕子抄水式

Extend the right hand out from under the left forearm. Form a fist and circle it up then right, then down and right then again up, passing in front of the body to scoop up. Form a fist with the left hand and, as the right fist turns right, bend the left elbow and bring the fist in and across the chest to the lower left, extending out to the left, crossing wrists with the right. The left fist rotates internally (turn the fist heart down) under the right fist (which has its fist heart left). Turn the body first right then left. Keep the weight evenly balanced, then shift more forward onto the left knee and lift the right heel with the knee bent. Look straight ahead (figures 8-2, 8-3).

Main points: Keep the body erect when turning. Rotate from the centre of the body (the lumbar area, waist area). Move quickly and follow the movement with the eyes.[40] Keep the lumbar area flat and the shoulder settled. Push the ball of the right foot hard into the ground.

Push off forcefully to jump forward with the right foot. Bend the knee in a half-squat on landing, and follow in with the left foot, placing it dorsi-flexed at the right ankle. Keep the legs tight together. Separate and lift the arms up to left and right, circling the fists up then down to shoulder height (fist eyes up) elbows bent. Look to the left (figure 8-4).

Main points: Separate the hands at exactly the same time as you advance forward. Jump for distance while keeping under control. Keep the lumbar area flat and the head up.

8.3 Enter with right drive   jìnbù yòu bēngquán   进步右崩拳

Step the left foot forward. Follow with the right, bringing it in near the left heel with both knees bent. Bring the right fist in to the waist then drive punch forward (fist eye up). Open the left hand and inwardly rotate it to slap onto the right wrist. Look at the right fist (figure 8-5).

Main points: The right punch hits at exactly the same time as the left foot lands. Keep the shoulder settled and the lumbar area flat.

8.4 Left split   zuǒ pīzhǎng   左劈拳

Advance the left foot a half-step without moving the right foot. Slide the left hand out from the right with a split to shoulder height (palm diagonally down and forward). Open the right hand and bring it back to the abdomen. This stance is the same as *santishi*. Look at the left hand (figure 8-6).

---

[40] Translator's note: Follow the right fist with the eyes and head until the last instant, then snap the head to look forward to the left fist.

TWELVE ANIMALS

Main points: All the important points of this technique are the same as split. See the description in the five elemental phases in this chapter.

8.5   Swallow turns around   huíshēn shì   回身式

Lower the hands and make fists. Bring them in to either side of the waist (fist hearts up). Turn the left foot in on its heel and turn the body around to the right, pivoting the right foot around on its ball. This is the same as the split turn. Look forward (figure 8-7).

8.6   Enter with left split   jìnbù zuǒ bēngquán   进步左劈拳

Step the right foot forward, hooked out. Extend the right fist up past the chest then forward to eye height (fist heart in). Step forward with the left foot and follow the right forearm with the left fist. Finish with a left split technique. Look at the left hand (figure 8-8).

8.7   Swallow skims the water   yànzi chāo shuǐ shì   燕子抄水式

This move is the same as the first *swallow skims the water* (move 8.2) but in the opposite direction.

8.8   Enter with right drive   jìnbù yòu bēngquán   进步右崩拳

This move is the same as the first *enter with right drive* (move 8.3) but in the opposite direction.

8.9   Left split   zuǒ pīzhǎng   左劈拳

This move is the same as the first *left split* (move 8.4) but in the opposite direction.

8.10 Swallow turns around   huíshēn shì   回身式

This move is the same as the first *swallow turns around* (move 8.5) but in the opposite direction.

8.11 Enter with left split   jìnbù zuǒ pīzhǎng   进步左劈拳

This move is the same as the first *enter with left split* (move 8.6) but in the opposite direction.

Practise back and forth in this way.

8.12 Swallow closing form   shōu shì   收式

On arriving back at your starting place, turn around with the *swallow turns around* (see move 8.5) and do another *advance left split* (see move 8.6) Then bring the left foot in beside the right, bring the left hand down the chest, and place both hands by your side. Stand up.

9. SNAKE   shé xíng   蛇形

The snake form imitates the actions of the snake as it coils, flexes, and extends. In the past this talent to coil tightly in and strike out was described as the snake "having the spirit of dividing the grass." To train this you should keep actions soft and agile, and make clear the differences between closing in and striking out. The whole body needs to be coordinated, so that there is a solid force even while coiling in tight. The snake form repeats to left and right, and the footwork follows a wavy line.

9.1 Ready stance   yùbèi shì   预备式

The same as *santishi* (figure 9-1).

9-1

9.2 Snake form (right) shéxíng yòu shì 蛇形右式

Step the left foot forward with the knee bent. Follow in with the right foot, heel off the ground and knee bent pointing down.[41] Put the weight on the left leg. Stab the right hand down across the abdomen to the lower left so that the back of the hand sticks in front of the left hip (palm out and fingers down). Bend the left elbow and bring the hand in to in front of the right shoulder (palm in and fingers up).[42] Look to the forward right (figure 9-2).[43]

Stride the right foot to the right front. Follow a half-step in with the left. Keep the weight on the left leg. Form fists and swing the right arm to the right and up to waist height (fist eye up). Pull the left fist back to beside the left hip (fist eye up). Lean forward slightly. Look at the right fist (figure 9-3).

Main points: Keep the hands tight to the body when doing the right lower stab with the left upper thread. The switching up and down of the hands matches the time of the left step. Keep the hips relaxed, the shoulders settled, and the head up.

The right upward strike matches the time of the right advancing step. As the right foot steps forward it passes by the left foot then steps out with the arm swing. Don't straighten the right arm too much. Keep the head up and the lumbar area flat.

---

[41] Translator's note: You may drop the left thigh parallel to the ground to make the coil more tight. If you do so, remember that this is not a cross-sit stance, so the right knee does not tuck in behind the left.

[42] Translator's note: The action of the stab is more sinuous or 'snakey' than the stab in the chicken form, which is crisp and direct. Also, the placement of the lower hand is different from that in the monkey form. The monkey covers the groin while the snake crosses the body.

[43] Translator's note: Figure 9-2 has an error. The right hand should be on the other side of the body, outside the left hip, as in figure 9-4 (on the opposite side).

9.3   Snake form (left)   shéxíng zuǒ shì   蛇形左式

Step the right foot forward with the knee bent and weighted. Follow a half-step in with the left foot, placing it with the heel up and the knee bent (kneecap points down). Open the hands and slide the left down past the abdomen to stab down by the right hip (palm out and fingers down). Bend the right elbow to bring the hand in front of the left shoulder (palm in and fingers up). Look forward left (figure 9-4).

Step the left foot forward and follow in a half-step with the right, keeping the weight on the right leg. Form fists and swing the left arm left and up to waist height (fist eye up). Bring the right fist back to the right hip (fist eye up). Lean slightly forward. Look at the left fist (figure 9-5).

Main points: Points of importance are the same as the *right snake form*, but applied to the other side.

9.4   Snake form (right)   shéxíng yòu shì   蛇形右式

This move is the same as the first *snake form* (right) (move 9.2). (See figure 9-2).

9.5   Snake turns around   huíshēn shì   回身式

After completing the right snake form, open both hands. Bend the right elbow and place the hand in front of the left shoulder (palm in, fingers up). Stab the left hand down by the right hip (palm out, fingers down). Lift the right foot, step it around to the outside of the left foot (toes hooked in), and pivot on the ball of the left foot. This turns the body one-eighty degrees to the left. Sit down with the weight more on the right

leg, and raise the left heel slightly off the ground. Look to the forward left (figure 9-6).

9.6   Snake form (left)   shéxíng zuǒ shì   蛇形左式

This is the same as the first *snake form* (left), but in the opposite direction (figure 9-7).

9.7   Snake form (right)   shéxíng yòu shì   蛇形右式

This is the same as the first *snake form* (right), but in the opposite direction (figures 9-8, 9-9).

Go back and forth until you arrive back at your starting point.

9.8   Snake closing form   shōushì   收式

Do another *snake turns around* (move 9.5, see figure 9-6) into a *left snake form* (move 9.3, see figures 9-4, 9-5). Bring in the left foot beside the right foot while bringing in and lowering the left fist down the chest. Stand up.

10. WEDGE-TAILED HAWK   tài xíng   鸟台形

The tai bird is a mythical bird[44] similar to an ostrich [tuó 鸵]. Classical writings admired the way the bird could stiffen its tail – soar into the skies – and the strength with which it could drop down to pounce on its prey. The Xingyi form imitates the wedge-tailed hawk's form by training the agility of the shoulders and elbows and the spring of the arm, chest and upper back muscles. The footwork is the same as that of the tiger form, but the hand technique is different. While the palms pounce forward in the tiger form, in the wedge-tailed hawk form the arms circle back then strike forward. The main point to emphasize in practising the wedge-tailed hawk form is to generate power from the body and transfer it to the arms. The path of the footwork is the same as the tiger, back and forth in a wave pattern.

10.1   Ready stance   yùbèi shì   预备式

The same as *santishi* (figure 10-1).

10-1

10.2   Wedge-tailed hawk form (left)   tàixíng zuǒ shì   鸟台形左式

Step the left foot forward. Lower the left hand to the abdomen while making a fist. Close the right hand at the abdomen as well (fist heart in). Step the right foot forward and follow in with the left foot – placed on the right ankle with the foot dorsi-flexed. Bring the fists up the centre, circle to separate them outwards as they pass in front of the head, circle around and bring them back to the waist (fist centers up). Look forward left (figure 10-2).

---

[44] Translator's note: I have seen, again in a Nature show in China, a bird referred to as *tai* which was a wedge-tailed hawk. It was smaller than a rabbit, but could fly in behind one and use its tail and wings as scoops to catch it. In this way it would encircle the rabbit, sometimes rolling over in a ball with the rabbit in its grasp. This action is so much like the *tai* form that I don't see the point in imagining some mythical bird that I've never seen fight. This is why I've called the *tai* form the wedge-tailed hawk.

Advance the left foot to the forward left and follow in a half-step with the right, knees bent, weight more on the right leg. Punch straight forward from the waist (fist heart up). Keep the arms slightly bent, and the fists about ten to twenty centimetres apart. Look at the left fist (figure 10-3).

Main points: Separate and circle the hands back to the waist as you step the right foot forward. The landing must be balanced and stable, with the elbows tight to the ribs, the shoulders settled, and the lumbar area flat.

The strike must be at exactly the same time as advance of the left leg. Don't over-extend the arms. Keep the line of the wrists to fist hearts straight, make sure you don't cock the wrists up or down. Keep the lumbar area flat and the head up.

10.3   Wedge-tailed hawk form (right)   tàixíng yòu shì   鸟台形右式

Step the left foot forward and bring in the right foot to hang by the left ankle (foot dorsi-flexed). Circle the fists up, separate them in front of the head, and circle around to pull in at the waist (fist hearts up). Look to the forward right (figure 10-4).

Punch straight forward. This move is the same as the *left wedge-tailed hawk form* (move 10.2) just transposing right and left (figure 10-5).

Main points: All important points are the same as the first *left wedge-tailed hawk form* (move 10.2).

10.4   Wedge-tailed hawk turns around   huíshēn shì   回身式

10-6

Lift the right foot and pivot on the ball of the left foot to turn the body around to the left. Step the right foot beside the left (about twenty to thirty centimetres from the left). As soon as the right foot touches down, raise the left to place it at the right ankle (foot dorsi-flexed). Circle the hands up, separate them in front of the head, and circle them around to the waist (fist hearts up). Look to the lower left (figure 10-6).

Main points: Turn quickly – the hands must finish the complete circle and be at the waist as the right foot lands. The left foot must pop up the instant the right touches down. The body must remain steady, the lumbar area flat, the shoulders set, and the elbows must stick to the ribs. The left foot steps out after the turn into the double strike, in the same way as the left wedge-tailed hawk described above – just going in the opposite direction.

Keep going back towards your starting point, alternating left and right.

On arrival at your starting point in a *right wedge-tailed hawk form*, perform another *wedge-tailed hawk turns around*.

10.5   Wedge-tailed hawk closing form   shōushì   收式

After wedge-tail hawk turns around at your starting point, do another *left wedge-tailed hawk form*. Stop, then lower the hands, bring the left foot in, and stand up.

11, 12.   EAGLE AND BEAR

yīng xíng xióng xíng héyǎn   鷹形熊形合演

This form imitates both the exactitude and ferocity of an eagle grasping its prey and the simple erectness of a bear protecting the emperor. The rising moves are the bear, so the body needs to show an erectness and superb rising strength. The dropping moves are the eagle, so the arms need to rotate and drop with the ferocity of grasping prey. The rising and dropping, rotating and turning, and right and left change-overs train the limbs, trunk and head.

This form also has the spirit of the eagle fighting the bear. The classics said that this form came from watching an eagle fight a bear. The two techniques combine *yin* and *yang* and show how Xingyi never abandons the concepts of *yin* and *yang* – attack and defense. Xingyi techniques also never abandon the alternation of rising and falling, extending and contracting which are exemplified in the eagle and bear form. The [Chinese] words for eagle [yīng 鹰] and bear [xióng 熊] also sound the same as those for hero [yīng xióng 英雄], which is another reason they are practised together as one form.

It is important in the eagle and bear form to coordinate breathing with the extension and contraction and the rise and fall of the moves. The extension, or opening, and the contraction, or closing, must be closely coordinated with breathing in order to have full power. This footwork follows the same type of stepping and the same line as the tiger form, except that the rear foot moves in towards the front foot and raises its heel.

11.1   Ready stance   yùbèi shì   预备式

The same as *santishi* (figure 11-1).

11.2   Eagle lands (right)   yòu yīngxíng luòshì   右鹰形落式

Close the left hand, lower it to the abdomen, then slide it up the chest to the lower jaw and extend it forward to eye height (fist center in). Close the right hand and, as the left extends, stretch it up inside the left forearm. As the fists approach each other, open the hands and turn them over to pull down, the right forward at waist height and the left beside the waist (palms down). Bring the left foot back to touch the toes down by the right as the right hand reaches up. Quickly step the left foot to the forward left as the hands drop down, and bring in the right foot a half-step. The weight is even in the final stance – the right heel slightly raised and the knees bent. Look at the right hand (figure 11-2).

110   CHAPTER TWO: BASIC TECHNIQUES

Main points: When first bringing the left hand down, both hands close to fists at the same time. The left foot comes back at the same time that the left hand draws in. When the right hand presses down the arm should not over-extend. The hands are like eagle claws grasping prey. The knees have a closing-in power and the body leans forward a bit. The hands drop at exactly the same time as the left foot lands.

11.3   Bear enters (right)   yòu xióngxíng qǐshì   右熊形起式

Close the right hand to a fist, lower it, then slide up the abdomen and chest to come out from below the jaw, extending to eye height (fist centre in). Close the left hand (fist heart down). Step the left foot forward without moving the right, just raising the heel and shifting more weight to the left leg.[45] Look at the right hand (figure 11-3).

Main points: Extend the right hand up at exactly the same time as you step the left foot forward. The left foot is turned in and the knees have a rolled-in force. The ball of the right foot pushes into the ground, to drive the power up. Keep the lumbar area flat and the shoulders settled down.

11.4   Eagle lands (left)   zuǒ yīngxíng luòshì   左鷹形落式

Bring the right foot in past the left, then step out to the right front. Follow in a half-step with the left foot, keeping the weight even between the two legs. Slide the left fist along inside the right forearm to extend up and forward. As it reaches the right fist, open both hands, turn them over, twist, and pull down. The left hand presses down in front at waist height and the right pulls in to the waist (both palms down). Look at the left hand (figure 11-4).

Main points: The important points are the same as the *eagle lands* (right) (move 11.2), just right and left are transposed.

---

[45] Translator's note: The eagle-bear advancing may also be done with a large step forward with the front foot and a follow-in with the back foot. This flows better when practising fast advancing. Also, the bear may be done more upright, and the eagle may drop with the supporting thigh parallel to the ground

11.5   Bear enters (left)   zuǒ xióngxíng qǐshì   左熊形起式

This form is the same as the *bear enters* (right) (move 11.3), just transposing right and left (figure 11-5).

11.6   Eagle lands (right)   yòu yīngxíng luòshì   右鹰形落式

This form is the same as the first *right eagle lands* (move 11.2) (figure 11-6).

11-5   11-6

11.7   Bear and eagle turn around   huíshēn shì   回身式

After reaching a left eagle lands, turn the body around to the left one-eighty degrees by pivoting on the balls of both feet. As you turn, bring the left hand down then slide it up the body to extend up and forward from under the jaw to eye height (fist heart in). Keep the right fist at the waist (fist heart down). After you have turned, step the right foot forward with the knee bent and the weight more on the right leg. Raise the heel of the left foot and bend the knee. Look at the left fist (figure 11-7).

Main points: Extend the left fist at the same time as you step forward with the right foot. Turn quickly, keeping balance.

11-7

11.8   Eagle lands (right)   yòu yīngxíng luòshì   右鹰形落式

Keep moving the left foot to the forward left and extend the right fist up and out from inside the left forearm. As the fists come close, open them, rotate the forearms and pull down. All the actions are the same as the first *right eagle lands* (move 11.2), but in the opposite direction (figure 11-8).

112 CHAPTER TWO: BASIC TECHNIQUES

Alternate right and left until you get back to where you started. Repeat to and fro depending on your stamina and the size of your training area (figures 11-9, 11-10).

11.9 Eagle and Bear closing form   shōushì   收式

When you get back to your starting position in a *left eagle lands*, perform *bear and eagle turn around* to the left into a *right eagle lands*. Then extend the left hand out under the right and bring the right back to the abdomen, settling into *santishi*. Pause then stand up.

Translator's note: Please note the difference in hand and leg positions for these three similar defensive maneuvers in the animal forms.

Monkey scrambles up a pole   Golden rooster blocks up   Snake form

CHAPTER THREE

SOLO FORMS

3.1 FIVE ELEMENTAL PHASES CONNECT

wǔ xíng lián huán quán   五行连环拳

This form is based on the five elemental phases. It repeats itself back and forth with a short, compact, lively style. As the basic form in Xingyi, it is very widespread in China.

1.   Ready stance   yùbèi shì   预备式

The opening is exactly the same as for *santishi*. See the description of *santishi* (figure 1).

2.   Enter with right driving punch   jìnbù yòu bēngquán   进步右崩拳

Form fists, drive the left foot forward from the right leg then bring up the right foot, keeping the weight back on the right leg. The heels are in line about twenty to thirty centimetres apart. Punch straight forward with the right fist, following the line of the left arm, and pulling the left fist back to the side (right fist eye up with the fist surface slightly tilted forward, left fist heart up). Look at the right fist (figure 2).

Main points: Hit with the left foot and the right fist at exactly the same time. Don't lift the foot too high. Keep the body steady and the lower back area flat and solid.

3. Step back, left driving punch   Green dragon shoots out of the water

tuìbù zuǒ bēngquán, qīnglóng chū shuǐ   退步左崩拳，青龙出水

Without moving the left foot or right fist, draw the right foot a half-step to the back, then slide the left foot back along the same line as the right, dropping behind the right foot with the legs crossed, the left foot on line and the right foot turned out. The left heel is slightly raised, forming a half-squat sitting stance. As the left foot withdraws, drive forward with the left fist and pull the right fist back to the side (left fist eye and right fist heart face up). Look at the left fist (figures 3, 4).

Note: This move is optionally done as a left wringing punch, in two different ways. Keeping the same footwork, either twist the fists into a wringing punch – left fist heart up and right fist heart down – or leave the left fist eye up but swing the punch slightly in a circle, giving it a wringing force.

Main points: Don't move the body or turn the right shoulder as you withdraw the right foot. When you withdraw the left foot, first hit hard with the heel, then raise the heel to set into the stance. Put the knees tightly together (the left knee nestled in the hollow of the right). Punch at exactly the same time you stamp the left heel.

FIVE ELEMENTAL PHASES CONNECT 115

4. Aligned right driving punch   Black tiger shoots out of its cave

   shùnbù yòu bēngquán, hēihǔ chū dòng   顺步右崩拳, 黑虎出洞

Drive the right foot forward, and then follow in with the left. Drive the right hand out in the direction of the right foot to chest height (fist eye up). Bring the left fist back to the side (fist heart up). This forms an aligned driving punch, with both right foot and right fist forward. Look at the right fist (figure 5).

Main points: The right foot and fist hit at exactly the same time. Keep the shoulders settled. Keep the left forearm tight on the ribs. Keep the head straight and the lumbar area flat.

5. Step back, hold   White crane flashes its wings

   tuìbù bàoquán, báihè liàngchì   退步抱拳, 白鹤亮翅

Draw the left foot back to the rear and a bit to the left. Flex the right arm and stab down near the abdomen (fist heart up). The left fist is under the right (fist centre down) (figure 6).

from behind

Turn to the right and circle the hands (right in a fist, left open) in front of the head, then separate and circle out and down, coming together in front of the abdomen. Nestle the right fist in the left palm. Draw the right foot back in front of the left. Look forward (figures 7, 8).

Main points: Stab the right fist down at exactly the same time that you withdraw the left foot. Keep the forearms tight to the sides, and make sure you don't shrug your shoulders.

When separating the arms, look at the right fist. Hit the right fist into the left hand at exactly the same time as you bring the right foot back, and make a sound as you hit. This sound shows that the whole body is working together – you don't have to make a sound, as long as you do the movement all together. Keep the head up, the shoulders set, and the lumbar area flat. Keep the forearms tight to the abdomen – don't let them move away. Settle your *qi* down.

6.   Enter with cannon punch   jìnbù pàoquán   进步炮拳

Stride the right foot forward and a bit to the right, then follow with the left. Form a fist with the left hand and punch forward. Drill the right fist up past the chest then rotate and block up to the right side of the head. This forms a reverse stance punch, with the right foot and left fist forward. Look at the left fist (figure 9).

Main points: Hit with the right foot and the left fist at exactly the same time. As the right arm blocks, the fist heart should follow the rotation of the body and roll in then forward, drilling first up then turning out – make sure you don't block straight up. Keep the shoulders settled and the lumbar area flat.

7.   Step back, left splitting palm   tuìbù zuǒ pīzhǎng   退步左劈掌

Lower the right fist in front of the body and bring the left fist to the left side (both fist hearts up). Draw the right foot back. Look at the right fist (figure 10).

Extend the left fist forward along the top of the right forearm, turning it over and opening to a palm to strike forward in a split. As the left hand strikes, open the right as well and press down in front of the abdomen. Look at the left hand (figure 11).

Main points: Do this all as one movement, without a pause. When lowering the right fist, first roll in the elbow. When extending the left arm, first turn the fist heart up then open the hand and rotate it. Keep the shoulders settled, the elbows dropped, and make sure not to over-extend the arms.

8.   Reverse stance, right drilling punch   àobù yòu zuānquán   拗步右钻拳

Pause, then turn to the right without moving the right foot, and bring the left foot back to the right ankle. Lower the palms down the left side to in front of the abdomen, forming fists with the forearms stuck to the sides (fist hearts up). Look ahead (figure 12).

Turn left, drill the left fist up in front of the chest then step the left foot forward and follow a half-step in with the right. Drill the right fist out along the left arm to nose height. Turn over the left fist, rotate and bring it down in front of the abdomen (fist heart down). Look at the right fist (figure 13).

Note: This move may alternatively be done as a wrapping posture [bāoguǒ shì 包裹式] as follows: drill the hands out in a character eight palm, and change the stance to forward-weighted dragon-riding stance with the left leg bent and the right heel raised.[46]

Main points: Bring the hands and left foot back at exactly the same time. Hit with the right hand and left foot at exactly the same time. Keep the lumbar area flat and the head up.

9.   Hop, double splitting palm   Leopard cat climbs up a tree
     tiàobù shuāng pīzhǎng, límāo shàng shù   跳步双劈掌, 狸猫上树

Step the left foot forward with the knee flexed without moving the hands (figure 14).

---

[46] Translator's note: This version allows you to charge into the following jump with good momentum.

118   CHAPTER THREE: SOLO FORMS

Lift the right knee with the foot hooked up (figure 15).

Push off from the left foot to hop forward, driving the right to kick forward then down with the foot turned out to stamp the ground. Follow in with the left foot, heel raised, forming a half-sitting stance (right foot turned, left foot straight). Slide the left fist out alongside the right arm then turn it over and hit with a splitting palm forward and down, no higher than the mouth. Open and pull the right hand back to the abdomen. Look at the index finger of the left hand (figure 16).

Main points: As you lift and kick the right foot, don't over-extend the left leg – keep your balance. The left palm strikes exactly when the right foot lands. In the cross-sit stance the rear knee is nestled into the concavity of the front knee. Keep the head up, the shoulders settled and the lumbar area flat.

10.   Enter with right driving punch   jìnbù yòu bēngquán   进步右拳

Form fists and step the right foot forward, then take a further step forward with the left. Follow in with the right a half-step, keeping the weight on the back leg. Punch the right fist out along the line of the left arm (fist eye up) and pull the left fist back to the side (fist heart up). Look at the right fist (figure 17).

Main points: Don't change your body position as you take the first step forward with the right foot. The left foot should step a good distance, steady and fast. Keep the body steady – do not rise or drop suddenly.

FIVE ELEMENTAL PHASES CONNECT 119

11. Turn around   Leopard cat climbs down a tree

huíshēn shì, límāo dào shàng shù   回身式, 狸猫倒上树

Turn the left foot in and pivot on the ball of the right foot. Turn around a full one-eighty degrees and sit onto the left leg. Bring the right fist back to the right side (fist heart up). Look ahead (figure 18).

Drill the right fist up past the chest then out from under the jaw to drill forward at nose height. Lift the right knee with the foot hooked up then kick with the heel forward and down, land with the foot hooked out. Bring the left foot in a half-step with the heel raised, settling the knee into the hollow of the right knee – this forms a half sitting cross-sit stance with the front foot hooked out and the back foot on the line of action. Extend the left fist out along the right arm then open it and turn it over – strike with a splitting palm forward and down no higher than the mouth. Bring the right hand back to the abdomen. Look at the index finger of the left hand (figures 19, 20).

Main points: Turn around quickly without rising or falling. Keep your left leg bent as you lift the right knee, to maintain balance. Hit with the right foot and the left hand at exactly the same time. When sitting into the half crouch, settle the rear knee tightly into the concavity of the front knee. Keep the head straight, the shoulders settled, and the lumbar area flat.

12. Closing of the form   shōu shì   收式

To get back to the starting place repeat the whole line of moves just described (moves 2 through 10). First step the left foot forward a bit then step the right foot forward and punch with the right fist as in the first advance right driving punch (move 2). Then follow the rest of the sequence of moves in the opposite direction (moves 3 through 10).

When you get back to your starting place in a *right driving punch* (figure 21), turn around as in move 11 (figures 22, 23, 24). Then close the form the

CHAPTER THREE: SOLO FORMS

same as the closing in the *driving punch form* described in chapter two (figures 25, 26, 27, and 28).

3.2 THE MIXTURE OF MOVES FORM

záshìchuí   杂式捶

The Mixture Of Moves form is a traditional form. Although it has been called 'the five elemental forces and twelve animals combined form,' it does not actually include all the animals. This form is so widespread that it is performed differently in different areas of China. It is one of the more complex of the traditional forms.

1.   Ready stance   yùbèi shì   预备式

Stand up straight, turned a bit sideways, heels together (left foot pointing along the line of action and the right foot turned out forty-five degrees). Let the arms hang at the sides with the hands on the thighs. Look ahead along the line of action (figure 1).

Main points: Keep the body straight with the shoulders set down, the lumbar area flat, and the jaw pulled in. Concentrate. Breathe naturally.

2.   Left driving punch on the spot

       yuándì zuǒ bēngquán   原地左崩拳

Bend the knees and shift the weight onto the right leg. Cross the hands in front of the abdomen. Form fists with the right on top (right fist heart up and left fist heart in). Keep the forearms tight to the sides of the body. Look ahead (figure 2).

Step the left foot forward without moving the right. Keep the knees bent and the weight on the right leg. Punch the left fist forward to waist height (fist eye on top). Draw the right fist back at the side of the waist (fist heart up). Lean forward slightly. Look at the left fist (figure 3).

Main points: When you sit down keep the weight mostly back on the right leg. Make sure the elbows are tight to the ribs, without shrugging the shoulders. First lift the right fist then pull it back as the left punches, to give equal power to both fists.

Hit with the left fist and foot at exactly the same time. Roll the knees in slightly, keep the head up, the lumbar area flat, and the buttocks tucked in.

3.　　Shin rubbing step, right driving punch　　Sparrow hawk folds its wings

　　　tíbù yòu bēngquán, yàozi shù shēn　　　提步右崩拳, 鹞子束身

Step the left foot forward, and then take a big step forward with the right. At the instant the right foot lands (almost before, but without jumping) lift the left foot and quickly bring it in to stick onto the right ankle, foot dorsi-flexed. This forms a right one-legged stance. Punch the right fist forward at sternum height (fist eye up) and pull the left fist back to the waist (fist heart up). Look at the right fist (figure 4).

Main points: As soon as the left foot steps forward, push off strongly from it to drive the right foot forward quickly. Keep the body balanced as you drive forward. The right foot and right fist hit at exactly the same time. Don't over-extend the right arm. Keep the shoulders down, the elbows settled, and the back steady.

4.　　Aligned cannon punch　　Sparrow hawk enters the woods

　　　shùnbù pàoquán, yàozi rù lín　　　顺步炮拳, 鹞子入林

Step the left foot forward. Follow in with the right foot, keeping the weight back on the right leg. Punch the left fist forward at sternum height (fist eye up), elbow slightly bent. Bend the right elbow, rotate the forearm and block up, the fist ending up by the right temple (fist eye down). Look at the left fist (figure 5).

Main points: The foot and hands hit at exactly the same time. Keep the knees bent and slightly rolled in. Keep the lumbar area flat and steady and the shoulders settled.

MIXTURE OF MOVES FORM, *ZASHICHUI*

5.   Left step back, pull   Tiger washes its face

    zuǒ tuìbù lǚ zhǎng, hǔ xǐliǎn   左退步捋掌, 虎洗脸

Lower the right fist to the waist. Pause, then open and raise the hand again to brush across the right side of the face (palm in, fingers up). As the right hand comes up, bring the left fist back to the left side (fist heart up). Turn the body quickly to the left and step the left foot back. Shift quickly onto the left leg, lift the right knee slightly, and lean forward slightly. Look to the lower left (figure 6).

Main points: Bring the left fist back, extend the right hand and step the left foot back all at the same time. Turn from the centre of your body. Lower and raise the right arm from the shoulder – do not use the elbow, and especially do not let the elbow stick out.[47] Keep the hip joint closed and the shoulder set down.

6.   Right step back, pull   Tiger washes its face

    yòu tuìbù lǚ zhǎng, hǔ xǐliǎn   右退步捋掌, 虎洗脸

Open the left hand and brush across the left face (palm facing right, fingers up). Close the right hand and bring the fist back to the waist (fist heart up). Turn right and step the right foot back. Shift immediately onto the right leg and lift the left knee slightly. Lean forward slightly. Look to the lower right (figure 7).

Main points: The main points for attention are the same as for the *left step back pull* (move 5), just transposing left and right.

7.   Left press down, right block up   Black dragon draws water

    zuǒ yā yòu jiàquán, wūlóng qǔ shuǐ   左压右架拳, 乌龙取水

Turn quickly to the left without moving the feet. Open the right hand and brush again across the right side of the face. Bring the left fist back to the waist as

---

[47] Translator's note: But do apply power to the elbow as well as the hand. This technique can either grab or brush aside with the palm, or knock down with the elbow.

before, but this time shift the weight forward (onto the left leg). Stop for an instant then continue to brush block with the right hand in front of the face (close to a fist). Quickly extend the left fist out and up above the right fist at eye height (fist heart diagonally up). Stop the right fist under the left elbow (fist heart down). Look at the left fist (figure 8).

Block up from under the left arm with the right arm, bending the elbow so that the fist ends up by the right side of the head (fist heart forward). Rotate the left fist and bring it down in front of the abdomen (fist heart down). Move the body back – draw the left foot back and shift onto the right. Look forward (figure 9).

Main points: As soon as you lower the left fist, extend it out above the right fist – this must be done quickly. The lowering of the left fist and blocking of the right are done while sitting back.

Starting out from the left step back and pull, this sequence of moves (moves 5 through 7) is all connected without hesitation. Maintain a clear rhythm. Each move has a distinct point of completion that is its power application. Stop for only an instant on reaching the last move (move 7). Always make sure that the power flow between moves is not broken – flow from one move to the next.

8.   Step back, plant fist down   Stretch out one wing

    tuìbù xià záquán, dān zhǎn chì

    退步下砸拳, 单展翅

Draw the left foot to the back then draw the right foot back beside the left (right heel near the left instep). Quickly rotate the right fist outward and lower it to the abdomen (fist heart up). Place the forearm tight onto the abdomen. Rotate the left fist up. Look forward (figure 10).

Main points: Bring the right fist down and the right foot back at the same time, both moving quickly. Use the hip joint to pull the right foot back with force, and lean slightly forward. As the right hand drops down, quickly look ahead. Keep the head up, the shoulders settled, the hip joints closed, and the forearms tight to the abdomen.

9. Left driving punch   zuǒ bēngquán   左崩拳

Stride the right foot forward and follow in with the left – keep the weight on the left leg. Drive forward with the left fist at sternum height (fist eye up). Pull the right fist back to the right side of the waist (fist heart up). Look at the left fist (figure 11).

Main points: Extend the left shoulder into the punch, but don't straighten the arm. Hit with the right foot and the left fist at exactly the same time.

10. Right aligned driving punch   yòu shùnbù bēngquán   右顺步崩拳

Stride the right foot forward again, following in a half-step with the left – keep the weight on the left leg. Punch forward at sternum height with the right fist (fist eye up). Pull the left fist back to the left side (fist heart up). Look at the right fist (figure 12).

Main points: The main points for attention are the same as the *left driving punch* (move 9) just transposing left and right.

11. Step back, hold   White crane flashes its wings

   tuìbù bàoquán, báihè liàngchì   退步抱拳, 白鹤亮翅

Draw the left foot back to the rear and a bit left. Bend the right elbow and stab the fist down, sliding it down the abdomen (fist heart up). Keep the left fist under the right (fist heart down) crossing the forearms tight to the abdomen. Look at the right fist (figure 13).

Raise both arms in front of the head then separate to left and right (right hand in a fist and left hand open). Drop them to either side then in front of the abdomen, right fist nestled in the left palm. Draw the right foot back to in front of the left (close to the instep). Look forward (figures 14, 15).

Main points: Stab the right fist down at exactly the same time you withdraw the left foot. Keep the arms tight to the body but do not allow that to lift your shoulders.

When opening the arms, follow the right fist with the eyes. Hit the right fist into the left hand at exactly the same time as you bring the right foot back. You can hit with a smack, to show that the foot and hand arrived at the same time, but it is all right not to make a sound as long as the actions are completed together. Keep the head straight, the shoulders set and the lumbar area flat. Keep the forearms tight to the body – don't let them move away. Lower the *qi*.

12.   Enter with cannon punch   jìnbù pàoquán   进步炮拳

Stride the right foot forward and a bit to the right. Follow a half-step in with the left. Form a fist with the left hand and drive straight forward while drilling the right fist up the chest to block out and up with the forearm by the right side of the head. This is a 'right foot – left fist reverse stance' position. Look at the left fist (figure 16).

Main points: Hit with the right foot at exactly the same time as the left fist. Be sure to rotate the right forearm – rotate the fist heart in as you lift and drill up then rotate the fist heart out to face forward as you block across. Make sure you do not simply block across the body with no arm rotation. Keep the shoulders set down and the lumbar area flat.

MIXTURE OF MOVES FORM, *ZASHICHUI* 127

13. Aligned cannon punch Sparrow hawk enters the woods

    shùnbù pàoquán, yàozi rù lín 顺步炮拳, 鹞子入林

Lower the right fist forward and down to meet the left, then bend both elbows and bring the fists in to either side of the waist (fist hearts up). Place the forearms tight to the body. Bring back the right foot to take the place of the left. Lift the left foot to switch places quickly and stick it dorsi-flexed by the right ankle (figure 17).

Stop for an instant then quickly step the left foot forward. Follow a half-step in with the right, keeping the weight back on the right leg. Drive forward to sternum height with the left fist. Drill the right fist up the chest then block up with the elbow bent; fist at the right side of the head (fist heart out). Look at the left fist (figure 18).

Main points: Pull the hands down open – form fists only as they come together into the waist. Bring the right foot in as the hands come in, and prepare to switch the feet before they arrive, so that the left lifts immediately. Keep the left foot tight to the right, which helps the whole body keep tight and united.

Hit with the left foot at exactly the same time as the left punch and the right block. There must be no time lag.

14. Left step back, pull Tiger washes its face

    zuǒ tuìbù lǔ zhǎng, hǔ xǐliǎn 左退步掳掌, 虎洗脸

This is the same as move 5 (figure 19).

15. Right step back, pull Tiger washes its face

    yòu tuìbù lǔ zhǎng, hǔ xǐliǎn 右退步掳掌, 虎洗脸

This is the same as move 6 (figure 20).

16. Left press down, right block up — Black dragon draws water

    zuǒ yā yòu jiàquán, wūlóng qǔ shuǐ 左压右架拳, 乌龙取水

This is the same as move 7, except this time do not stop, but go on immediately to *swallow skims the water* (figures 21, 22).

17. Jump, separate fists — Swallow skims the water

    zòngbù shuāng fēnquán, yànzi chāo shuǐ 纵步双分拳, 燕子抄水

Step the left foot quickly a half-step forward without moving the right foot. Lower the right fist and extend the left fist forward and up over the top of the right fist, to eye height (fist heart diagonally up). Stop the right fist under the left elbow (fist heart down). Look at the left fist (figure 23).

MIXTURE OF MOVES FORM, *ZASHICHUI*

Extend the right fist out under the left arm, then rotate and circle it up and back. Bend the left elbow and lower the fist down the chest to the left hip. Turn quickly right and to the back, pushing the left heel back. Turn left, pivoting the left foot to straighten the leg to the line of action. Extend the left fist forward and lower the right fist to the rear right, down, then scoop up to the front, crossing the wrists at shoulder height (right fist on the outside). Next swivel the left wrist (turn the fist in, down, then forward) to arrive on the outside of the right fist. Shift the weight forward to the left leg with the knees bent and the right heel raised, pushing into the ground with the ball of the right foot. Look forward (figures 24, 25).

Push off with the right foot to jump forward. Land with the knee bent and bring in the left foot – lift it to stick on the right ankle, dorsi-flexed. Keep the legs tightly together. Lift the arms and separate them to right and left at shoulder height with the elbows slightly bent (fist eyes up). Look ahead (figure 26).

Main points: Drill the left fist out as the left foot strides out.

Don't lean too much when you turn, use the waist and lower back area to snap left and right quickly. Go along with the rotation of the body with the eyes looking to the line of movement. As the wrists cross, quickly twist the left wrist in and down to the outside of the right. Keep the lumbar area flat and the shoulder settled down. Push strongly off the ground with the right foot.

Jump quickly and go for a good distance. Keep the body stable and the arms equally balanced. Keep the head up and the lumbar area flat.

18. Right driving punch   yòu bēngquán   右崩拳

Advance the left foot. Follow a half-step in with the right, keeping the weight on the right. Bend the right elbow and bring the fist to the waist to drive straight forward at sternum height (fist eye up). Draw the left fist back to the waist (fist heart up). Look at the right fist (figure 27).

19. Aligned cannon punch   Sparrow hawk enters the woods

shùnbù pàoquán, yàozi rù lín   顺步炮拳, 鹞子入林

Step the left foot again and bring the right foot a half-step in. Punch straight forward with the left fist and block up with the right, coming up from the chest then up and out beside the head. This is the same as the *sparrow hawk enters the woods* as described above in move four (figure 28).

20. Left step back pull   Tiger washes its face

zuǒ tuìbù lǚ zhǎng, hǔ xǐliǎn   左退步捋掌, 虎洗脸

This is the same as *tiger washes its face* – move 5 as described above (figure 29).

21. Right step back pull   Tiger washes its face

yòu tuìbù lǚ zhǎng, hǔ xǐliǎn   右退步捋掌, 虎洗脸

This is the same as *tiger washes its face* – move 6 as described above (figure 30).

MIXTURE OF MOVES FORM, *ZASHICHUI* 131

22. Enter with right driving punch   Golden rooster pecks a grain of rice

jìnbù yòu bēngquán, jīnjī shímǐ   进步右崩拳, 金鸡食米

This move starts out the same as *black dragon draws water* – move 7 as described above (figure 31).

Extend the right fist out under the left arm then rotate and circle it up then to the right. Bend the left elbow and lower the left fist down past the chest. Turn the body quickly to the right and back and bring the left foot in by the right with the turn without touching down. Turn to the left and stride the left foot forward, following in a half-step with the right. Drive the right fist from the waist forward at waist height. Open the left hand and circle out and forward, rotating to slap down on top of the right wrist. Keep the legs bent. Look at the right fist (figure 32).

Main points: Bring the left foot in and circle the right fist up and to the right at the same time as the body turns right and back. Land the left foot at exactly the same time as the right punch. The move must be done quickly. Keep the lumbar area solid and the head up. Don't over-extend the right arm.

23. Withdraw, left splitting palm   chèbù zuǒ pīzhǎng   撤步左劈掌

Draw the right foot back a half-step. Extend the left hand forward and open the right. Close the fists as the hands pull back to the sides (fist hearts up). Bring the left foot back beside the right, dorsi-flexed sticking on the right ankle. Look to the forward left (figures 33, 34).

Without moving the right foot, advance the left to sit into a *santishi*. Open the fists and extend the arms to split – the left to chest height the right to the abdomen (palms down). Look at the left hand (figure 35).

Main points: When splitting, both fists drill up, then come out from the mouth and open to strike forward and down. The hands must strike at exactly the same time as the foot lands.

24.   Advance, left push   Push the window to gaze at the moon

   jìnbù zuǒ tuīzhǎng, tuīchuāng wàngyuè   进步左推掌, 推窗望月

Lower the left hand to form a fist in front of the abdomen (fist heart up). Form a fist with the right hand and rotate it up, so that the fists are at either side of the *dantian*. Bring the left foot back beside the right without touching down (figure 36).

Without a pause, quickly brace the left hand toward the left and out at shoulder height (thumb down, palm out). As you do this, push off with the right foot and land with the left hooked in across the line of action (parallel to the right foot). Slide to bring the right towards it a bit to sit into a half-horse stance. Look at the left hand (figure 37).

MIXTURE OF MOVES FORM, *ZASHICHUI*

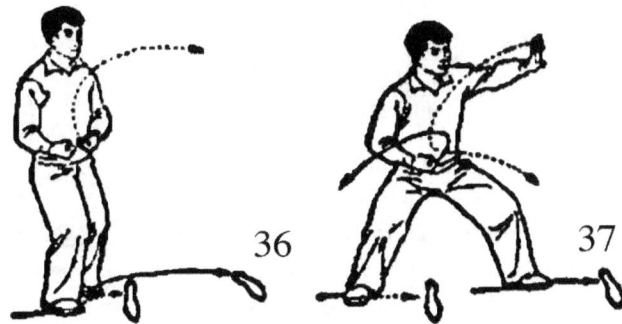

Main points: Don't lift the feet while moving first the left, then the right – slide in with both close to the ground. Use the power of the whole body to brace the arm – don't allow any segments to relax. Keep the shoulders level.

25. Horse stance, double brace   Three basins land on the ground

    mǎbù shuāng chēngzhǎng, sānpán luòdì   马步双撑掌, 三盘落地

Stop for an instant, then quickly turn the left hand in and lower it down the chest, crossing with the right hand in front of the abdomen (open the right fist). Brace out with both hands (palms down). As you brace out, push off with the right foot and step forward with the left turned across the line of attack again. Again slide in with the right foot. Sit down with the weight more on the right leg, the left foot turned out a bit (compared to a horse stance) to form a half-horse stance. Look at the left hand (figure 38).

Main points: The arms keep rounded as they brace out. Keep the lower back area flat and steady, the hip joints rolled in and the shoulders settled. The hands brace out at the same time that the feet move to the left, the whole body working as a unit.

26. Cross-sit stance, stab down   Lazy dragon lies in the road

    zuòpán xiàchāquán, lǎnlóng wò dào   坐盘下插拳, 懒龙卧道

Step the right foot across in front of the left, turned across the line of action to form a half-sitting stance. Form fists and bring the right fist across in front of the abdomen then cross in front of the left arm to stab down (right fist heart up, left fist heart down). Keep the arms tight to the body. Look forward and down (figure 39).

Main points: Keep the right arm tight to the body as it stabs down. Tuck the left knee tightly into the hollow of the right knee. Don't lean forward too much and don't shrug the shoulders. Keep the lumbar area flat.

27. Advance, left wringing fists   Black dragon overturns the waves

jìnbù zuǒ héngquán, wūlóng fān jiāng   进步左横拳, 乌龙翻江

Roll and twist the left fist forward and up, snapping with a wringing power, fist heart up and elbow bent. Pull the right fist back to the side (fist heart down). Advance the left foot at the same time with the knees bent. Look at the left fist (figure 40).

Main points: Twist the left arm forcibly to the left. Don't overextend the elbow. Keep the lumbar area flat and the head straight.

28. Right driving punch on the spot   yuándì yòu bēngquán   原地右崩拳

Punch the right fist forward (fist eye up) and pull the left fist back to the side (fist heart up). Shift the weight forward a bit but don't move the feet. Look at the right fist (figure 41).

29. Left hit and right kick   Dragon and tiger make friends

zuǒ chōng yòu dēng, lóng hǔ xiāngjiāo   左冲右蹬, 龙虎相交

Stand steady on the left leg. Lift the right knee and kick forward with the heel (foot pulled back). Punch the left fist forward with the kick (fist eye up). Pull the right fist back to the waist (fist heart up). Look forward (figure 42).

Main points: Kick and punch quickly. Keep the left leg slightly bent and kick the right straight. Keep the body balanced and steady. Pull the right foot back so that you can apply power through the heel.

30. Aligned right driving punch   shùnbù yòu bēngquán   顺步右崩拳

Land the right foot forward with the knee bent. Follow a half-step in with the left, also with the knee bent, and keep the weight back on the left leg. Punch the right fist straight forward at sternum height (fist eye up) and pull the left fist back to the waist (fist heart up). Look at the right fist (figure 43).

Main points: Punch at exactly the same time as you land. Keep the lumbar area flat and the head up. Don't hit the ground too hard when you land.

31. Step back, hold   White crane flashes its wings

     tuìbù bàoquán, báihè liàngchì   退步抱拳, 白鹤亮翅

This move is the same as the first *white crane flashes its wings* – described in move 11 (figures 44, 45, 46).

136 CHAPTER THREE: SOLO FORMS

32.   Advance, cannon punch   jìnbù pàoquán   进步炮拳

This move is the same as *advance cannon punch* – described in move 12 (figure 47).

33.   Aligned cannon punch   Sparrow hawk enters the woods

     shùnbù pàoquán, yàozi rù lín   顺步炮拳, 鹞子入林

This move is the same as *sparrow hawk enters the woods,* described in move 13 (figures 48, 49).

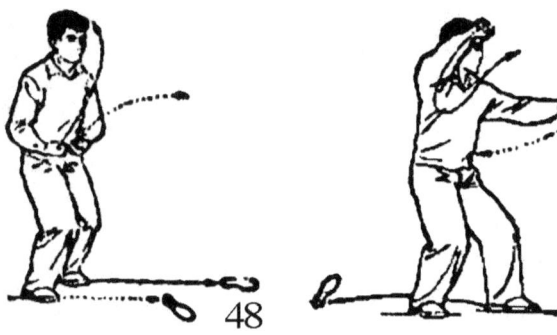

34.   Left step back, pull   Tiger washes its face

     zuǒ tuìbù lǔ zhǎng, hǔ xǐliǎn   左退步将掌, 虎洗脸

This move is the same as *tiger washes its face* – described in move 5 (figure 50).

35.   Right step back, pull   Tiger washes its face

     yòu tuìbù lǔ zhǎng, hǔ xǐliǎn   右退步将掌, 虎洗脸

This move is the same as *tiger washes its face,* described in move 6 (figure 51).

MIXTURE OF MOVES FORM, *ZASHICHUI*

36. Left press down, right block up   Black dragon draws water

zuǒ yā yòu jiàquán, wūlóng qǔ shuǐ   左压右架拳, 乌龙取水

This move is the same as *black dragon draws water,* described in move 7 (figures 52, 53).

37. Step back, plant fist down   Stretch out one wing

tuìbù xiàzáquán, dān zhǎn chì   退步下砸拳, 单展翅

This move is the same as *stretch out one wing*, described in move 8 (figure 54).

38. Left driving punch   zuǒ bēngquán   左崩拳

This move is the same as *left driving punch*, described in move 9 (figure 55).

39. Right aligned driving punch   yòu shùnbù bēngquán   右顺步崩拳

This move is the same as *right aligned driving punch*, described in move 10 (figure 56).

40. Turn around double swinging palms   The wind sways the lotus leaves

 zhuǎnshēn shuāng bǎizhǎng, fēng bǎi héyè   转身双摆掌, 风摆荷叶

Turn to the left, stepping the left foot back. Circle both fists left and up, then open them and push out to the right behind the body. Twist the body around to the rear right. The right hand is extended at shoulder height and the left is beside the right shoulder (both palms turned right). As the hands swing around to push out behind, step the right foot across in front of the left with the foot turned across the line of action – this forms a cross stance. Look at the right hand (figure 57).

Main points: Swing the arms around in a vertical circle. When you push out, twist the body forcibly to the right. Step the right foot across as you swing the arms. Land exactly when you push.

41.   Enter with left splitting palm

 jìnbù zuǒ pīzhǎng   进步左劈掌

Turn the body left and step the right foot forward. Close the right hand and bend the elbow, bringing the fist in to the waist, then extend the arm forward and up (fist centre up). Close the left hand and bring the fist in to the waist (fist heart up). Quickly and forcibly stride the left foot forward, following in a half-step with the right, keeping the weight on the right leg. Slide the left fist along the right up and forward until it approaches the right fist, then open both hands and strike out in a splitting palm. The left splits to sternum height, the right draws back to the abdomen (palms forward and down). Look at the left hand (figure 58).

Main points: All important points are the same as split, as described in Chapter Two.

42. Enter with right drilling fist   Sparrow hawk pierces the sky

    jìnbù yòu zuānquán, yàozi zuān tiān   进步右钻拳, 鹞子钻天

Close both hands. Bring the right fist up the chest then extend it out over the left fist to eyebrow level (fist heart up). Bring the left fist to under the right elbow (fist heart down). Step the left foot a half-step forward (foot hooked out) then step the right foot forward, knees bent. Look at the right fist (figure 59).

Main points: Close the fists as the left foot steps forward. Strike as the right foot steps forward.

43. Sparrow hawk flips over   yàozi fān shēn   鹞子翻身

Turn around to the left, hooking the right foot in. Bend the right elbow as the arm comes around with the left turn. The left fist stays by the right elbow with the turn. On completion of the turn extend the left fist out in front of the left shoulder and lower the right fist to under the left elbow (left fist heart in, right fist heart down). Continue to rotate the arms across the face to the right and back. As the right fist turns to the back, bend the elbow and bring the fist in to the waist (fist heart up). Bring the left fist down across the body, turning the fist to the left side and extending it at waist height (fist eye up). Quickly turn the body left and pivot the left foot to form a *santi* stance. Look at the left fist (figures 60, 61).

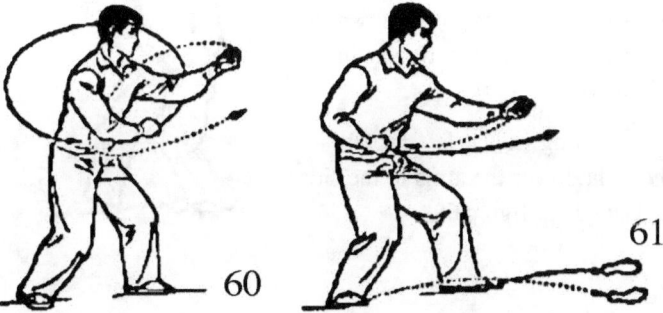

Main points: The body turns first left then right, then left again. This must be done without any breaks. The head must also follow the movement of the body so that the eyes can watch what is happening in front of the body as it turns. The whole action must be connected. On the final turn, turn the head, flatten the lumbar area, and sit down a bit.

44. Lift step, right driving punch   Sparrow hawk folds its wings

tíbù yòu bēngquán, yàozi shù shēn   提步右崩拳, 鷂子束身

This move is the same as the first *sparrow hawk folds its wings* – as described in move 3 (figure 62).

45. Aligned cannon punch   Sparrow hawk enters the woods

shùnbù pàoquán, yàozi rù lín   順步炮拳, 鷂子入林

This move is the same as the first *sparrow hawk enters the woods* – as described in move 4 (figure 63).

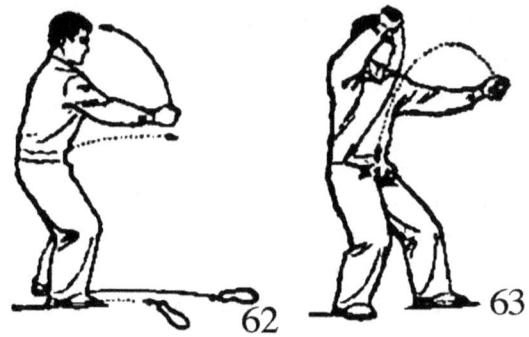

46. Close the form   shōu shì   收式

Without moving the feet or body, lower the fists down the body in front of the abdomen (fist hearts down). Bring your power down into your centre and stop for an instant (figure 64).

Bring in the left foot beside the right, lower the arms to the sides and stand up (figure 65).

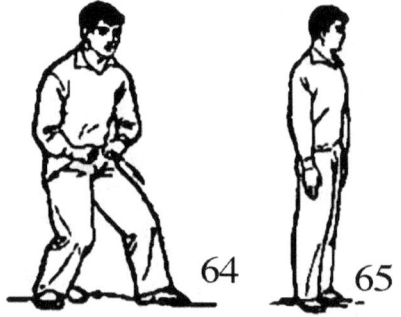

3.3 COMPREHENSIVE XINGYI FORM
xíngyì liánquán, zōnghé xíngyìquán
形意连拳、综合形意拳

This Comprehensive Xingyi form has been developed recently, and combines all of the basics of the five elemental phases and the twelve animals. It uses moves and combinations from Five Elemental Phases Connect, Twelve Cannon Fists, Mixture Of Moves and other traditional forms. It also has new moves and combinations, which aim to give Xingyiquan practitioners a complete reference form.

The reasons behind the creation of this form are as follows:

1) To increase both athletic intensity and difficulty, and to satisfy the desire of athletes for a challenge.

2) To increase rotational movement, jumps, rising and falling actions, and quick attacks and withdrawals. This increases the training effect and makes practice more interesting.

To keep the characteristics and fully develop the unique flavour of Xingyi – the clarity of hard/soft, solid/empty, movement/stillness, and the solid simplicity of the style. Many familiar moves from traditional forms have been used to ensure that new students will still learn the traditional combinations.

To keep the excellent Xingyi method of practice – the form can be broken into parts, so you can practise a long form or a short, as a whole or in sections.

Makeup of the comprehensive Xingyi form

The whole form contains seventy-seven moves, broken into six sections which go back and forth with much variety (see the chart of the path of movement). It has over thirty moves more than a traditional form such as Mixture Of Moves. The whole form can be split into three short forms for convenience: section one and two make up one form; section two and three make up another form; and section three, four, five and six make up a third form. Each short form can be practised alone, which makes it easier for beginners, and helps advanced players to perfect sections. In more detail, the three short forms are:

First short form (sections one and two):

> Start from opening of the form and continue on to *left turn, snake form* (move 45). Then bring the left fist in front of the abdomen (first turn the fist heart up then bend the elbow and turn the fist down), so that the fists are together with the fist hearts down. Settle your power down then bring in the left foot and stand up. This short form is forty-six moves, and emphasizes the basic moves and handwork and footwork of Xingyi. It has twenty-four fist techniques, twenty palm techniques, one elbow technique, one distance jump, one high jump, two on the spot jumps, two turns, and most basic stances (pouncing, horse, cross sit, high one-legged, rub shin one-legged, and *santishi*).

Second short form (sections two and three):

> Start by standing straight, half sideways, and move into *left driving punch* on the spot (the first two moves – figures 1, 2, and 3 – of the Mixture Of Moves form – *opening of the form, left driving punch on the spot*). Then open the hands and extend the right hand out under the left arm, threading forward and up into the *swallow enters the clouds* (move 21). Continue from there to *advance left splitting palm* (move 66). Then bring the left hand back and stand up, as in the usual closing of the form. This short form has forty-nine moves and is a bit more difficult than the first short form, calling for quite a bit more coordination.

Third short form (sections three, four, five and six):

> Start with *opening of the form* and *left driving punch on the spot* from the Mixture Of Moves form, but punch a bit lower than usual. This resembles the snake form, so you continue as if from the *left snake form* (move 45) to *sparrow hawk folds its wings* (move 46), then through to move 77, finishing with the *closing of the form*. This short form has thirty-four moves, which, although not numerous, require quite a bit of agility and demand a solid foundation in the basics.

In summary, the Comprehensive Xingyi form can be practised as a unit or split into short forms, giving a bit of freedom in training. You can also practise each section repeatedly on its own as many times as you wish.

COMPREHENSIVE XINGYI FORM, *XINGYI LIANQUAN*

SECTION ONE

1. Ready stance yùbèi shì 预备式

Stand with the body half facing the direction of action with the heels together; the left foot along the intended line of action and the right foot turned out forty-five degrees. Place the arms naturally at the sides. Look forward (figures 1 and from the side).

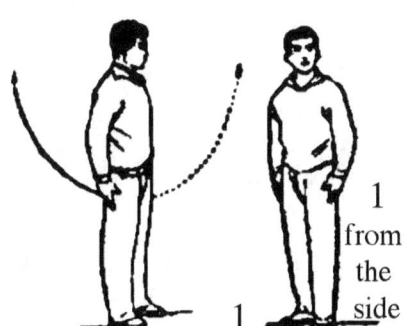

Main points: Keep the body naturally erect with the shoulders settled down, the chest relaxed and comfortable, the head and neck erect and the jaw pulled in. Focus, and breathe naturally.

2. Starting position (*santishi*) sāntǐshì 三体式

Outwardly rotate the arms and bend the elbows slightly, lifting the hands up the sides. As the forearms come to shoulder height, bend the elbows more to bring the palms in, inwardly rotating (palms face down). Bring the hands down either side of the abdomen, closing gradually to fists after they pass the face (fist surfaces face each other). Bend the knees to lower the body as the hands come down. Keep looking forward (figures 2, 3).

Outwardly rotate the right forearm to drill the fist up the chest then forward from the jaw at nose height (fist heart diagonally up). The forearm is outwardly rotated, the little finger twisted upward, and the elbow pulled down. Turn over the left fist in its original position so that the fist heart faces up. Advance the right foot, hooked out, with the knee bent. Raise the left heel slightly and push into the ground with the ball, putting the weight equally on both legs. Look at the right fist (figure 4).

Advance the left foot without moving the right, keep the knees bent and grip the ground with the toes. Drill the left fist up past the chest and out from the jaw, extending it along the right forearm. As it approaches the right fist, open both hands and apply splitting power, the left forward and down to sternum height, the right back to the abdomen, both palms forward and down (see *santishi*). Look at the index finger of the left hand (figure 5).

Main points: Don't shrug the shoulders when lifting with the hands. Make sure you keep the arms a bit bent and the elbows rolled under. When lowering the hands, wait until they come down the chest before closing them. When they arrive at the abdomen, make sure to keep the elbows tight to the ribs. Keep the head lifted and the energy lowered.

Make sure you don't turn the right foot out too much or too little – forty-five to sixty degrees is just right. Otherwise the *santishi* won't be steady.

See the main points in the *santishi* description in Chapter Two for more details on the left splitting palm.

3. Lifted step right driving punch   Sparrow hawk folds its wings

   tíbù yòu bēngquán, yàozi shù shēn   提步右崩拳, 鷂子束身

Form fists (left fist eye up and right fist heart up). Step the left foot a half-step forward, hooked out, and take a strong and long step forward with the right. Bring the left foot in quickly to place the heel at the right ankle as soon as the right foot lands (almost before, but don't jump). This forms a right one-legged stance, the left foot dorsi-flexed (also called lifted stance or chicken pose stance). Rotate the right fist and punch straight forward at sternum height (fist eye up). Draw the left fist back to the side (fist heart up). Look at the right fist (figures 6, 7).

Main points: Do not hesitate as the left foot steps forward, but push off strongly, advancing the right foot a long step. When you advance, make sure not to lift the foot too much – concentrate on speed and keeping the body steady. Punch at exactly the same time as the foot hits. Check in the final posture that the arm is not over-extended into the punch, the shoulders are settled down, the elbows are rolled under, the head is upright, the lumbar area is flat and solidly held, and the body is erect without leaning in any direction whatsoever.

4.   Aligned left cannon punch   Sparrow hawk enters the woods

       shùnbù zuǒ pàoquán, yàozi rùlín   顺步炮拳, 鹞子入林

Land the left foot forward and follow a half-step in with the right, keeping most of the weight on the right leg. Punch the left fist out with the elbow bent at sternum height (fist eye up). Rotate the right arm and block up, the fist by the right temple (fist eye down). Look at the left fist (figure 8).

Main points: Hit with the front foot, drive out one fist, and block with the other at exactly the same time. Roll the knees in slightly. Keep the lumbar area flat and the shoulders set down.

5.   Right turn around, left drill   Sparrow hawk pierces the sky

       yòu zhuǎnshēn zuǒ zuānquán, yàozi zuān tiān   右转身左钻拳, 鹞子钻天

Hook the left foot in and the right foot out, turning one-eighty degrees around to the right, then step the right foot forward (in the new, opposite, direction of action) with the foot hooked out. Outwardly rotate the right forearm and lower the fist, bringing it back to the chest (fist heart up), then as the body turns, circle it right, out and forward to in front of the body at shoulder height, forearm inwardly rotated to turn the fist heart down. Keep the arm slightly bent and tuck down with the wrist [kòu jìn 扣劲]. Bring the left fist back to the waist (fist heart up). Look at the right fist (figure 9).

     Advance the left foot and follow with the right in behind the left. Drill the left fist out along the right forearm at nose height – fist heart diagonally up, little finger side rotated up, elbow tucked down, and arm bent. Place the right fist under and inside the left elbow (fist heart still down). Stand up as the left fist drills out, with the legs naturally parallel. Look at the left fist (figure 10).

Main points: Keep the forearm stuck to the body as you lower the right fist – rotate the arm and bring it around to the back, so that the hand slides around without leaving the body at all (slide around the chest and ribs). Step the right foot as you circle down and tuck in the right fist. Turn quickly, and keep your power in the whole body connected.

Hit with the left drilling fist at the same time as with the left advancing foot. Don't over-extend the arm, shrug the shoulders, or rooster the head.

This whole sequence is done as one movement, with no hesitation, making a complete one-eighty degrees about face. Put the power of the body into the arms.

6.   Turn around, double separation   Sparrow hawk turns around

   zhuǎnshēn shuāng fēnquán, yàozi huíshēn   转身双分拳, 鹞子回身

Turn right, turning the left foot in and sitting down on the left leg. Straighten the right leg and extend it to the right, keeping both feet firmly on the ground in a drop stance. Slide the right fist out along the thigh (fist eye turns down). Inwardly rotate the left arm as well (fist eye also turns down) and extend it out to the left. Form a straight line with the arms. Look at the right fist (figure 11).

Main points: Extend the right leg and arm together. Keep a twisting power in the arms as they extend, don't relax them. Lean a bit forward but keep the head up and the lumbar area flat. Make sure you don't hump over the upper back or shrug the shoulders.

COMPREHENSIVE XINGYI FORM, *XINGYI LIANQUAN* 147

7. Left driving punch   zuǒ bēngquán   左崩拳

Shift forward from the drop stance and extend the right leg. Turn right and step the left foot forward. Follow immediately in a half-step with the right foot, landing twenty centimetres behind the left with most of the weight on the right leg. Outwardly rotate the arms. Bring the left fist in to the waist (fist eye up) then punch forward at sternum height. Turn the right fist and bring it back to the waist (fist heart up). Look at the left fist (figures 12, 13).

8. Right driving punch   yòu bēngquán   右崩拳

Continue to drive the left foot forward and follow in a half-step with the right. Punch the right fist forward in an upright fist and bring the left fist back to the waist in a face up fist. Look at the right fist (figure 14).

9. Left driving punch

    zuǒ bēngquán   左崩拳

Drive the left foot forward again and follow in again a half-step with the right. Punch the left fist forward in an upright fist and bring the right fist back to the waist in a face up fist. Look at the left fist (figure 15).

148 CHAPTER THREE: SOLO FORMS

Main points: These three punches (moves 7, 8, and 9) should hit in succession with no breaks. Check the main points in the driving fist description of chapter two for more details. These three punches have also been called "one horse three arrows" and "continuous stepping three punches". Keep the body steady and drive the fists from the legs. There can be no slacking off between or during the punches. Keep the weight back on the driving leg (the rear leg).

10.   Cover with elbow, jump, cannon punch   Horse stance roll the elbow, enter the woods

yǎnzhǒu tiàobù pàoquán,   mǎbù chánzhǒu rù lín

掩肘跳步炮拳   马步缠肘入林

Turn right. Outwardly rotate the left arm and bend the elbow to roll it in, causing the fist heart to turn in. Then push off from both legs to jump while snapping the waist to turn around to the left – switch the place of the feet in the air so that you land in a horse stance after rotating a full one-eighty degrees. Punch the right fist straight out to the right and bring the left fist back to the left upper side of the head (fist heart out). Look at the right fist (figures 16, 17, and 18).

Main points: Turn on the spot when you jump, and when you turn keep the body upright. Snap the whole body together; don't release pressure in the arms or body just because you are in the air. Land on both feet solidly at the same time. You will be facing the opposite direction.

11.   Enter with tiger form   jìnbù hǔxíng   进步虎形

Turn slightly right and step the left foot a bit to the rear left, lifting the right foot to bring it back to the left ankle, foot dorsi-flexed. Open the hands. Reach the left hand forward and up, then pull it down beside the right wrist (palms face

COMPREHENSIVE XINGYI FORM, *XINGYI LIANQUAN*   149

each other). Then pull the hands together to the sides (fist hearts face up). Look to the forward right (figures 19, 20).

Step the right foot diagonally forward to the right, following in a half-step with the left, so that the heels are in line about twenty to forty centimetres apart. Keep the weight back on the left leg in a right empty stance. Turn the fists in, drill them up past the chest, then extend them out from the jaw. Quickly rotate and open the hands to press down to the front. The palms face forward at sternum height, tiger mouths facing each other and arms bent. Look at the right hand (figure 21).

Main points: Lower the left hand at the same time as you step the left foot back. Pull the hands back at the same time as you bring the right foot back to the ankle. Pounce the hands at the same time as you advance the right foot.

12. Enter with left wedge-tailed hawk form   jìnbù zuǒ tàixíng   进步左驼形

Step the right foot a half-step forward. Follow with the left bringing it onto the right ankle, foot dorsi-flexed, legs tight together, half-sitting in a right one-legged stance. Circle the hands to either side, withdrawing them to the waist as they close (fist hearts up). Keep the forearms tight to the sides. Look forward left (figure 22).

Advance the left foot forward left and follow a half-step in with the right, keeping the weight on the right in a left empty stance. Hit straight forward from the waist with both

fists, fist hearts up, arms slightly bent, fists about ten to twenty centimetres apart. Look at both fists (figure 23).

Main points: Bring the fists back at the same time as you lift the left foot. Hit at the same time as you advance the left foot. Keep the elbows tight to the ribs as you hit.

13.   Change-over step, right horse   huànbù yòu mǎxíng   换步右马形

Draw the left foot back to the rear. Bring the right foot in to the left ankle as soon as the left foot touches down, if not before. Keep the legs tight together and the right ankle dorsi-flexed in a left one-legged stance. Open the hands, inwardly rotate and tuck in the wrists and close the hands again to face-down fists. Pull the fists back to either side of the abdomen, elbows tight to the abdomen (fist hearts down). Look ahead (figure 24).

Advance the right foot and follow in a half-step with the left, keeping the weight back on the left leg. Hit forward with both fists, the right forward and the left inside the right forearm. Hit with both arms naturally bent (fist hearts down). The right fist is at shoulder height. Look at the right fist (figure 25).

Main points: Bring the hands back as you withdraw the left foot. Keep the body steady, the head up, and the energy settled down.

Hit at exactly the same time as you land the forward foot. Don't overextend the arms.

14.   Enter with left horse   jìnbù zuǒ mǎxíng   进步左马形

Step the right foot forward then advance the left, following a half-step with the right. Turn the right fist over (fist heart up) then hit forward to shoulder height with the left fist sliding out from under the back of the right fist. As the left fist passes the right, turn the right over again (fist heart down) and pull it back to inside the left forearm. Keep both arms naturally bent. Look at the left fist (figures 26, 27).

Main points: As the left fist hits out from under the right forearm, rotate, rooster and pull back the right fist with some force. This gives more power to the forward strike of the left fist. Don't bring the right foot in too close to the left foot. Keep the lumbar area flat, the head straight, and the shoulders settled. Keep a rolled-in force around the knees.

15.   Advance, right alligator   jìnbù yòu tuóxíng   进步右鼍形

Draw the left foot back to the rear left. Rotate the right hand, open it, and extend it forward and right over the left forearm (palm turned first up then down). Open the left fist as well (turn the palm up). Watch the right hand as it turns. Without hesitation, change to unicorn horn palms and pull both hands quickly to the side (palms up). Lift the right foot to place it by the left ankle. Keep a level watch, following the turning of the body (figures 28, 29).

Return the right foot to the forward right. Following with the left foot to beside the right, touching down the toes in a T stance. Brace the right arm horizontally to the right – bring the right unicorn palm across the chest (palm up) then rotate it in front of the mouth (palm down). Keep the arm bent. Leave

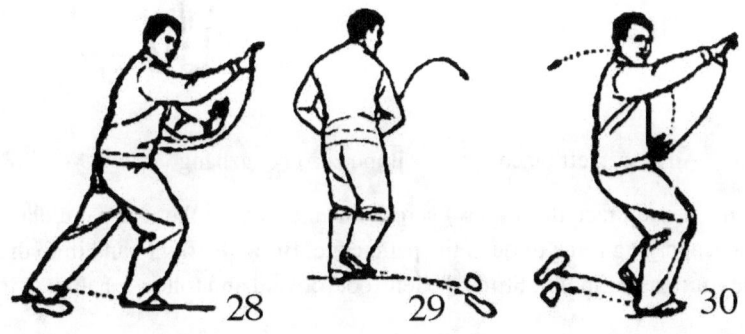

the left hand in the unicorn horn palm (palm up). Look at the right hand (figure 30).

Main points: Open the hands as the left foot steps back. Pull in with the hands as the right foot comes in. Brace out with the right arm as the right foot steps out. Don't pause between these actions, but use the rotation of the body, first right, then left, then right again, to move the arms. Use the power of the body to drive the arm, don't wave randomly. This trains the agility and coordination of rotational body technique.

16. Step back, left alligator   tuìbù zuǒ tuóxíng   退步左鼍形

Stop for an instant then quickly draw the left foot back to the rear left, turning the body left and bringing the right foot back beside the left, touching down the toes in a right T stance. Bring the left hand across the chest and mouth, rotating the palm down with a rolling force. Brace out to the left at mouth height with the arm rounded. Rotate and bring in the right hand, in a unicorn horn palm, turning the palm up in front of the abdomen. Look at the left hand (figure 31).

Main points: The important points are the same as the *right alligator form*, just transposing right and left.

17. Step back, right alligator   tuìbù yòu tuóxíng   退步右鼍形

This move is the same as the *step back, left alligator form*, just transposing right and left (figure 32).

18. Advance, left brace out   jìnbù zuǒ chēngzhǎng   进步左撑掌

Turn left and brace the left arm across the chest out to the left, palm diagonally down, applying force through the palm edge. Bring the right hand in to the right side (turn the palm up). Stride the left foot forward and follow a half-step in with the right, keeping the weight mostly on the right leg. Look at the left hand (figure 33).

Main points: Work with the left foot and hand together. Keep the head up and the lumbar area flat. Keep the hands in the unicorn horn palm even while moving.

19. Lift knee, right drilling fist   tíxī yòu zuānquán   提膝右钻拳

Step the left foot forward then stride the right foot forward. Lift the left knee with the foot hooked in and down. Keep the right leg slightly bent, in a raised knee stance. Close the fists and drill the right fist up and forward at eye height from over the left forearm (fist heart diagonally up). Bring the left fist to under the right elbow (fist heart down). Look at the right fist (figures 34, 35).

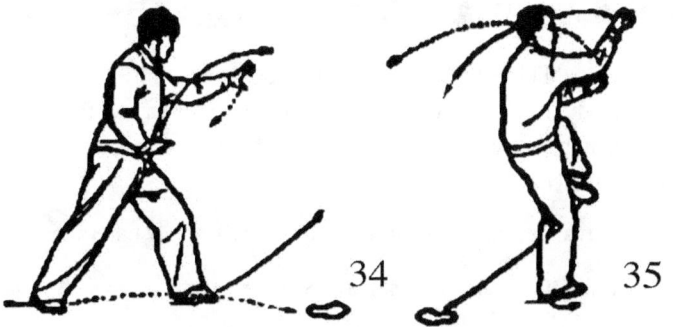

Main points: Drill the right fist at the same time as you advance the right foot. Press down with the left fist with equal force as you drill up with the right to get a more complete power. Don't lean forward or to the right too much. Keep the head straight and the lumbar area flat.

SECTION TWO

20. Turn around, left drilling fist   Sparrow hawk flips over

zhuǎnshēn zuǒ zuānquán, yàozi fān shēn   转身左钻拳, 鹞子翻身

Land the left foot behind you and turn one-eighty degrees around to the left, pushing the right heel back to form a left bow stance. Drill the left fist up inside the right forearm, lowering the right fist to under the left elbow. Look at the left fist (figure 36).

Immediately turn quickly right into a right bow stance. Rotate the right hand to brace out, bringing it outside the left forearm and up to extend in front of the head (fist heart out). Lower the left fist past the face and extend it out to the left along the outside of the thigh, fist heart facing the rear (figure 37).

Turn immediately left again and with the weight on the right leg form a left empty stance. Lower the right fist to the waist (fist heart turning up). Outwardly rotate the left fist and extend it forward in front of the body to chest height (fist eye up). Look at the left fist (figure 38).

Main points: This whole move must be done as a unit without any hesitation. As the body and arms rotate, they work together to use the power of the body. Although the feet help the turn by turning in or out, don't let them throw you off balance.

21. Advance, raise knee, thread up   Swallow enters the clouds

  jìnbù tíxī shàng chuānzhǎng, yànzi rù yún   进步提膝上穿掌, 燕子入云

Advance the right foot and lift the left knee, straightening the right leg into a raised knee one-legged stance. Open the hands and thread the right up outside the left forearm, lifting it above the head (fingers up, palm in, elbow slightly bent, and little finger side rolled in). Bend the left arm and slide the hand along the right arm to tuck into the hollow of the elbow (palm in). Look ahead (figure 39).

Main points: Lift the knee and hand at the same time. Outwardly rotate both arms with a twisting force – don't leave them relaxed. Keep the shoulders set and the head straight.

COMPREHENSIVE XINGYI FORM, *XINGYI LIANQUAN*

22. Leap, double separation   Swallow plays over the water

    yuèbù shuāng fēnzhǎng, yànzi xì shuǐ   跃步双分掌, 燕子戏水

Stop for an instant then land the left foot forward. As soon as it lands push off to spring the whole body up, jumping forward while bending both legs (right then left) in the air. As you land, drop onto a full squat on the right leg and extend the left straight to the left, foot turned in. Keep both feet flat on the ground and lean the body slightly forward, forming a left drop stance. Lower the hands down the body then separate them to either side, extending diagonally down and out, inwardly rotating the forearms to turn the palms over to face up. Look to the left (figures 40, 41, 42).

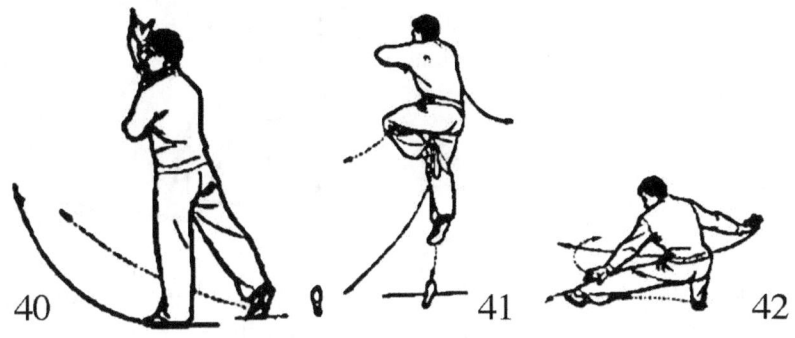

Main points: Land quickly and push off hard with the left leg. Jump for both height and distance. Land lightly but steadily. Use the power of the whole body – don't relax just because you are in the air.

23. Right stab   Swallow gathers mud

    yòu chāzhǎng, yànzi xián ní   右插掌, 燕子衔泥

Move up and forward. Turn the left foot straight and bring the right foot behind the left heel in a half-squat with the weight mostly on the right leg. Turn the right hand over and stab down to the front (palm diagonally up). Turn the left hand and bring it in above the right forearm (palm down). Look at the right hand (figure 43).

Main points: Stab at the same time that you bring the right foot in. Don't stab any higher than the waist. Twist the hand with an upward force from the little finger.

24.　　Turn around, elbow strike　　　　　White tiger shows off its prowess

　　　huíshēn dǐngzhǒu, báihǔ dǒu wēi　　　回身顶肘, 白虎抖威

Turn the left heel out and turn the body to the right. Stride the right foot forward and sit into a half horse stance (weight six-tenths on the back leg and four-tenths on the front leg). Turn the hands over and cross them, then close the right hand and strike forward with the elbow. Stop when the right fist is in front of the right abdomen (fist heart down). Bend the left elbow as well and brace out with it (palm up in front of the chest). Look at the right elbow (figure 44).

Main points: Keep the chest relaxed, the shoulders set, and the head straight. Strike with the right elbow, brace out with the left elbow, and land the right foot all at the same time. The power must be solid and full. Make sure you don't puff up the chest.

25.　　Parallel stance, thread the palm　　Swallow enters the woods

　　　bīngbù chuānzhǎng, yànzi rù lín　　　并步穿掌, 燕子入林

Step the right foot forward, hooked out. Open the right hand and swing it down then forward (palm upside down). Step the left foot forward – follow quickly with the right foot to a parallel stance – turn right, and stand up with the shoulders aligned to the line of attack. Thread the left hand along under the right forearm diagonally up to head height (palm diagonally up) and slide the right hand into the hollow of the left elbow (palm down). Look at the left hand (figure 45).

Main points: Thread the palm and step into the parallel stance at the same time. Keep power in the whole body when you stand up, don't slack off. Extend the shoulder into the hand strike while keeping the elbow down.

26. Turn around, slice up   Black tiger slashes its tail

huíshēn liāozhǎng, hēihǔ yáo wěi   回身撩掌, 黑虎摇尾

Turn the left foot in and turn the body to the right. Stride the right foot forward, keeping the weight back on the left leg in a half-horse stance. Roll the left hand in to the waist (palm up). Swing the right hand down to the right, then forward to strike with the edge of the arm at abdomen height (fingers forward, thumb down). Look at the edge of the right hand (figure 46).

Main points: Keep the chest relaxed and the lumbar area solid. Step and slice at the same time.

27. Recoil, change-over step, lift   Tiger lifts up

suōshēn huànbù tuōzhǎng, hǔ tuō   缩身换步托掌, 虎托

Extend the left hand to the front and right then thread out under the right forearm to sweep horizontally left. Turn the right hand up and, when both arms reach the same level, bend the elbows and pull the hands in to the waist (fingers diagonally down). Draw the right foot back just behind the left foot as the hands pull back. As the right foot touches down, immediately pick up the left to place it at the right ankle to form a right one-legged stance (figure 47).

Pause slightly then advance the left foot forward and left, following a half-step in with the right. Keep the weight on the right leg to form a left empty stance. Lift both palms forward in front of the abdomen (arms half bent, palms diagonally up) (figure 48).

158 CHAPTER THREE: SOLO FORMS

28.   Pull, driving punch   lǔshǒu bēngquán   将手崩拳

Stride the left foot forward again and follow in a half-step with the right foot. Form a fist and extend the left hand slightly then turn it over to pull and cover (fist heart down, fist eye in). Bend the right arm slightly, make an upright fist, then punch out over the left wrist, as with an advance driving punch. Bend the left arm and bring the left fist back under the right forearm (fist heart down) (figures 49, 50).

Main points: When pulling, rotate and roll in the forearms, connecting the power from the lumbar area. Move forward and punch in the same direction as in the previous move, *tiger lifts up*.

29.   Step back, wringing punch   tuìbù héngquán   退步横拳

Draw the right foot a half-step back. Then bring the left foot behind the right so that the legs cross with the right foot across the projected line of action and the left foot along it. The left heel is slightly raised to form a half-squat sitting stance. Twist the left fist out from under the right forearm – circle and strike with force both to the left and forward (fist heart rotates up at mouth height). Rotate the right fist and pull it back in front of the abdomen (fist heart down). Look at the left fist (figure 51).

Main points: Strike with the left hand as the left foot hits the ground. The wringing strike must have a force both hitting forward and twisting left. Tuck the left knee tightly into the hollow of the right knee in the cross-sit stance.

COMPREHENSIVE XINGYI FORM, *XINGYI LIANQUAN*   159

30. Aligned right driving punch   Black dragon shoots out of its cave

shùnbù yòu bēngquán, hēilóng chū dòng   顺步右崩拳, 黑龙出洞

Advance the right foot and follow a half-step in with the left. Drive the right fist forward at chest height (fist eye up). Pull the left fist back to the waist (figure 52).

Main points: Hit with the right foot and fist at exactly the same time. Keep the shoulders set, the head up, and the lumbar area flat. Keep the left forearm tucked into the ribs.

31. Step back, hold   White crane flashes its wings

tuìbù bàoquán, báihé liàngchì   退步抱拳, 白鹤亮翅

Draw the left foot back a half-step to the rear left to form a right bow stance. Bend the right elbow and, keeping the right fist tight to the body, stab down to the left (fist heart up) above the left fist. Rotate the left arm to turn the fist heart down, and cross the two wrists tightly. Look at the right fist (figure 53).

Turn right, lift the arms, separate in front of the head, then lower them in a vertical circle, closing in front of the abdomen. Open the left hand as it lifts and set the right fist into it when they close. Draw the right foot back just in front of the left (figures 54, 55).

Main points: Stab down with the fists at exactly the same time that the left foot steps back. Keep the arms tight to the body. Keep the power down and lower the shoulders.

When separating the hands, the body and eyes follow the movement of the right hand. Look straight ahead once the hands connect.

Drop the hands in together at the same time as the foot comes in, making a sound with both (although as long as the intention is there, the sound is not necessary). In the final position, keep the head up, flatten the back, settle the shoulders, lower the *qi*, and hold the forearms tight to the body.

32.   Advance, cannon punch   jìnbù pàoquán   进步炮拳

Stride the right foot forward and to the right, following a half-step in with the left. Punch forward with the left fist. Drill the right fist up the chest then turn it to block up by the head (figure 56).

Main points: Hit with the right foot and left fist at exactly the same time. Make sure to first drill the right fist up and then rotate out, don't block straight up. Other points are the same as in the cannon punch form described in chapter two.

33.   Step back pull   tuìbù lǚ shǒu   退步捋手

Turn left, outwardly rotate the forearms – extend the right fist forward in front of the body and bring the left fist back to the waist (both fist hearts turn up, the right angled) (figure 57).

Draw the right foot back to form a left bow stance and turn again to the left. Open the left hand and stretch it out over the right forearm (palm turning down). As the left hand turns and presses down, open and turn the right down as well. Look at the left hand (figure 58).

Shift back, turn right, and bring back the left foot, lifting it to place it at the right ankle. Pull in from the left until the fists face up at the abdomen. Look forward (figure 59).

COMPREHENSIVE XINGYI FORM, *XINGYI LIANQUAN*

Main points: This sequence must flow without hesitation. Rotate the body to move the arms.

As the right fist extends and drops (figure 57), the forearm must use rolling-in force. As the left hand extends (figure 58) the arm must circle (from in outward).

Pull in with the hands and left foot at the same time. Pull the hands in tightly to the body, so that the forearms end up snug to the abdomen.

34. Advance, wrapping posture   jìnbù bāoguǒ shì   进步包裹式

Open the left fist to a unicorn horn palm and drill it up the chest (figure 60).

Advance the left foot, follow in a bit with the right and bend the knees in a half-crouch with the weight more on the left leg and the right heel raised in a dragon riding stance. Open the right fist to a unicorn horn palm as well, and drill up inside the left forearm, outwardly rotating (little finger side twists up) – stop in front of the face at nose height. Lower the left hand to the abdomen (palm down). Look at the right hand (figure 61).

Main points: Don't step forward until the left hand has completed the drill – wait until the right hand comes out. Step the left foot forward to the forward left with the toes hooked in. The right arm twists – the little finger turns up, the forearm outwardly rotates, and the elbow rolls in. Keep a rolled-in force around the knees and push the back foot into the ground. Keep the left forearm tight to the body. Hold the neck straight, the lumbar area flat, the shoulders down, and the chest relaxed and open. Lean forward slightly.

35. Advance, left dragon form   jìnbù zuǒ lóngxíng   进步左龙形

Without moving the hands, step the left foot forward with the knee slightly bent and lift the right foot with the foot hooked up (figure 62).

Kick forcibly down and forward with the right heel as it lands, turning the foot out across the line of action. Follow in a half-step with the left foot, pushing against the ground with the ball of the foot. Turn sharply right; squat into a cross step in a full cross-sit stance with the right foot turned across and the left foot aligned with the line of action. Drill the left unicorn horn palm up along the right forearm. As it reaches the right hand, quickly open both hands, inwardly rotate them, then press down. The left presses down twenty to forty centimetres from the ground in front of the body, the right back to the right hip. Look at the left hand (figure 63).

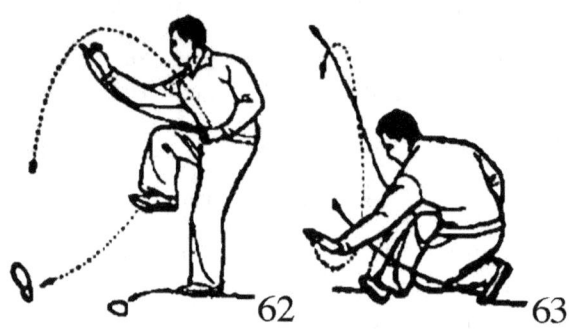

Main points: Use the body's drop into the squat to get power and speed into the hand technique. In the cross-sit stance keep the knees tightly together, raise the left heel off the ground, lean forward slightly, and sit the buttocks back almost on the left heel. Keep the head straight and the lumbar area flat.

36. Jump, right dragon form   tiàobù yòu lóngxíng   跳步右龙形

Close the hands and bring them in to drill up the chest – the left leading and the right following along the left forearm and up. Jump up, and at the highest point of the jump quickly switch the position of the legs and open the hands. Start to rotate the hands to prepare for the press down (figure 64).

On landing, turn the trunk left and squat into a full cross-sit stance – left leg forward, right hand pressing down in front (about twenty to forty centimetres off the ground) and left hand back at the hip. Look at the front hand (figure 65).

COMPREHENSIVE XINGYI FORM, *XINGYI LIANQUAN*

Main points: The jump and the landing must be timed together with the hand movement – use the jump to extend the right fist up, and use the landing to get power into the press down. The legs switch places in the air, so must move quickly. The main points of the final posture are the same as the previous dragon form.

37.   Enter with bear   jìnbù xióngxíng   进步熊形

Close the right hand. Bring it in and drill up the chest then forward and up from the jaw at eye height (fist heart diagonally up). Take a big stride forward left with the left foot. Follow in a small step with the right foot. Raise the back heel off the ground, half-bend the knees, and put the weight on the front leg to form a dragon-riding stance. Close the left fist and bring it to the waist (fist heart down). Look at the right fist (figure 66).

Main points: Step the left foot on a diagonal line with the foot hooked in. Push into the ground with the ball of the rear leg. Twist the little finger of the right hand up and outwardly rotate the forearm. Roll in the power around the knees. Keep the lumbar area flat and the head up. Lean forward slightly.

38.   Advance, eagle   jìnbù yīngxíng   进步鹰形

Step the left foot forward with the foot hooked out. Advance the right foot diagonally to the forward right with the foot hooked in. Bring the left foot in slightly with the heel raised and half-crouch in a dragon-riding stance. Outwardly rotate the left arm and drill up along the right forearm. As the left fist extends to meet the right, open and rotate the hands, pressing down. The left presses down in front of the body, the right back to the waist (both palms down). Look at the forward hand (figure 67).

Main points: Be attentive when pressing down – like an eagle grasping its prey. Use the action of the legs to get power to the hands. Don't over-extend the arms. Lean forward slightly. Roll in around the knees. The stance is the same as in the bear form.[48]

39.   Withdraw, chicken   Golden rooster stands on one leg

chébù jīxíng, jīnjī dúlì   撤步鸡形, 金鸡独立

Shift back and draw the right foot back, threading the right hand forward from under the left and bringing the left back to the side (figure 68).

The instant the right foot lands, quickly and forcibly lift the left foot (dorsi-flexed) to settle at the right ankle in a right one-legged stance. Thread the left hand forward under the right to chest height, and bring the right back to the waist. Look at the forward hand (figure 69).

---

[48] Translator's note: Although the author describes the eagle and bear dragon-riding stances as the same, the bear is often done more erect, with rising power, and the eagle stance more crouched, with dropping power.

Main points: Draw the foot back quickly and land solidly. Coordinate handwork with the footwork – hands and feet arrive together at the final position. In the one-legged stance, keep the head up, the lumbar area flat, and lean forward slightly.

40. Drive forward, chicken stance   Golden rooster stands on one leg

  zòngbù jīxíng, jīnjī dúlì   纵步鸡形, 金鸡独立

Take a strong step forward with the left foot without moving the arms[49] (figure 70).

Advance the right foot further forward, then instantly bring the left foot forcibly in – snap it to the right ankle in a right one-legged stance (figure 71).

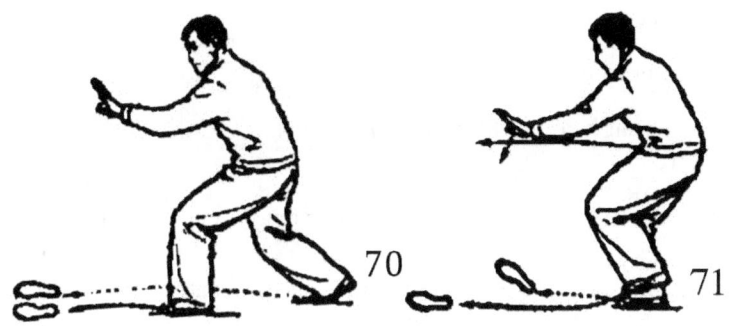

Main points: Take quick and connected steps, also going for distance. Keep the legs tight together in the stance. Don't rise, fall, or sway when you step. Look at the forward hand.

41. Advance, right driving punch   Golden rooster pecks a grain of rice

  jìnbù yòu bēngquán, jīnjī shí mǐ   进步右崩拳, 金鸡食米

Advance a full step with the left foot and a half-step with the right – leave most of the weight back on the right leg. Close the right hand and punch an upright fist forward under the left hand. Pull the left hand back a bit, slapping it to clasp the right wrist. Look at the right fist (figure 72).

---

[49] Translator's note: This may also be done with a left hand movement – press into the back of the hand (palm up) as the left foot steps forward, then turn the palm over to press forward and down as the right foot lands. This is done softly but firmly, and the hand does not change position relative to the body.

Main points: Hit with the foot and fist at the same time. Extend the shoulder into the punch, keep the elbow down, and the arms slightly bent.

SECTION THREE

42. Turn around, left brace out   Golden rooster shakes its tail

   zhuǎnshēn zuǒ chēngzhǎng, jīnjī dǒu líng   转身左撑掌, 金鸡抖翎

Draw the right foot back, turn the body about ninety degrees right, and slide the left foot back – end up feet parallel, knees in a half-squat, and weight mostly on the right leg. Brace out and down above the left knee with the left hand (palm down). Brace up with the right fist, elbow bent, fist at the temple (fist heart out). Look at the left hand (figure 73).

   Stop for an instant then pivot on the ball of the left foot and the heel of the right – push into the left foot to turn sharply ninety degrees to the right, into a right bow stance. Continue to brace the left hand back, stopping at the hip, and keep force in the right arm as it turns with the body. Look ahead (figure 74).

COMPREHENSIVE XINGYI FORM, *XINGYI LIANQUAN* 167

43. Stand on one leg, stab down   Golden rooster blocks up

dúlì xià chāzhǎng, jīnjī shàng jià   独立下插掌, 金鸡上架

Advance the left foot with the knee half bent, and push off the right foot, lifting it to perch on the left ankle in a left one-legged stance. Open the right hand and stab it down strongly – slide by the chest down to the lower left and stop by the left knee (back of hand on leg). Bend the left elbow and thread up to the right – slide by the chest to finish in front of the right shoulder (palm in). The arms cross with the left on the inside. Look straight ahead (figures 75, 76).

(image 76 is 75 from behind)

44. Advance, right flicking up strike   Golden rooster heralds the dawn

jìnbù yòu tiǎozhǎng, jīnjī bào xiǎo   进步右挑掌, 金鸡报晓

Advance the right foot and follow in a half-step with the left to sit on the left leg in a *santi* stance. Flick the right arm up forward right at eye height with a sideways upright palm (fingers up). Rotate the left hand and press down to the left hip (palm down). Keep the arms naturally bent. Look at the index finger of the right hand (figure 77).

Main points: For important points to bear in mind for the preceding three moves, see moves 6, 7, and 8 of the chicken form in Chapter Two.

45. Left turn around, snake   zuǒ zhuǎnshēn shéxíng   左转身蛇形

Pivot on the ball of the left foot to turn quickly around to the left, lifting the right foot as you turn and landing it hooked in behind the left foot. Half crouch, shifting the weight onto the right leg with the left heel raised. Cross the hands into a hugging position, right hand at the left shoulder (palm down) and left hand at the right waist (palm up). Use the quick drive and twist of the arms to increase the rotational speed of the body. Look ahead to the lower left (figure 78).

Stop for an instant, then step forward with the left foot a half-step, sitting mostly on the right leg (in a *santi* stance). Close the hands and slice the left arm down from the waist then forward to waist height (fist eye up). Bring the right fist back to the hip (fist eye diagonally up). Look at the left fist. Lean a bit into the strike (figure 79).

Main points: Turn around quickly, with a tight twisting back force in the body, looking around to the left back. Close the hands in as the body turns, so that everything arrives together. Hold the knees tightly together to help keep the body steady. Stride and slice out at exactly the same time – the left hand and foot hit together. Don't hold the arm stiff after you hit. Keep the head up, the lumbar area flat, and be attentive.

46. Shin rubbing step, right driving punch   Sparrow hawk folds its wings

    tíbù yòu bēngquán, yàozi shù shēn   提步右崩拳, 鷂子束身

Step the left foot a half-step forward then advance the right. As the right foot lands, quickly settle the left foot on the right ankle in a right one-legged stance. Drive the right fist straight forward from the hip to chest height (fist eye up). Pull the left fist back to the waist (fist heart up). Look at the right fist (figure 80).

COMPREHENSIVE XINGYI FORM, *XINGYI LIANQUAN*   169

47. Aligned cannon punch   Sparrow hawk enters the woods

shùnbù pàoquán, yàozi rù lín   顺步炮拳, 鹞子入林

Advance the left foot and follow in a half-step with the right, sitting on the back leg. Hit with the left fist straight forward at chest height with the elbow slightly bent (fist eye up). Bend the right elbow and rotate to block up, fist at the temple (fist eye down). Look at the left fist (figure 81).

48. Left step back, pull   Tiger washes its face

zuǒ tuìbù lǔ zhǎng, hǔ xǐliǎn   左退步捋掌, 虎洗脸

Lower the right fist to the waist (figure 82).

    Pause. Open the right hand and bring it up then block across the right side of the face (palm left, fingers up). Bring the left fist back to the waist (fist heart up). Step the left foot back and turn quickly left as you block, shifting to the left leg into a *santi* stance. Lean slightly forward. Look to the lower left (figure 83).

49. Right step back, pull   Tiger washes its face

yòu tuìbù lǔ zhǎng, hǔ xǐliǎn   右退步捋掌, 虎洗脸

Open the left hand and bring it up then in to sweep across the left side of the face (palm right, fingers up). Close the right hand and bring it down to the waist (fist heart up). Step the right foot back as you block. Turn right and shift your weight onto the right leg into a *santi* stance, leaning forward slightly. Look to the lower right (figure 84).

50. Left press down, right block up   Black dragon draws water

zuǒ yā yòu jiàquán, wūlóng qǔ shuǐ   左压右架拳, 乌龙取水

Push from the right foot to shift forward onto the left foot and quickly twist left. Block across the right face with the right hand (open from a fist) and bring the left hand to the waist (closing into a fist) (figure 85).

    Pause, then close and lower the right hand, drilling the left fist quickly forward and up (fist heart diagonally up) over the right at eye height. Stop the right fist under the left elbow (fist heart down). Look at the left fist (figure 86).

    Without hesitation, block up with the right fist – slide up from under the left forearm and bend the elbow to put the fist beside the head (fist eye down, fist heart forward). Inwardly rotate the left fist and press down to in front of the abdomen (fist eye in, fist heart down). Sit back and bring in the left foot, touching the ball of the foot down in front of the right foot. Look forward (figure 87).

COMPREHENSIVE XINGYI FORM, *XINGYI LIANQUAN* 171

51. Turn around, drive forward, double separation   Swallow skims the water

zhuǎnshēn zòngbù shuāng fēnquán   yànzi chāo shuǐ

转身纵步双分拳   燕子抄水

Replace the left foot forward where it was. Lower the right fist and again drill the left fist forward and up over the right fist at eye height (fist heart diagonally up). Stop the right fist under the left elbow (fist heart down). Look at the left fist (figure 88).

Extend the right fist under the left forearm, rotating out, up, then back, stopping at the temple (fist eye down, fist heart out). Turn quickly around to the right, turning the left foot in to form a right bow stance. Bend the left elbow and slide the left fist down the chest to the hip. Look to the lower front (figure 89).

Without pause, turn around one-eighty degrees to the left back, twisting the left foot on line and bending the left knee. Shift forward, bend the right knee, raise the heel and push into the ball. Extend the left fist forward and swing the right fist down, forward, then up, ending up crossing the wrists – the fists are at shoulder height, right arm on the outside. Then leave the right fist where it was and circle the left wrist with force, back and under the right arm so that the left arm ends up on the outside. The fist eyes face in during both cross hands (figures 90, 91).

Push off strongly with the left foot and drive forcibly forward with the right to jump forward – land in a half squat. Just as the right foot lands, quickly lift the left foot to perch by the right ankle. Raise the arms and separate them forward and back at shoulder height (fist eyes up). Keep the elbows slightly bent and the body sideways to the line of attack. Look to the front (figure 92).

172   CHAPTER THREE: SOLO FORMS

91   92

Main points: The preceding sequence of six moves (moves 46 through 51, figures 80-92) is taken from the traditional Mixture Of Moves form. Refer to the main points for moves 3 through 7, and move 17 (figures 4, 5, 6, 7, 8, 9, 23, 24, 25) in the Mixture Of Moves form descriptions in this chapter.

52.   Right driving punch   yòu bēngquán   右崩拳

Advance the left foot and follow in a half-step with the right. Bend the right elbow, bring the fist in to the waist, then punch straight forward at chest height (fist eye up). Bring the left fist back to the waist (fist heart up). Look at the right fist (figure 93).

Main points: The forward foot and fist hit together. Keep the elbow bent when you punch – gain distance by extending the shoulder and turning the body into the punch.

53.   Aligned cannon punch   Sparrow hawk enters the woods

shùnbù pàoquán, yàozi rùlín

顺步炮拳, 鷂子入林

This is described above in move 47 (figure 94).

COMPREHENSIVE XINGYI FORM, *XINGYI LIANQUAN*

54. Left step back, pull   Tiger washes its face

zuǒ tuìbù lǚ zhǎng, hǔ xǐliǎn   左退步捋掌, 虎洗脸

This is described above in move 48 (figures 95, 96).

55. Right step back, pull   Tiger washes its face

yòu tuìbù lǚ zhǎng, hǔ xǐliǎn   右退步捋掌, 虎洗脸

This is described above in move 49 (figure 97).

56. Turn around, right driving punch   Golden rooster pecks a grain of rice

zhuǎnshēn yòu bēngquán, jīnjī shí mǐ   转身右崩拳, 金鸡食米

This starts the same as move 50, *black dragon draws water*. Push with the right foot, shift forward, and quickly twist left. Open the right hand and block across the face while the left fist closes and draws back to the waist (figure 98).

    Stop for an instant, then close and lower the right hand while the left fist drills quickly forward and up over the right at eye height (fist heart diagonally up). Stop the right fist under the left elbow (fist heart down). Look at the left fist (figure 99).

    Turning the right fist, bring it outside the left forearm, up and back to position in front of the temple (fist eye down, fist heart out). Quickly push the left leg and turn the body around to the right – lift the left foot to bring it in to the right ankle, shins together. Bend the left elbow; lower the fist past the chest and swing it back behind the hip (fist eye back). Go along with the body's rotation with the eyes, then look to the lower front (figure 100).

174 CHAPTER THREE: SOLO FORMS

Stop for an instant. Turn left again, stride the left foot to the forward left and follow with the right foot a half-step. Lower the right fist down the side then punch forward to waist height. Open the left hand and outwardly rotate the forearm, circling forward at the left side, to hook in the palm on top of the right wrist. Look at the right fist (figure 101).

57. Withdraw, left splitting palm chèbù zuǒ pīzhǎng   撤步左劈掌

Draw the right foot back a half-step into a left bow stance. Extend the left hand to eye height (palm forward). Open the right hand and leave it inside the left forearm (palm faces left) (figure 102).

Pull both hands down and in to in front of the abdomen, then close the hands into face-up fists. Push off and lift the left foot to dorsi-flex at the right ankle. Twist right and sit on the right leg. Follow the rotation of the body with the eyes, keeping a level gaze (figure 103).

Don't move the right foot – step the left forward into a *santi* stance. Drill both fists up, out from the jaw, then rotate and open to split forward and down. The left finishes at chest height, the right under the left elbow (both palm hearts diagonally down). Look at the left hand (figure 104).

COMPREHENSIVE XINGYI FORM, *XINGYI LIANQUAN*

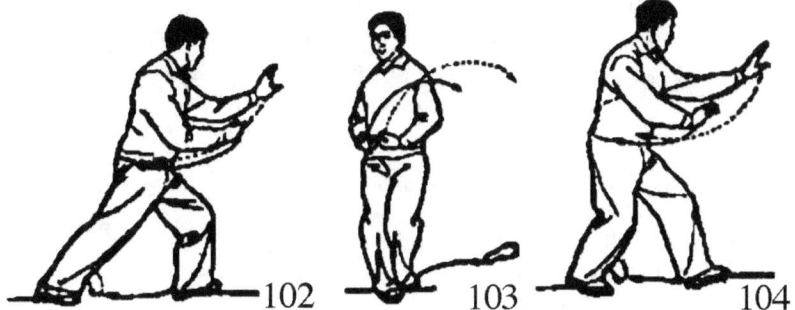

58. Advance, left push   Push the window to gaze at the moon

jìnbù zuǒ tuīzhǎng, tuīchuāng wàngyuè   进步左推掌, 推窗望月

Lower and bring in both hands, closing to face-up fists in front of the abdomen. Bring in the left foot to the right ankle (figure 105).

Without a pause, open the left hand and quickly push up and left at shoulder height (thumb down, palm out). Step the left foot out sideways with the hand (foot turned across the line of push) and slide the right foot in. Sit down a bit, more weight on the right leg, into a half-horse stance. Look at the left hand (figure 106).

59. Horse stance, double brace out   Three basins land on the ground

mǎbù shuāng chēngzhǎng, sānpán luòdì

马步双撑掌, 三盘落地

Roll the left hand in across the chest to the abdomen. Open the right hand and cross it above the left (palm up). Then brace out to the sides with both hands outside the knees (tiger mouths in, palms

down). Shift the left foot out sideways another half-step and slide the right foot in to form a half-horse stance again, a bit lower than the first. Lean a bit forward into the move. Look at the left hand (figure 107).

60.　　Cross-sit, stab down　　　　　　　Lazy dragon lies in the road

　　　　zuòpán xià chāquán, lǎn lóng wò dào　　坐盘下插拳, 懒龙卧道

Do a front crossover step with the right foot in front of the left. Turn the body a bit left with the legs crossed in a cross-sit stance. Close both hands; stab the right fist forward and down over the left forearm (fist heart up). Bring the left fist under the right forearm (fist heart down). Keep the forearms close to the body. Look to the lower front (figure 108).

61.　　Advance, left wringing fists　　　Black dragon overturns the waves

　　　　jìnbù zuǒ héngquán, wūlóng fān jiāng　　进步左横拳, 乌龙翻江

Advance the left fist and left foot together – twist the left fist forward and left to shoulder height with the elbow bent (rotate the fist heart up); bend the knee. Bring the right fist back to the waist (fist heart down). Look at the left fist (figure 109).

62.　　Right driving punch on the spot

　　　　yuándì yòu bēngquán　　原地右崩拳

Push from the right leg to shift forward into a left bow stance. Punch the right fist straight forward from the waist at sternum level (fist eye up). Pull the left fist back to the waist (fist heart up). Look at the right fist (figure 110).

63. Left punch, right kick   Dragon and tiger make friends

zuǒ chōng yòu dēng, lóng hǔ xiāngjiāo   左冲右蹬, 龙虎相交

Bend the left knee to hold balance. Lift the right thigh then extend the leg to kick to waist height, pulling the foot back to put force into the heel. Pull the right fist back to the waist (fist heart up) and punch the left fist straight forward (fist eye up). Look ahead (figure 111).

64. Aligned right driving punch   shùnbù yòu bēngquán   顺步右崩拳

Land the right foot forward, follow in a half-step with the left, then half sit on the back leg. Drive the right fist straight forward from the waist at sternum height (fist eye up). Pull the left fist back to the waist (fist heart up). Look at the right fist (figure 112).

Main points: The preceding nine moves (56 through 64, figures 98-112) are the same as moves 22 through 30 (figures 31-43) in the traditional Mixture of Moves form. See the main points in the Mixture of Moves form descriptions in this chapter.

SECTION FOUR

65. Turn around, double swing   The wind sways the lotus leaves

zhuǎnshēn shuāng bǎizhǎng, fēng bǎi héyé   转身双摆掌, 风摆荷叶

Shift back and pivot on the heel of the left foot and the ball of the right to turn the body around to the left. Inwardly rotate the forearms and lower the fists close to the body (figure 113).

Keep circling the fists left then up, opening as they pass the head, swinging right and pushing to the back. Turn the body right and to the back as well. The palms finish facing out – fingers up, the right at shoulder height, the left under the right elbow. As the arms swing around and push back, step the right foot quickly across in front of the left, then bring the left foot in. The legs end up crossed – the front leg bent, the rear leg naturally bent with the heel raised, and the body twisted to the back – in a twisted scissors stance. Look at the right hand (figure 114).

Main points: Swing the hands in a vertical circle tight to the body. The swing of the hands, twist of the body, and the cross step are done simultaneously. Make sure the knees are not held stiff and straight.

66. Advance, left splitting palm   jìnbù zuǒ pīzhǎng   进步左劈掌

Turn left , close the right hand and bring it in to the waist, then drill up to nose height (fist heart diagonally up). Step the right foot forward and shift the weight forward to form a right bow stance (with the foot hooked out). Close the left hand and bring it in to the waist as well (fist heart up). This is the right split entry (figure 115).

Take a big step forward with the left foot and follow in a half-step with the right. Outwardly rotate the left forearm, twisting [níngjìn 拧劲] and extending it over the right forearm. Open the left hand and split down to sternum height. Open the right hand and bring it back in front of the abdomen. This is the left split landing (figure 116).

67. Drive forward, thread palm   Golden rooster stands on one leg

zòngbù qián chuānzhǎng, jīnjī dúlì   纵步前穿掌, 金鸡独立

Advance the left foot a half-step, shifting the weight forward and bending the knee into a half-squat. Lean forward slightly and raise the right heel, knee bent. Thread the right hand out under the left, forward to sternum height, and bring the left hand back to beside the hip (both palms down and fingers forward). Look at the forward hand (figure 117).

Spring off the left leg and forcibly advance the right, landing in a half-squat. Bring the left foot immediately up to the right ankle in a one-legged stance. Thread the left hand out under the right, forward to sternum height, and bring the right hand back to the waist (both palms still down, fingers forward). Look at the forward hand (figure 118).

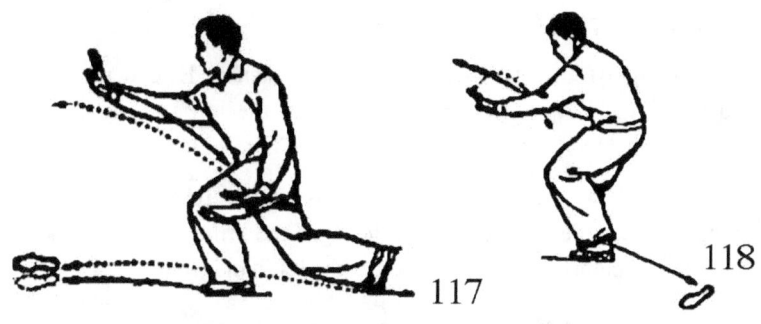

Main points: Drive forward for distance, but keep your balance. Don't jump at all – drive the body forward, not up. Be attentive as you thread each hand forward. Bring the other hand back to cover the knee. When lifting the foot, keep the lumbar area flat and the head up. Don't lean forward too much.

68. Monkey grabs the leash in its mouth (right)

yuánhóu diāo shéng yòu shì   猿猴叼绳右式

Draw the left foot back to the rear left to form a right bow stance. Thread the right hand forward under the left hand at sternum height, and bring the left back in front of the abdomen (palms down). Look at the right hand (figure 119).

Shift back and draw the right foot back a half-step, touching the toes down in front of the left foot to form a right T stance. Bring the right hand in and stab down, sticking inside the right thigh (palm out, fingers down). Extend the left hand in front of the right shoulder, pressing out with the palm forward. Look forward, sighting along the line of the left fingers (figure 120).

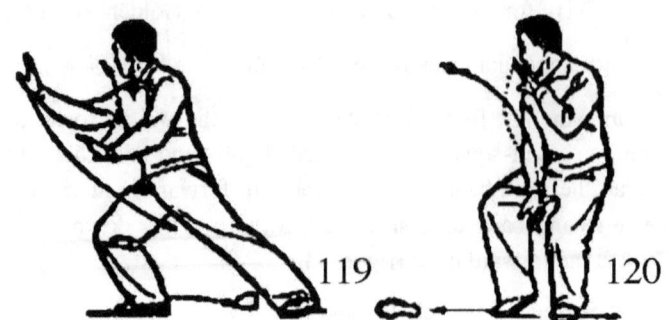

Main points: To scrunch the body in, close in the chest, keep the lumbar area flat, lift the neck, and be attentive. Don't just relax and curl in.

69. Monkey scrambles up a pole (right)

   yuánhóu pá gān yòu shì   猿猴爬竿右式

Advance the right foot a half-step, into a *santi* stance. Extend the right hand forward under the left at eye height, and bring the left back in front of the abdomen (palms down). Look at the right hand (figure 121).

Step the right foot forward again, shifting the weight forward into a right bow stance. Thread the left hand under the right and bring the right back in front of the abdomen (palms still down). Look at the left hand (figure 122).

Advance the left foot and extend the right hand forward under the left (figure 123).

Without pause after the previous action, quickly push off with the left foot and forcibly lift the right knee to bring the thigh up (foot dorsi-flexed). Lean forward. Hop forward on the left foot. Thread the left hand under the right and bring the right back in front of the abdomen (palms still down). Look at the forward hand (figures 124, 125).

When the left foot lands, stride strongly forward with the right. As the right foot lands follow a half-step in with the left, sitting on the rear leg in a *santi* stance. Extend the right hand out under the left to eye height, and bring the left back in front of the abdomen (palms down). Look at the front hand (figure 126).

Main points: Link this whole sequence together smoothly. Step and extend the hands quickly without hesitations between each action. Push off and up to hop with the left leg, and lift the right knee high, raising the centre of gravity. Jump for distance but maintain balance. Coordinate the left hand strike with the jump. As you lean forward make sure not to shrug the shoulders or scrunch up the neck. Watch what the hands are doing, switching the eyes to whichever hand is in front.

SECTION FIVE

70. Turn around monkey scratches its mark

   zhuǎnshēn yuánhóu guà yìn   转身猿猴挂印

Bring the right foot back and touch the toes down. Twist the body left. Lower the hands in front of the abdomen, forming unicorn horn palms (palms up). Turn the head with the body, watching straight ahead (figure 127).

Stride the right foot (hooked out) out to the rear right and twist the body right. Inwardly rotate the right forearm, bringing the palm horizontally past the chest to brace out at shoulder height (thumb down, palm out). Look at the right hand (figure 128).

Hook the left foot in beside the right, about a foot length away, forming the character eight 八 with the feet. Continue to turn the body right around to the back. Don't change the position of the hands. Keep watching the right hand (figure 129).

Draw the right foot back, following the line of the left heel. Turn around to face the same direction that the ready stance faced, shifting forward into a left bow stance. Open the hands to face-down palms, extend the left under the right to eye height, and bring the right back to in front of the abdomen. Look at the left hand (figure 130).

Main points: Stop for an instant in the position of figure 127, then do not pause between the rest of the moves (figures 128-130), completing the whole sequence as one move. Bring the right hand and foot in together then brace the right hand out as the right foot steps around. Hook out, hook in, and twist the body quickly around to the right – use the feet to get the body around and use the body to give power to the legs.

71. Monkey grabs the leash in its mouth (left)

yuánhóu diāo shéng zuǒ shì   猿猴叼绳左式

Sit back and bring the left foot back a half-step, touching the toes down in front of the right foot in a left T stance. Bring the left hand in and stab down inside the left thigh (palm out, fingers down). Place the right hand in front of the left shoulder with a patting action (palm down, fingers forward). Look ahead (figure 131).

Main points: The main points are the same as move 68, right side *monkey grabs the leash in its*

mouth, just transposing left and right.

72. Monkey scrambles up a pole (left)

   yuánhóu pá gān zuǒ shì   猿猴爬竿左式

The actions and main points are the same as move 69, *monkey scrambles up a pole* (right), just transposing left and right. This move also travels in the opposite direction from move 69 (figures 132, 133, 134, 135, 136, 137).

184 CHAPTER THREE: SOLO FORMS

SECTION SIX

73. Turn around, right thread palm

   zhuǎnshēn yòu chuānzhǎng   转身右穿掌

Draw the left foot back behind the body and pivot on the ball of the right foot to turn around one-eighty degrees to the left. Outwardly rotate the arms (turning the palms up) and bring them around with the body. Look at the left hand as before (figure 138).

Advance the right foot strongly and follow in with the left, to stand up with the feet together, the body side on to the line of action. Extend the right hand forward along under the left arm at eye height, and bring the left hand back beside the right elbow (both palms up). Look at the right hand (figure 139).

Main points: Turn and step into the closed stance quickly. Outwardly rotate both forearms when you thread the hand out, creating a rolling in force in the elbows. In the final position, keep the arms and knees naturally bent, not rigid.

74. Turn around, drop stance, cover

   zhuǎnshēn pūbù gàizhǎng   转身仆步盖掌

Turn left again, pivoting on the ball of the right foot and quickly drawing a big step to the back with the left foot. Lean forward and drop down – squat on the right leg with the knee over the toes and extend the left leg straight. Bend the right elbow and lift the hand, rolling it around the head to cover in front of the body. Roll the left wrist to stick the back of the hand on the ribs, then stab down behind the body by sliding the back of the hand along the back of the ribs (palm out). Look at the front hand (figures 140, 141).

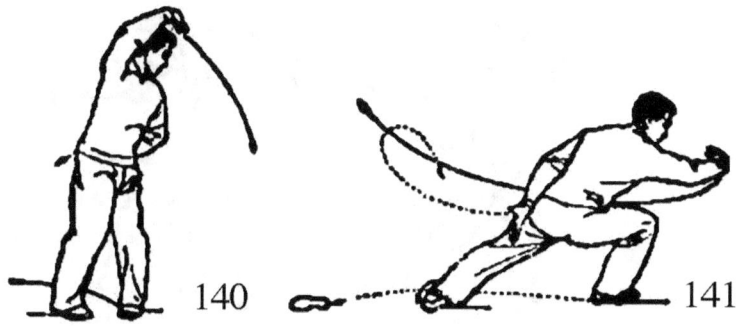

Main points: Turn with agility. Roll the arms tightly around the body. Drop and cover at the same time.

75.   Advance, right thread palm   jìnbù yòu chuānzhǎng   进步右穿掌

Shift back, turn around to the left, and advance the right foot, rising up into a *santi* stance. Outwardly rotate the right forearm (to turn the palm up) and thread it up past the chest at eye height. Extend the left hand to the rear then outwardly rotate the forearm (to turn the palm down) and bring it back along under the right forearm to the elbow. Look at the right hand (figure 142).

Main points: Rotate the forearms with an opposing twisting force [níng jìn 拧 劲]. As the left hand extends out to the rear, rotate and put force into the palm, spiraling out.

Step the right foot forward and thread the right hand at the same time.

76.   Turn around, *santishi*   huíshēn sāntǐshì   回身三体式

Hook the right foot in and turn around to the left, pivoting the left foot straight. Sit on the right leg in a *santi* stance. Bend the right elbow to lift the hand up, then lower the hand in front of the face to the front of the abdomen. Turn the left hand over to face up and roll the wrist to stick the back of the hand on the ribs. Then circle the hand (palm up) to the back, left, forward and up, finally outwardly rotate the forearm (to turn the palm down) and drop the wrist in front of the body at sternum height in a *santi* stance (figures 143, 144).

Main points: Roll the arms around tight to the body. Put dropping force into the hands at the same time as the left foot straightens out, transferring the force of the leg into the hands. Make sure to settle the shoulders, drop the wrists, straighten the neck, flatten the lumbar area, and lower the *qi* at the same time.

77.   Close the form   shōu shì   收式

Without moving the feet, turn the palms up and circle the right hand up and in. When the hands reach the same height, lift both hands to head height. Then form fists and press them down in front of the abdomen (fist surfaces face each other, fist eyes in). Look straight ahead (figure 145).

Bring the left foot back beside the right, feet at a forty-five degree angle. Relax the hands to open and lower beside the body. Stand up with the body facing almost sideways to the line of action (figure 146).

Main points: Breathe in as you raise the hands, and out as you lower them, sinking your energy, showing the completeness of the final move. You can also turn the body with the hand movement. Stand up gradually and remain alert – don't relax right away.

COMPREHENSIVE XINGYI FORM, *XINGYI LIANQUAN* 187

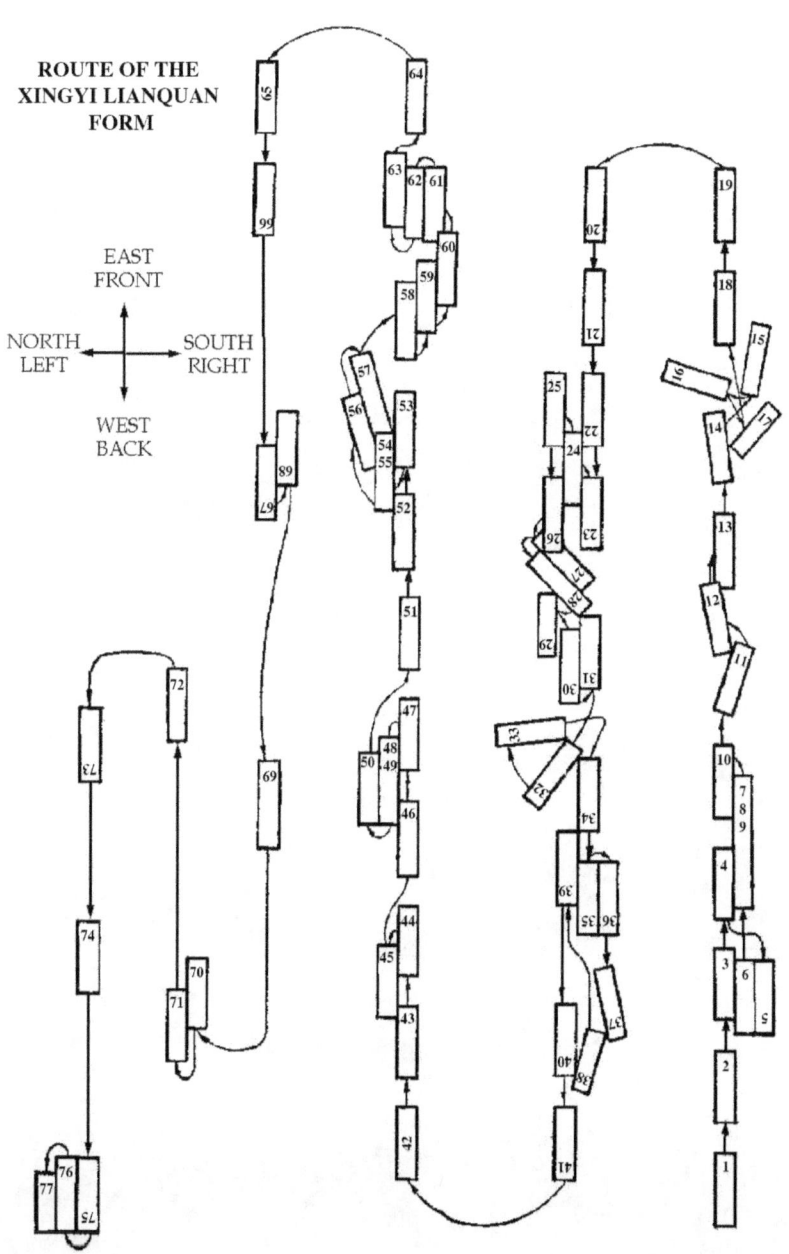

CHAPTER FOUR

PARTNER FORMS

4.1 FIVE ELEMENTAL PHASES CONTEND

wǔxíng xiàngkè 五行相克

The partner training form for the five basic techniques is called the Five Elemental Phases Contend. Xingyi uses metal, wood, water, fire, and earth to signify the techniques of split, drive, drill, cannon punch, and wring. The attack and defense are thus: metal controls wood, wood controls earth, etc.[50] This partner form is a way to train continuous fighting applications, and train the correctness and agility of body, hand and foot techniques.

1. Ready stance

    yùbèi shì 预备式

Partners A and B[51] stand in *santishi* facing each other; left hands about thirty to sixty centimetres away from each other (figure 1).

---

[50] Translator's note: Metal controls wood, wood controls earth, earth controls water, water controls fire, and fire controls metal. Thus, split controls drive, drive controls wring, wring controls drill, drill controls cannon, and cannon controls split. This interprtation of applications is not absolute.

[51] Translator's note: Usually in partner forms, the one who initiates the form is called partner A [jiǎ 甲], and the one who responds is called partner B [yǐ 乙]. In this form, the partner in the black shirt is A.

190   CHAPTER FOUR: PARTNER FORMS

2.   Partner A: Advance, right driving punch   jìnbù yòu bēngquán   进步右崩

Form fists and advance your left foot a half-step, drawing the right up a half-step. Drive your right fist directly towards partner B's left ribs. Bring your left fist back to the waist (fist heart up) (figure 2).

Partner B: Withdraw, parry   chèbù àn   撤步按

As partner A punches, quickly step your right foot back, following with the left a half-step back. Turn over your left hand and roll it in to tuck onto his right wrist. Close your right hand and bring it back to the waist (fist heart up). Look at your left hand (figure 2).

Main points: When partner A punches, his fist hits at exactly the same time as his front foot lands. The punch must be fast, driven strongly forward from the back leg, without popping the body up or dropping.

Partner B has to step back relative to the speed and distance of partner A's attack. His left hand should parry at the same time as the left foot draws back. Both partners should extend the shoulders into their moves, keep the lumbar area solid, and be attentive.

3.   Partner A: Advance, left driving punch   jìnbù zuǒ bēng   进步左崩

Continue another half-step forward with your left foot, following in a half-step with the right. Bring your right fist back to the waist (fist heart up) and drive your left fist towards partner B's left ribs (figure 3).

Partner B: Right splitting palm   yòu pī   右劈

Quickly step the right foot back, drawing your left a half-step in. Dodge partner A's left fist, quickly form a fist with your left hand, and roll it under his left fist (drilling up slightly) to press on the outside edge of his left wrist (figure 3).

Then step your left foot forward (hooking out) while opening your left hand to press down on his left wrist. Quickly step the right foot to the outside of his left foot, opening the right hand to chop his shoulder. Hit with your foot and hand at the same time and with the same speed (figure 4).

Main points: After partner B gets away from partner A's left split, he must step in and punch quickly. The right foot lands at exactly the same time as the right hand strikes.

4. Partner A: Cannon punch   pào quán   炮拳

As partner B tries to strike your shoulder, turn left without moving the feet. Quickly turn over your left fist (drilling then turning), bringing it up to the left side of the head (fist eye down). This makes his split fall away. While you do this, quickly drive your right fist towards the pit of his stomach (figure 5).

    Partner B: Right drilling fist   yòu zuān   右钻

As you see partner A's punch coming, quickly draw your right foot back beside the left (turn the foot out). Drop your left hand and hook onto his right wrist. Close your right hand and bring it back to the waist. Then advance your left foot and drill your right fist out over your left hand towards his jaw. Look at his face (figure 6).

Main points: As partner A cannon punches, he should rotate to put power into the punch. The upper block must first drill up then turn over and out, in order to slide off partner B's chop.

    Partner B's left hand should have a rolling in force as it drops onto partner A's right fist. Then the right drill punch must strike at exactly the same time as the step in. The partners must cooperate closely with each other, which demands attentiveness.

5.   Partner A: Withdraw, rolling deflection   chèbù jiézhǒu 撤步截肘

Withdraw both feet and turn right, quickly bringing your right fist back to the waist (fist heart up). Strike sideways at the outer edge of partner B's right elbow with your left forearm (fist heart up) (figure 7).

Main points: Partner A's strike to partner B's elbow has a rolling in force. The shoulder must be set down, elbow tucked in, and lumbar area solid.

6.   Partner B: Enter with left driving punch   jìnbù zuǒ bēng 进步左崩

As partner A tries to deflect your right arm, quickly withdraw that arm to the waist. Form a fist with your left hand and quickly punch his chest, advancing with the left foot and following in a half-step with the right (figure 8).

    Partner A: Step back, right splitting palm   tuìbù yòu pī   退步右劈

As you see partner B's left fist approaching, quickly draw your left foot back a big step and follow with the right. Turn left; open your right hand and press down on his left wrist. Bring your left fist back to the waist (fist heart up) (figure 9).

Main points: Partner A must step back quickly and adjust the size of his step by judging how far partner B has driven in the punch.

7.   Partner B: Enter with right driving punch   jìnbù yòu bēng 进步右崩

As your left punch is brushed off, quickly take your left fist back to the waist (fist heart up) and punch partner A's chest with your right fist. Step forward your left foot a half-step, following with the right (figure 10).

Partner A: Step back, left splitting palm   tuìbù zuǒ pī   退步左劈

As you see partner B's punch coming, quickly take a big step backward with your right foot, then the left. Open your left hand and extend it to press down on his wrist. Close your right hand and bring it back to the waist (fist heart up) (figure 10).

Main points: This move is the same as the preceding *punch and parry*, just transposing left and right.

8. Partner B: Enter with left driving punch   jìnbù zuǒ bēng   进步左崩

As your right punch is brushed off, quickly bring your right fist back to the waist (fist heart up) and punch again to his chest with your left fist. Advance a half-step in with your left foot and follow a half-step in with the right. Look at the left fist (figure 11).

Partner A: Withdraw, left drilling punch   chèbù zuǒ zuān   撤步左钻

Step the right foot back quickly, following a half-step with the left. Dodge partner B's left punch, quickly close your left hand, and encircle the fist underneath. Drill out and up to press down on partner B's left wrist (figure 11).

This routine may be practised back and forth repeatedly. Partner A steps in again; hooks out the left foot and steps the right outside partner B's left foot; opens his right hand to chop B's shoulder and opens his left hand to turn out and over to press down on B's left wrist in a splitting palm (see figure 4, but A now playing B's role and visa versa). Then B uses cannon punch to hit A's chest, A uses split then drill to hit B's face, B retreats as A advances, and they can carry on back and forth as they wish.

9. Close the form   shōu shì   收式

When either partner gets to the last left drill, both can stop, bring back the forward foot, and lower the hands to the sides, then stand up.

4.2 THREE HANDS CLASH   sān shǒu pào   三手炮

THREE HANDS CLASH: STATIONARY PRACTICE

1. Ready stance   yùbèi shì   预备式

Partners sit in horse stances facing each other about an arm length apart, fists by the waist (fist hearts up). To measure an arm length extend the arms with fists closed – you should just be able to reach your partner's stomach (figure 1).

2. Partner A: Right driving punch   yòu bēng   右崩

Drive your right fist towards partner B's stomach with your arm slightly bent (fist eye up) (figure 2).

Partner B: Left splitting palm   zuǒ pī   左劈

As partner A punches, quickly open your hands and press down his right arm on the wrist with your right hand. Strike and press down his upper arm with your left hand (figure 2).

3. Partner A: Left driving punch   zuǒ bēng   左崩

As partner B presses down your right arm, drive your left fist towards his stomach (fist eye up) arm slightly bent. Pull your right fist back to your waist (figure 3).

Partner B: Right splitting palm   yòu pī   右劈

As you see partner A's left punch coming, extend your right hand forward and up to strike and press down on his upper arm. Press down on his left wrist with your left hand (figure 3).

4. Partner A: Right cannon punch yòu pào 右炮

As partner B presses down your left arm, just as you are about to lose your advantage, quickly drill the forearm up and block out (first rotate outwardly then inwardly), crossing to the left of your head (fist eye down). Quickly punch towards his chest with your right fist (figure 4).

Partner B: Left pull, right driving punch zuǒ lǚ yòu bēng 左捋右崩

As your split loses its effect, quickly get away from partner A's left arm and drop onto the outside of his right elbow, pressing it from left to right, (with both pushing and pulling force). Bring your right hand back, form a fist, and slide in under your left hand to punch at his stomach (fist eye up) with your arm slightly bent (figure 5).

Partner A: Left splitting palm zuǒ pī 左劈

As your right arm is pressed away by partner B, losing its effectiveness, quickly bring your left hand down to chop his right arm. Press down his right wrist with your right hand (figure 6).

Continue on in this way, switching sides.

Partner B will next do the *left driving punch*, partner A the *right splitting palm* (move 3); partner B will then do the *right cannon punch*, partner A the *left pull and right driving punch* (move 4).

When just learning, start out slowly and gradually add speed. As you get faster make sure you don't get wild. Be sure to cooperate closely with each other.

196 CHAPTER FOUR: PARTNER FORMS

THREE HANDS CLASH: MOVING PRACTICE

1. Ready stance   yùbèi shì   预备式

Partners stand facing each other. Sit down and step into the left foot forward *santishi*, front hands about ten to twenty centimetres apart (figure 7).

2. Partner B[52]: Advance, left press, right pull, high driving punch

jìnbù zuǒ yā yòu lǚ gāobēng   进步左压右捋高崩

Close your left hand to a fist and press down partner A's left wrist by outwardly rotating your forearm. Step a half-step forward with the left foot as the left hand presses. Then change hands, placing your right hand on top of his wrist to pull it down. Advance your right foot as your right hand pulls, landing just outside his left foot. Sit mostly on the back leg. Once your right hand has pulled his arm down, bring your left fist back then punch to the face (fist eye up, fist surface forward). Look at partner A's face (figures 8, 9).

---

[52] Translator's note: In this instance the person in the white shirt initates the form. Since he was called partner B in the preceeding form, the author has just kept the labels.

Partner A: Withdraw, right pull   chèbù yòu lǚ   撤步右捋

As partner B's punch nears your face, quickly draw the left foot back and turn left, pulling on his left wrist with your right hand hooked onto the wrist. Bring your left fist back to the waist (fist heart up). Sit down a bit. Look at partner B (figure 10).

3. Partner B: Advance, right press, left pull, high punch

jìnbù yòu yā zuǒ lǚ gāobēng   进步右压左捋高崩

As partner A grabs your left wrist, go along with the direction of the press down and bring your fist back in. Quickly slide your right fist along the line of your left arm to get onto the outer edge of his right forearm, pressing down his wrist by outwardly rotating your forearm (fist heart up) (figure 11).

Step the right foot forward then the left, pulling down partner A's right wrist with your left hand. Bring back your right fist, then punch towards his face (fist eye up, fist surface forward). Look at partner A's face (figure 12).

Partner A: Withdraw, left pull   chèbù zuǒ lǚ   撤步左捋

Just before partner B's punch arrives, quickly draw your right foot back and turn right. Hook onto his right wrist with your left hand and pull. Bring your right fist back to the waist (fist heart up). Drop down a bit. Look at partner B (like figure 10, but transposing left and right).

198   CHAPTER FOUR: PARTNER FORMS

In this practice when partner B attacks, partner A defends – when partner B advances, partner A withdraws. You can go back and forth switching roles. For example, on arriving at one side of the practice area, B changes to defend and A attacks, B withdraws and A advances. The number of repetitions depends on the size of the practice area and the energy of the players.

4.   Close the form   shōu shì   收式

On finishing the sequence for the last time, both players will have the right foot forward. Both pull in the right foot to sit into the *santishi* and close.

When first starting out, practise slowly. Try to get the footwork and hand techniques correct and the cooperation smooth. Gradually increase speed but don't get hard and rigid.

Partners need to cooperate – the advance and retreat need to be just right; hands and eyes must work together. Such practice this way will improve total hand-eye-body-foot coordination and reaction skills.

4.3 PROTECT THE BODY FIGHTING FORM

ān shēn pào　　安身炮

The Protect the Body fighting form is the more complex and complete of Xingyi's partner forms. Practised often, and continually worked on, it can train coordination of hands, eyes, body, and feet, reaction skills, and help train self defense skills and understanding.

1. Ready stance　　　　yùbèi shì　　预备式

Partners A and B stand facing each other, then sit down into a *santishi* ready stance, front hands about thirty to sixty centimetres apart (figure 1).[53]

2. Partner A: Advance, right driving punch

   jìnbù yòu bēngquán　　进步右崩拳

Form fists and advance strongly with your left foot, following a half-step in with the right. Drive your right fist towards partner B's chest, and pull your left fist back to the waist.

   Partner B: Step back, left pull, right driving punch

   tuìbù zuǒ lǚ yòu bēng　　退步左捋右崩

As partner A's fist approaches, quickly withdraw your right foot and lift your left knee. Pull his right wrist down with your left hand and push it to your right (figure 2).

Land the left foot forward and follow in with the right. Follow the line beside partner A's right forearm with your right fist to punch at his right ribs. Close your left fist and bring it back to the waist (figure 3).

---

[53] Translator's note: In the illustrations, partner A is now wearing the white shirt, and partner B is in the black shirt.

3. **Partner A: Left splitting palm   zuǒ pīzhǎng   左劈掌**

Quickly open your right hand and pull partner B's right wrist down. Chop to his face with your left hand as your left foot steps in (figure 4).

Partner B: Aligned left cannon punch   shùnbù zuǒ pàoquán   顺步左炮拳

As you see partner A's left hand coming, quickly bring your right arm up, back, and turn it out, bending your elbow just beside your head. Punch at his chest with your left fist, moving your left foot forward (figure 5).

4. Partner A: Switchover step, right splitting palm

   huànbù yòu pī   换步右劈

As partner B strikes, quickly withdraw your left hand to press down on his left fist. Bring your left foot back and quickly advance the right, stepping to the outside of his left foot. Strike at his left shoulder with your right hand (figure 6).

PROTECT THE BODY FIGHTING FORM: *ANSHENPAO*

Partner B: Left hook, right splitting palm   zuǒ guà yòu pī   左挂右劈

As you see partner A's right hand coming, quickly draw your left foot back and advance the right foot. Open your left hand and bring it back then up, hooking his right hand. Strike to the left side of his face with your right palm (figure 7).

5.   Partner A: Double deflection to the left   zuǒ shuāng jiéquán   左双截拳

As partner B strikes, quickly turn left and form fists. Hit and stick your right fist onto his right forearm and clamp your left fist onto his wrist (figure 8).

    Partner B: Left splitting palm   zuǒ pīzhǎng   左劈掌

As partner A rolls your right hand away, his right side is open. Quickly chop to the right side of his face with your left hand. Close your right hand and bring it back to the waist (figure 9).

Main points: As partner A deflects partner B's right arm, his forearms should rotate (the left inwardly, the right outwardly) and the arms should use the power of the body's rotation. Don't use force to knock the arm away. Roll the arm back and out to lead it away. Move quickly, and use the power of the whole body.

6. Partner A: Right hook, right driving punch

yòu guà yòu bēngquán　　右挂右崩拳

As you see partner B's left hand coming towards your face, quickly turn right and knock it aside with your right fist and left palm. Then quickly slide your right fist under your left forearm to punch towards partner B's chest (figure 10).

Partner B: Step back, right driving punch

tuìbù yòu bēngquán　　退步右崩拳

As you see partner A's right fist coming, quickly draw your left foot back and lift your right knee. Pull his right fist down with your right hand and encircle his right fist with your left hand to deflect it out. Then land your right leg forward and quickly punch at his chest with your right fist (figures 11, 12).

Main points: Deflecting with the left hand and punching with the right fist are done smoothly, without hesitation between them.

Partner B needs to step back quickly, pull with the right hand and deflect with the left, and hit forward without pause. The quicker these moves link together, the better.

7.   Partner A: Right strike to face   yòu pūmiànzhǎng   右扑面掌

As partner B's right fist comes towards your chest, quickly sit back and withdraw your right foot. Open your right hand and drop it onto his right fist to brush it back. Open your left hand and drop it in front of your right hand to continue to pull his right arm. This gives you the opportunity to strike at his face with your right hand. Move in with your right foot and follow with the left (figure 13).

   Partner B: Right thread palm   yòu chuānzhǎng   右穿掌

As partner A's strike comes, open your right hand and rotate it down and to your left – encircle outside his right arm and extend your arm up, sticking to his arm. Step both feet back a bit (figure 14).

Main points: The action as partner A deflects with the right then left hand and strikes partner B's face with the right must be fast and continuous without any hesitation – the faster the better.

8.   Partner A: Enter with cannon punch   jìnbù pàoquán   进步炮拳

As your right hand loses its effectiveness, form fists. Quickly lift up partner B's right arm with your left fist and punch at his chest with your right fist. Advance your left foot and follow in with the right (figure 15).

   Partner B: Step back, left press down   tuìbù zuǒ ànzhǎng   退步左按掌

As you see partner A's punch coming, quickly step your right foot back and press down his right wrist with your left hand. Form a fist with your right hand and bring it back to the waist (figure 16).

Main points: As partner A does a cannon punch, the upward block with the left hand must not be straight up and out, but must first drill up then turn out. The right punch and forward advance of the left foot must come together.

The degree to which partner B steps back depends on how far partner A comes in. The distance must be judged so that it is neither too far nor too close for the following move. Step back quickly. Press down with the left hand at the same time as you step back.

9. Partner A: Advance, right rolled backfist

   jìnbù yòu fānbèiquán   进步右反背拳

Open your left hand and allow partner B to push your arm down, then loosen his grip to get away. Step your right foot outside his left foot. Hit with your right fist rolled over to strike the left side of his face with the back of your fist (figure 17).

   Partner B: Step back, left thread palm

   tuìbù zuǒ chuānzhǎng   退步左穿掌

As partner A's punch comes, quickly step back – right foot then left foot – to evade the punch. Bring your left hand down and in, then thread it forward along inside his right forearm (figure 18).

PROTECT THE BODY FIGHTING FORM: *ANSHENPAO*

Main points: Partner A must step in and hit at the same time, and must move quickly. The foot and hand must not move independently.

Partner B must use the power from partner A's deflection and the pull down, in order to pull back to the chest, and only then thread forward quickly. He must not simply pull his hand straight out of the grip. The back step and threading of the left arm must be done at the same speed in order to work together.

10. Partner A: Advance, right splitting palm   jìnbù yòu pīzhǎng   进步右劈掌

Follow the direction of partner B's threading palm, opening your left hand to slap his left arm quickly to the right. Then open your right hand, circle under his left arm, and chop the left side of his face. Advance your right foot with the strike, following in a half-step with the left (figure 19).

Partner B: Right rolled backhand   yòu fānbèizhǎng   右反背掌

Slap partner A's right hand quickly to your left with your right hand and circle your left hand in from the outside to his right hand, knocking his right arm aside (when you do this, he will close his left hand and take his fist back to the waist). Slide your right hand along his right arm to hit the right side of his face with the back of your hand. Bring the left foot back and advance the right, switching places with your feet (figure 20).

Main points: Partner A must attack continuously, left hand slapping partner B's left arm and right hand striking his face at the same time.

Partner B must combine three moves quickly into one continuous motion: slap aside with the right hand, knock away with the left, then right backhand.

11. Partner A: Switchover step, left splitting palm

huànbù zuǒ pīzhǎng　　　换步左劈掌

Once partner B has knocked your right hand away, quickly draw your right foot back to avoid his right hand. Quickly circle your right hand under, inside, then around the outside of his right arm – pulling the arm back and down. Extend your left hand forward to chop at the right side of his face. Step the left foot in (figure 21).

Partner B: Right hook, strike at face

yòu guà pūmiànzhǎng　　　右挂扑面掌

As partner A strikes with the left split, quickly bend your right arm and bring it back, using your right hand to hook away his left hand. Slide your left hand under his left forearm and step your left foot back, lifting your right knee. Then quickly land your right foot forward and chop to his face with your right hand.

Partner A: As partner B chops to your face, quickly circle your left arm in and up around his right arm, extending your arm to deflect his arm (figures 22, 23).

Main points: When partner A pulls down partner B's right arm, he must first extend up then pull down and back. The left chop strikes at the same time that the left foot advances.

Partner B pulls back with the right hand and down with the left quickly. Hit with the right chop as the right foot lands.

PROTECT THE BODY FIGHTING FORM: *ANSHENPAO*

12. Partner A: Advance, slice up   jìnbù liāoquán   进步撩拳

Don't stop as you jam your left arm against partner B's right arm – forcefully push it to the outside. Bend your left arm and form a fist, bringing it back to your waist. Quickly step your right foot in. Close your right hand and swing the fist down then forward at his groin.

    Partner B: Step back, pull, splitting palm   tuìbù lǚ pī   退步捋劈

As partner A swings his right fist towards your groin, quickly draw your right foot back, pull his wrist down with your right hand, and chop at his neck with your left hand (figure 24).

Main points: As partner A swings the right fist, the body should drop to help swing the shoulder and arm forward with force.

    Partner B needs to step back just the right amount, according to how far partner A advances. Partner B must put equal force into pulling down with the right hand and striking forward with the left – applying force in opposing directions aids in getting more force to the front.

13. Partner A: Right hook, left splitting palm   yòu guà zuǒ pī   右挂左劈

Without moving your feet, quickly bend your right arm and open your hand to brush away partner B's left hand. Chop at the right side of his face with your left hand (figure 25).

    Partner B: Right thread palm   yòu chuānzhǎng   右穿掌

Quickly bring your left hand back to your waist and thread your right arm up along the inside of his left arm, jamming his left hand. Shift your feet back slightly (figure 26).

14. Partner A: Right strike at the face   yòu pūmiànzhǎng   右扑面掌

Without moving your feet, quickly bring your left hand back and down to brush away partner B's right hand. Quickly strike at his face with your right hand (figure 27).

Partner B: Horse stance, left driving punch

mǎbù zuǒ bēngquán   马步左崩拳

As you see partner A's right hand coming, quickly use your right hand to slap it to the left. Close your left hand and punch at his right ribs. Turn your left foot in to snap the body right and sit down into a horse stance (figure 28).

Main points: Partner B must snap the body and left foot to put power into the punch, so that all parts of the body drop into the horse stance punch at the same time.

15. Partner A: Continuous right strike to face

liánhuán yòu pūmiànzhǎng   连环右扑面掌

As you see partner B's punch coming towards your ribs quickly suck in your body. First press his left fist down with your right hand – he will then take his right fist back to his waist. Change hands to press down with your left hand. Step your right foot forward and quickly strike at his face with your right hand. (figure 29).

Partner B: Step back, thread palm   tuìbù chuānzhǎng   退步穿掌

Pull your left arm back quickly. Step your left foot back. Thread your right arm along outside partner A's right arm, dodging his right hand and jamming his arm (figure 30).

PROTECT THE BODY FIGHTING FORM: *ANSHENPAO*

16. Partner A: Trap arm, cut   xié bēi qiēzhǎng   挟臂切掌

Step your left foot outside partner B's right leg, swinging his right arm up and out with your left arm. Once you have swung around inside his arm, use your left arm to trap it and quickly strike to the left side of his face with your right hand (figure 31).

    Partner B: Double deflection to the left   zuǒ shuāng jiéquán   左双截拳

Go along with the rotational direction of partner A's left arm – bend your elbow and bring in your right arm – then use both fists to quickly knock his right forearm to the left. Don't move your feet, but twist quickly left. Keep your elbows down (figure 32).

Main points: As partner B intercepts partner A's arm, he must sit down and use the lower back to put a rolling force into the forearms (rotating the left inwardly and the right outwardly). This rolls the power to deflect left and back instead of using brute force to hit straight out.

17. Partner A: Left splitting palm   zuǒ pīzhǎng   左劈掌

As soon as partner B deflects your right hand, chop to the right side of his face with your left hand. Close your right hand and bring it back to your waist. Don't move your feet.

Partner B: Double deflection to the right   yòu shuāng jiéquán   右双截拳

As you see partner A's strike coming, quickly turn right and deflect his left arm with both fists (figure 33).

Partner B: Punch at partner A's left ribs with your right fist. As you pull your left fist back to your waist, step your right foot forward.

Partner A: As partner B punches, shift both feet back a bit – sit back, pulling his right fist back with your left hand (figure 34).

Main points: Once partner B has knocked aside partner A's arm he must punch immediately.

18. Partner A: Advance, crushing kick   jìnbù cǎijiǎo   进步踩脚

Continuing on without pause from the last attack, pull and press partner B's right forearm with your right hand, then switch to press down his right wrist with your left hand. Lift your right foot without changing the height of your stance, then stamp towards his right shin and extend your right palm forward and up. Drive forward off the left foot and land the right foot into an aligned stance with your chop.

Partner B: Step back, deflect and hit   tuìbù jié jī   退步截击

Quickly step your right leg back and bring your right fist back. Then circle your right fist around the outside of partner A's right arm to extend up to deflect his right hand (figures 35, 36).

PROTECT THE BODY FIGHTING FORM: *ANSHENPAO*

Main points: Partner A must switch the hands, pull down, and strike all as one move.

    Partner B must first bring the right arm back before he extends it outside partner A's right arm.

19.   Partner A: Left flick, right splitting palm   zuǒ tiǎo yòu pī   左挑右劈

As your right arm is deflected by partner B, bring your left arm out under your right forearm to swing up his right arm. Bring your right arm back then chop to the right side of his face. Advance your left foot and withdraw your right slightly.

    Partner B: Left grab shoulder   zuǒ zhuā jiān   左抓肩

Quickly bring your right fist back to your waist and slide your left hand forward inside partner A's right arm to grab his right shoulder (figure 37).

20.   Partner A: Pluck off the shoulder, right splitting palm

    zhāi jiān yòu pīzhǎng   摘肩右劈掌

Brush aside partner B's left hand with your right, then push it away with your left. After that, chop to the left side of his face with your right hand. During this exchange, lift your left foot slightly then replace it on the ground.

Partner B: Left brush aside, right splitting palm

zuǒ lōu yòu pī　　左搂右劈

Bend your left elbow quickly to bring your arm in. Turn your arm under partner A's right arm and extend it up to brush aside his right hand. Chop to the left side of his face with your right hand (figure 38).

21.　Partner A: Double deflection to the left

zuǒ shuāng jiéquán　　左双截拳

Without moving your feet, quickly turn your body left to deflect partner B's right forearm with your fists (figure 39).

　　　Partner B: Left splitting palm　　zuǒ pīzhǎng　　左劈掌

Bring your right arm back in quickly, then chop the right side of partner A's face with your left hand.

　　　Partner A: Turn right, deflecting partner B's left forearm with your fists (figure 40).

Main points: This move is the same as the preceding *double deflect to the left* and *left split*. Compare to the main points for move 17.

PROTECT THE BODY FIGHTING FORM: *ANSHENPAO*   213

22. Partner A: Right driving punch   yòu bēngquán   右崩拳

Continue straight on to quickly punch partner B's left ribs with your right fist, and pull your left fist back to your waist (figure 41).

Partner B: Step back, left pull, right driving punch

tuìbù zuǒ lǚ yòu bēng   退步左将右崩

When you see partner A's punch coming, quickly step your right foot back, and lift your left. Control his punch by sliding your left hand along his arm to stop at his right wrist (figure 42).

Land your left foot and punch with your right fist (figure 43).

Partner A: As partner B punches, step your right foot back and lift your left, pulling his right fist with your left hand (figure 43).

Then partner A pulls with the left and punches with the right so that the former B advances as the former A retreats, and the whole sequence repeats, switching roles until both arrive back where they started. You may go back and forth in this way as many times as you wish. There is no need to explain the moves again; just switch over.

23. Close the form   shōu shì   收式

You have a choice on how to close the form. You can turn and thread palm to return to the *santishi*, or you can change to *santishi* on the spot. The choice prevents the end of the form from getting too rigid.

CHAPTER FIVE

STANCE TRAINING FOR HEALTH

Post Standing practice [zhuāng gōng 桩功] is a static training used in the martial arts to increase strength, endurance and other types of body conditioning, and to learn and perfect form requirements. Each style uses its own stance practice. Long fist, for example, practises the horse stance, bow stance, and empty stance; Taijiquan stands in the pre *taiji* posture [wújí shì 无极势], and Xingyi stands in the *santishi*. These stance practices all develop the most basic skills of their styles, but they are not just for beginners. Even the most skilled players should practise them often and perfect them.

Xingyi's stance training for health is a form of health and physio-therapy training which has been developed fairly recently by masters and health professionals together, using the principles of Xingyiquan.

Although Xingyi itself is hard and strong, its basic requirements are remarkably similar to the soft and flowing style of Taijiquan. Both require an empty heart and a solid abdomen [xūxīn shífù 虚心实腹]; a hollow chest and a stretched upper back [hánxiōng bábèi 含胸拔背]; a suspended head and straight neck [xuántóu shùxiàng 悬头竖项]; and a centered, straight, relaxed and open body [zhōng zhèng ān shū 中正安舒]. Xingyi also requires alternating hard and soft [gāngróu xiāngjì 刚柔相济] and sinking energy to the centre of the body [qì chén dāntián 气沈丹田]. The master Sun Lutang studied the similarities of Xingyiquan, Baguazhang and Taijiquan, and combined their theories into one school. Sun stated that although Xingyi emphasizes stability, Bagua agility, and

Taiji tactics, their basic theory was the same – developing the interior and using it to its fullest. Experience has shown that Xingyi stance practice has the same therapeutic effects on elderly, weak, or chronically ill people as does Taijiquan.

The theory behind the Xingyi stance practice is to empty the mind and relax the body. Undertaking various static postures or gentle movement allows the practitioner's physiology to settle down and his mind to focus. This in turn regulates both the excitation and inhibition functions of the central nervous system – repairing confusion and fatigue of the brain. In addition, the central nervous system will emit many beneficial signals so this type of exercise enlivens the functions of every system of the body.

There are four main principles behind training Xingyi's stances for health: empty, relaxed, smooth, and settled. These are the rules for training. In addition, each specific body segment has specific position requirements, and people of various conditions or illnesses need different training plans–but these specific requirements and plans do not depart from these four essential principles. These rules are not just the foundation of Xingyi stance practice, but of all therapeutic standing and therapeutic *qigong* training.

1. Empty   xū   虚

The most important aspect of being empty is keeping the mind quiet during practice. Emptying the mind and clearing the spirit mean to concentrate on one thing, to keep the mind quiet and the breath easy, to avoid having a rushing mind and uneven breathing, and to avoid thinking of outside distractions. Of course at first beginners will have difficulty controlling their thoughts. They must go through a certain period of training until the practice becomes habitual. Once this is achieved, when the body takes its position the mind will quickly settle down, and the inner and outer aspects of the person can be united.

2. Relaxed   sōng   松

Relaxed means that when practising, the whole body must keep a natural open stance, allowing the *qi* and blood to flow unimpeded. Relaxed and empty are connected. The classics say "when the mind is peaceful the emotions are quiet, when the emotions are quiet there are no obstructions, and when there are no obstructions the *qi* can flow." This shows that only when you can settle and calm your thoughts can your body relax and allow everything to flow unobstructed. And the opposite is also true. If you can learn to relax this will help you to focus your mind and achieve your goal of regulating the breath and nourishing the spirit. Two main points involved in relaxing are opening and roundness.

2a   Open   shū   舒

Relaxation and openness are linked together. If you lose your openness, relaxing becomes soft and weak, lifeless and flaccid. In the past people often referred to an open and relaxed naturalness, bracing out to the eight directions. The meaning of opening includes your mind and your position. In your mind, you want to have a relaxed body and open spirit, an unimpeded mind and lifted spirit, emotions full; in your position you want to be open and large, standing naturally. Only in this way can you be truly relaxed.

2b   Rounded   yuán   圆

Sometime rounded refers to combining internal and external in a rounded body, but here it means mostly the outward position. The body should be relaxed and quiet, and every part must maintain a natural roundness. Stance practice has a holding stance with the arms held in front of the chest. The arms must be round and full, keeping the shoulders settled and the elbows down, the chest slightly closed. This opens the upper back and expands the diaphragm, allowing every joint to open naturally. The upper body can be relaxed, soft, settled and still, open, expansive, rounded and full. The lumbar area and buttocks are also relaxed, tucked in, and the *qi* can settle down easily. Other positions are the same – no matter how the feet or arms are placed, you can't ignore the requirement of roundness.

3.   Smooth[54]   shùn   顺

Smooth includes both the breathing and the body. Controlling breathing means that, with the principle of natural breathing understood, causing your breathing to be deep, even, fine, and steady, so that the air can get everywhere without blockage. During practice, avoid raising your *qi* or blood, which causes the top to be heavy and the bottom light. When controlling your breathing, you should think of leading the breath and avoid forcibly holding your breath, always remembering to breathe naturally.

---

[54] Translator's note: The word *shun* is used for a tailwind, moving downstream or with the flow of traffic, or when life in general is going along smoothly. In English, 'unobstructed' and 'go along with the natural flow' have some of this sense.

Controlling the body means that the light and heavy, empty and solid, movement and stillness are all controlled in each body segment – top and bottom, right and left, front and back. In this way the large and small muscles, the joints, every body part which takes part in the position will be coordinated and naturally balanced, and you will not create any stiffness. This will make the whole position open and rounded, light and steady, the outer form smooth and the inner at peace, so when you practise you will feel relaxed and calm.

4. Settled   chén   沈

One aspect is to settle the *qi* to the *dantian*, to avoid rough breathing and upsetting the mind. The other aspect is to send the *qi* down during practice. The method for this kind of settling is to control with the mind to relax the muscles and joints and open the posture, not to force the *qi*. Beginners often feel that when they don't master the posture the mind can't settle down, the body is hard to relax, and so they feel top heavy and the bottom light, as if their feet have no root. After practising for a while they gradually master clearing the mind and relaxing the body, and the inner and outer become smooth, then they feel that the upper body feels lighter and the legs feel more solid the longer they stand, and the breath becomes deep, long and even and the mind and spirit open and calm. At this time, the muscles and joints of the shoulders, elbows, lumbar area, hips, and all body parts are naturally open and relaxed, giving a feeling of being settled down. The whole body feels fused and unblocked. This kind of power, which is relaxed, settled, open and expansive shows the correct mastering of the standing practice. It is the result of persistent practice combined with controlled breathing.

1. DRAGON STANDING   lóng xíng gōng   龙形功

1. Dragon coils up   lóng pán shì   龙盘式

Stand naturally erect, heels together, feet open to ninety degrees (figure 1-1).

1-1

Place the left foot a half-step to the forward left, the heels in line, about a foot length apart. Keep the knees slightly bent, relax the hips, and sit the weight mostly – about seventy percent – on the right leg. Bend the left arm horizontally at chest height in front of your chest, forming a half circle (palm in and fingers naturally curved) with middle of the forearm above the foot. Place the right hand in front of the right waist, palm in, arm rounded, forearm bracing out. Settle your shoulders

STANCE TRAINING   219

and elbows down. Keep the chest in, the lumbar area relaxed, the spine straight, the buttocks rolled under, and anal sphincter lifted (contracted), the head and neck straight, the mouth lightly closed, the tongue lightly on the palate, the breathing natural, and watch the left forearm. The body should be naturally relaxed and smooth, the spirit empty and the mind focused (figure 1-2).

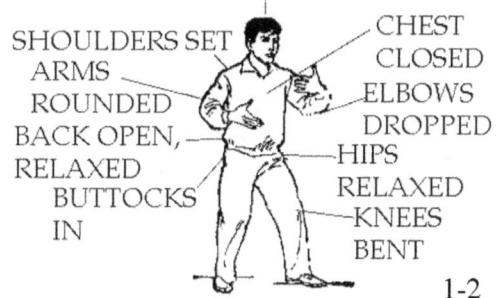

1-2

Figure 1-2 is the left stance. The right stance is the same, just transposing right and left (figure 1-3).

Alternate left and right stances. The length of time is determined by the situation of the individual. Wait until your legs get hot before changing stances.

1-3

2.   Dragon stretches out its claws (left)   tàn zhuā shì   探爪式

Stand erect, feet parallel and shoulder width, feet straight, shoulders hanging naturally, looking straight ahead (figure 1-4).

Turn left, push the right heel back, lift the right hand up and left, and inwardly rotate both forearms (figure 1-5).

Wait until the right hand is higher than the left shoulder, then turn the left foot out and lift the left hand (palm up) to thread it forward above the right wrist (figure 1-6).

After threading the left hand through, turn the palm slowly down and lower the hand to the chest (fingers slightly open, tiger's mouth rounded, wrist slightly set down).

Slowly rotate the right hand inwardly and bring it back to beside the right hip above the right foot (fingers forward, wrist slightly down, tiger's mouth in). Sit down slightly, rolling the knees in slightly, keeping both feet firmly on the ground, sit about seventy percent on the right leg. Keep the shoulders relaxed, elbows dropped, index fingers slightly lifted, and palms contained. Keep the spine straight, chest in, lumbar area relaxed, buttocks in, head and neck straight, spirit empty, breathing natural, and *qi* settled to the *dantian*. Look at the index finger of the forward hand (figure 1-7).

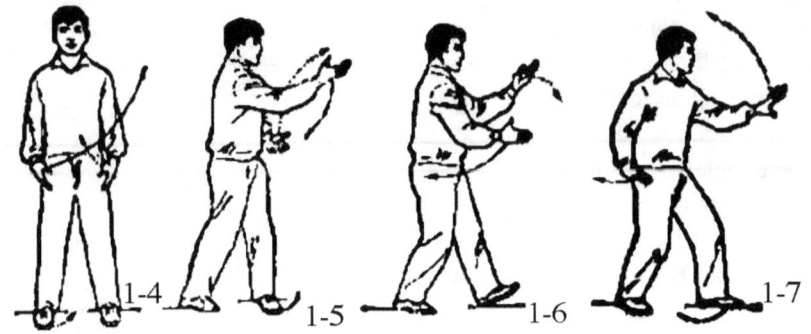

3. Dragon stretches out its claws (right)   tàn zhuā shì   探爪式

Turn right, pivoting first on the left heel to turn the foot in, inwardly rotating and lifting the left forearm, turning the palm right to head height. Turn the head right with the body, watching the right side (figure 1-8).

Turn the right foot out to point right and lower the left hand in front of the right shoulder. Outwardly rotate the right arm and lift the right hand (palm up) to thread over the left wrist (figures 1-9, 1-10).

Slowly turn the right hand down, lowering it as you push forward, to chest height, fingers slightly open, tiger's mouth open, wrist slightly cocked down. As you extend the right hand slowly bring the left hand back, inwardly rotating to press down in front of the left hip, fingers forward, tiger's mouth in, above the left foot. Sit down slightly, roll in slightly around the knees, keep both feet solidly on the ground, and sit mostly on the left leg (seventy percent). Look at the index finger of the right hand (figure 1-11).

STANCE TRAINING 221

All the other body positions are the same as the left stance.

Alternate left and right, changing from right to left in the same way (figure 1-12).

2. TIGER STANDING   hǔ xíng gōng   虎形功

1.   Tiger crouches   hǔ jù shì   虎踞式

Stand with your feet shoulder width apart, feet pointing straight forward or slightly out. Keep the hips relaxed, knees slightly bent, feet flat on the ground, and centre of gravity between the feet. Place the hands in front of the hips, arms rounded, palms down, fingers forward, tiger mouths in, wrists cocked to press down, fingers open and naturally bent, palms concave. Keep the shoulders relaxed and settled, elbows slightly opened, hands slightly pressing down (but unforced). Keep the head and neck straight, mouth lightly closed, face natural, tongue touching the palate lightly, and breathe through the nose. Keep the chest relaxed, the spine straight, the lumbar area settled, the abdomen relaxed, the buttocks pulled in, and the anal sphincter lifted. Focus, breathe naturally and evenly (even, slow, deep, and long). Look straight ahead (figure 2-1).

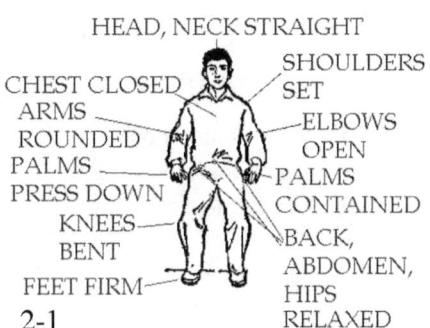

The three main goals of this stance are to calm the mind, relax, and regulate the breathing. The length of time depends on the individual.

2.   Tiger pounces (left)   yuè pū shì   跃扑式

Stand up with the heels together, feet turned ninety degrees to each other. Form fists and bend the elbows to place them at the waist (fist hearts up). Relax the upper body, look straight ahead (figure 2-2).

Sit down slightly and step the left foot to the forward left, touching the heel down. Drill the fists up the chest, fist hearts in (figure 2-3).

Shift forward, landing the whole foot into a left bow stance. Bring the fists out under your jaw and slowly open them, turning them over to push forward and down – pouncing (palms forward, tiger's mouths opposing, wrists slightly cocked down). Keep the arms rounded, shoulders relaxed, elbows dropped, palms concave, head and neck straight, chest relaxed, spine aligned, lumbar area settled, abdomen relaxed, buttocks tucked, and anus lifted. Breathe naturally. Look at the tip of the index finger of the left hand (figure 2-4).

Pause in the above stance then shift slowly back and bring the left foot back to its original place. Slowly close the hands and lower them to beside the waist. Stand up, returning to your original posture (see figure 2-2).

3. Tiger pounces (right)   yuè pū shì   跃扑式

The right stance is the same as the left, just stepping out to the right side into a right bow stance and pouncing to the forward right (figures 2-5, 2-6).

The number of repetitions and the stance height is open to the individual to determine, depending on conditioning. Change position softly and slowly, make sure not to stiffen up or hurry.

STANCE TRAINING   223

Keeping to the principles of natural and smooth, gradually introduce breathing practice. As you lift the fists breath in, and as you push forward and down breath out. Breathe naturally throughout the rest of the movement.

3.   APE STANDING   yuán xíng gōng   猿形功

1.   Ape cups its hands   yuán pěng shì   猿捧式

Open the feet to shoulder width, toes pointing forward (or slightly out). Relax the hips, bend the knees, keep the feet flat, and settle the weight evenly between the feet. Cup the hands in front of your *dantian* (two to three inches below your navel). One hand is half-closed (fist heart up) and sits lightly on the other palm (figure 3-1).

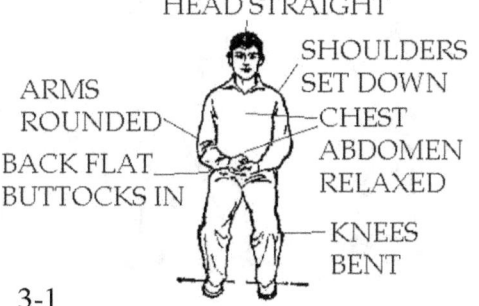

3-1

Keep the arms rounded, shoulder relaxed, elbows slightly opened, upper body naturally relaxed. Focus and look straight ahead. The details for the body in general are the same as tiger crouches.

2.   Ape clambers up a branch (left)   pān zhī shì 攀枝式

Stand up straight, heels together, feet turned ninety degrees to each other. Bend the elbows to place the fists at the waist (fist hearts up). Relax the upper body and look straight ahead. (See figure 2-2).

Step the left foot to the forward left, touching the heel down. Open the hands and bring them up the chest then extend to the forward left (palms up) with the arms slightly bent (figure 3-2).

Continue to extend the hands to the left and up (palms up) without fully extending the elbows. The left hand is ahead of the right. Shift slowly forward to the left leg, straightening the right leg and raising the right heel. Keep the head and neck straight, body open and relaxed, buttocks tucked and anal sphincter lifted. Although the right heel is raised, it should keep a pushing back force, pushing down to counter the upward push of the hands to involve the whole body. Look at the left hand (figure 3-3).

Sit back, shifting slowly to the right leg and raising the left toes. Turn the palms over to face each other and gradually close to fists (closing them as you lower them). Bend the elbows to bring the fists in as if pulling the branch of a tree. Look at the left fist (figure 3-4).

Pause then bring the left foot slowly back to its starting place and stand up. Bring the fists back to the waist and return to the ready stance (figure 3-5).

3.　　Ape clambers up a branch (right)　　pān zhī shì　　攀枝式

The right side is the same as the left, just transposing right and left (figures 3-6, 3-7, 3-8).

4.　　BEAR STANDING　　xiōng xíng gōng　　熊形功

1.　　Bear embraces　　xiōng bào shì　　熊抱式

Stand with the feet at shoulder width, body naturally erect, hands hanging, looking straight ahead.

Sit down slightly, holding the arms rounded in front of the stomach with the hands about ten centimetres apart (palms in, fingers opposing, tiger's mouths up). Keep the arms rounded to brace out, shoulders relaxed, elbows dropped,

STANCE TRAINING   225

fingers naturally opened, chest relaxed, spine erect, lumbar area relaxed, abdomen relaxed, buttocks tucked, and anus pulled in. Other details are the same as *tiger crouches* on page 201 (figure 4-1).

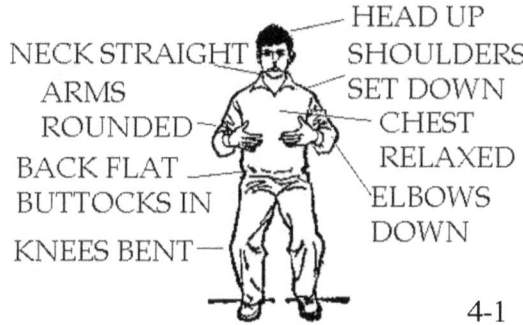

4-1

2.   Bear swings its arms   yáo bāng shì   摇膀式

Stand with the feet open slightly wider than the shoulders, arms naturally hanging, then sit slowly down, turning left. Raise the right arm and bring it left with the body, forearm outwardly rotating (palm in). Go along with the leftward turn with the eyes (figure 4-2).

Without pausing slowly turn right, turning the right hand and following along to circle to the right side of the body, chest height (palm down). Turn the left hand right and circle up to under the right elbow (palm up). Sit onto the right leg, knees bent, body half-turned right, left hip joint relaxed, right hip joint tucked back. Use the waist to lead the whole movement. Look at the right hand (figure 4-3).

Pause, then slowly turn left, shifting to the left leg. Raise the left hand to shoulder height (palm turning in) and lower the right hand. Look at the left hand (figure 4-4).

Using the waist, turn left. Circle the left hand left to chest height at the left side of the body, following the waist (palm turning down). Circle the right hand left and up (turning the palm up) under the left elbow. Finish with your body halfway turned to the left. Look at the left hand. Other details are exactly

the same as the right side (figure 4-5).

Use your waist and spine to turn. Connect the lower body to the upper. Do not just swing your arms. Use a soft, slow, even power, don't tighten up.

The four animal exercises described above each contain a standing portion and a moving portion. You may either practise all the standing portions then all the moving portions, or you may practise each animal (standing and moving) in order. You may also choose to practise any standing or moving stance of any animal separately. You may repeat the moving portions as you wish. You may, for example, change from right to left movement on the spot or moving, or you may repeat one side without bringing the foot back to change to the other side (shifting back and forth, bending and straightening the legs, changing the hand positions, whatever the moving portion is). Don't worry too much about how many repetitions you are doing, or how long you are practising, and don't fix a rigid pattern of practice. Rather, concentrate on performing every posture and action to your best ability according to the requirements. This is how to perfect the technique.

5. REGULATING THE HEALTH   tiāo yáng gōng   调养功

Stand with your feet parallel and shoulder width apart, arms hanging naturally, head and neck erect, face natural, mouth slightly closed, tongue lightly touching the palate, and upper body relaxed. Look straight ahead (figure 5-1).

Slowly lift the arms out to each side to shoulder height (figure 5-2).

Outwardly rotate the forearms to slowly turn the palms up, then bend the elbows to bring the palms in front of your temple (palms almost facing down). Keep looking straight ahead (figure 5-3).

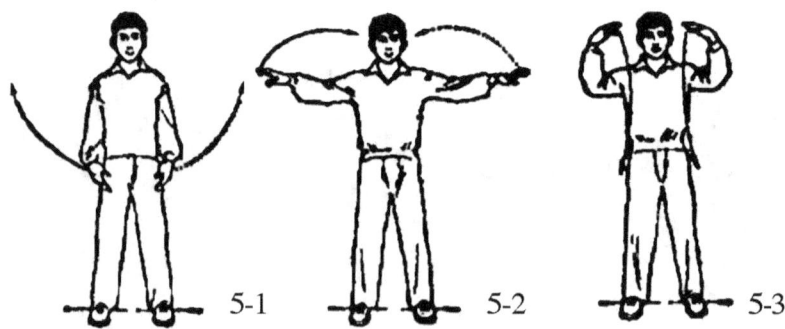

5-1   5-2   5-3

Without pausing, slowly lower the hands past your face and chest, bending the knees and relaxing the hips to sit down. Slowly bring the hands from in front of your stomach out to the side to in front of the hip joints, fingers forward, tiger mouths in, wrists slightly cocked down. Keep the body erect, chest settled, lumbar area relaxed, buttocks tucked in, anal sphincter raised, abdomen open and relaxed, and *qi* settled to the *dantian*. Look straight ahead (figure 5-4).

Pause, then slowly stand up, slowly bringing the hands up to repeat the whole move. Repeat a number of times.

This move can train upper body relaxation and leg strength. It can also be used by beginners to practise concentration on control of their actions. It also naturally trains coordination of breathing and uniting intention, *qi* and movement.

Beginners should breathe naturally for all of these standing exercises. As you get used to the stances and actions, gradually, and using an appropriate speed, introduce breath control. Without losing the basic principles of 'smooth' and 'natural,' breathe in as you do rising movement and out as you do lowering movement. In more detail for regulating health training: breathe in when you raise both arms; breathe out when you lower both arms past your chest and sit, caving your chest in and relaxing your shoulders. In addition, intentionally expand your abdomen as you breath out, settling your *qi* to your *dantian*, using the technique of reverse breathing.[55] Experience has shown that chronically ill get the best effects from this type of training. If you feel it is too difficult to coordinate breathing then keep using natural breathing – don't force anything.

The regulating health practice also works very effectively as a settling routine. Any time you feel out of breath after doing some training or forms, just use it to relax your body and regulate your breathing.

---

[55] Translator's note: In reverse breathing, expand the lower ribs and pull the belly in when you breathe in. Push into the belly when you breathe out, as you would naturally do if using force to push a heavy object. Do not over exaggerate this action, do just enough to move *qi* into the *dantian* and stabilize the body core.

APPENDIX

CLASSIC TEXTS[56]

These reference materials are copied from masters' hand copied books or books published before liberation.[57] Quotations are from the originals, but I have edited some places.

Some of the quotations have theory or poems that refer to fighting methods. These can help the player learn the requirements, power, and applied meaning of the style, and they have reference value for practical fighting. But some references have some viewpoints that are difficult to understand, some authors and sources are as yet unverified, and different publishers have published some materials slightly differently. I ask the reader to 'discard the dross and select the essential' and take this inheritance with a critical mind. Also, from the point of view of training the body, you mustn't seek a brave, fast and direct fighting method that causes death.[58]

---

[56] Translator's note: The texts here have been translated before, so I see my job to explain, clarify, and bring new meanings into consideration. Chinese words hold an abundance of connotations, and classical texts are concise and leave interpretation open to the reader. I often chose to translate one possible meaning into clear English rather than leave the Chinese terminology, because English is not Chinese and ambiguity does not really help. The texts were written by teachers to help students call to mind what is important, so I have usually chosen the most practical meaning in terms of performing Xingyi. I realize that there are other possible interpretations, and encourage the reader to find other translations of the same texts in order to sort out more meanings.

[57] Translator's note: 1949.

[58] Translator's note: At the time of publication, 1981, the author needed to include this disclaimer to protect himself in printing this old material referring to 'superstitions' or fighting. Also, due to the typeset at the time, the texts were printed in simplified characters, as I have copied them.

太极歌

心猿已动，拳势斯作，

刚柔虚实，开合起落。

Poem of the ultimate principle

As soon as you put your heart into it your fighting power is formed.

(And so is your potential to range fully between) hard or soft, empty or solid, open or closed, to rise or to land.[59]

两仪歌

鹰熊竞志，取法为拳，

阴阳暗合，形意之源。

Poem of the two primordial forms (*yin* and *yang*)

Eagle and bear compete, their techniques were taken to make a fighting style in which *yin* and *yang* secretly combine – this is the source of Xingyi.

---

[59] Translator's note: *Yin* and *yang* are not contradictory opposites, but are phases of the cycle of life that blend into each other. As one moves far into a phase, one will naturally move through into the other phase. There are a lot of sources that fully describe this theory in much more depth than is possible in these notes. For the relevant terms here:

Yin	soft	empty	closed	land	withdraw
Yang	hard	solid	open	rise	enter

两仪说

两仪者，拳中鹰熊之势，防守进取往来之理也。吾人俱有四体百骸，伸之而为阳（鹰势），缩之为阴（熊势），故曰阴阳暗合也。前人见有鹰熊竞志，因取法为拳，防守像熊，进取像鹰，越此二势，其拳失真。名为形意者，像其形而思其意也。

Explanation of the two primordial forms

The two primordial forms as they relate to a fist style are the theories of defense and attack, entry and counter, originally taken from the eagle and bear postures. People have four limbs and a hundred bones (i.e. they are neither eagles nor bears) – so extending out is considered *yang* (eagle) and withdrawing in is considered *yin* (bear), this is why we say *yin* and *yang* secretly combine. Someone in the past saw the eagle and bear fight and adapted the techniques into a fist style, using the defense of the bear and the attack of the eagle.[60] If one neglects these two postures the fist style loses its true meaning. The style called Xingyi (form and intent) copies both the form (of the eagle and bear) and their intent.

---

[60] Translator's note: The actual techniques may have changed since this text was written, since as we know them, the bear extends up and the eagle drops down. Note also the 'strength of uprightness' of the bear in 'The meaning taken from the twelve animals.' In keeping with the general principles of Xingyiquan, what is important from this text is that one must not neglect the interchange between the phases of *yin* and *yang*, not that one must stick to some specific techniques. Even the choice of which is *yin* and which *yang* is entirely dependent on context. Possibly the generally calm nature of the bear influenced the choice of *yin* for the bear, but in Western Canada the word *yin* does not pop into mind when faced with a charging grizzly.

六合歌

身成六式，鸡腿龙身，熊膀鹰爪，虎抱雷声。

六合者，鸡、龙、熊、鹰、虎、雷，形意拳之身法，六形合为一体也。又内三合，心与意合，意与气合，气与力合；外三合，手与足合，肘与膝合，肩与胯合，是为六合也。

Poem of the six combinations

The body can form six shapes: legs of a chicken, body of a dragon, shoulders of a bear, hands of an eagle, chest and arms of a tiger, and the sound of thunder.

The six combinations are these body techniques of the chicken, dragon, bear, eagle, tiger, and thunder. In Xingyiquan's bodywork, the six combine into one. In addition, the three internal combinations are heart (subconscious, mindset, engagement) with mind (consciousness, cognitive mind, will, commitment), mind with energy (vital energy, aliveness, activation), and energy with strength (motor control, power); and the three external combinations are hands with feet, elbows with knees, and shoulders with hips.

十二形取意

龙有搜骨之法,
虎有扑食之勇,
猴有纵山之能,
马有疾蹄之功,
鼍有浮水之灵,
鸡有争斗之性,
鹰有捉拿之技,
熊有竖项之力,
骀有崩撞之形,
蛇有拨草之精,
鹞有钻天之势,
燕有抄水之巧。

The meaning taken from the twelve animals

Dragons have the method of ransacking bones.
Tigers have the ferocity of pouncing on prey.
Monkeys have the ability to run over mountains.
Horses have the skill of quick feet.
Alligators have the suppleness of swimming in water.
Chickens have the instinct for fighting.
Eagles have the talent of grabbing.
Bears have the strength of uprightness.
Wedge-tailed hawks have the form of bracing out.
Snakes have the essence of sliding through grass.
Sparrow hawks have the power of spiraling into the sky.
Swallows have the agility of swooping over the water.

三节说

三节举一身而言，手肘为梢节，身为中节，脚腿为根节是也。分而言之，则三节之中亦各有三节也。如手为梢节，肘为中节，肩为根节，此梢节中三节也。脚为梢节，膝为中节，胯为根节，此根节中之三节也。头为梢节，心为中节，丹田为根节，此中节中之三节也。要不外乎起、随、追而已，盖梢节起，中节随，根节追之，庶不至有长短曲直参差俯仰之病，此三节之所以贵明也。

三节即三体也，手为梢节，身为中节，足为根节，三节不明，周身是空，上中下三节总要分明，上节不明手多强硬，下节不明足多盘跌，中节不明浑身是空。

Explanation of the three segments[61]

The three segments refer to the body – the whole arm is the tip, the body is the middle, and the whole leg is the root. Breaking it down further, each of the three segments has three segments. The three segments of the tip segment are: the hand is the tip, the elbow the middle, and the shoulder the root. The three segments of the root segment are: the foot is the tip, the knee is the middle, and the hip is the root. The three segments of the middle segment are: the head is the tip, the heart area is the middle, and the centre of gravity[62] is the root. This cannot be separated from initiating, following, and chasing – that is: the tip

---

[61] Translator's note: The body is divided this way in other styles as well, and is often likened to the branch, trunk and root of a tree. This division refers to the principle of summation of forces, or transferring power sequentially from the ground through the body to the point of power application. This is also described in the 'seven flows.' Power transfer differs according to the point of reference, which is why there is more than one 'three segments.'

[62] Translator's note: The *dantian*. The centre of gravity lies roughly in the lower *dantian* in most Xingyi stances. See the diagram on page 297.

initiates, the middle follows and the root chases. Knowing the three segments is important because that enables you to avoid the mistakes of too long and too short, too bent and too straight, unevenness, and leaning.

When the three segments refer to the body as three limbs (as in the *santi* stance), the hand is the tip, the body the middle and the foot the root. If the three segments aren't clearly distinguished then the whole body is empty. The upper, middle and lower segments must always be clearly distinguished. If the upper segment is not clear the hands will be too stiff. If the lower segment is not clear the feet will be all over the place. If the middle segment is not clear the whole body will be empty.

七顺说

肩要催肘，而肘不逆肩；

肘要催手，而手不逆肘；

手要催指，而指不逆手；

腰要催胯，而胯不逆腰；

胯要催膝，而膝不逆胯；

膝要催足，而足不逆膝；

首要催身，而身不逆首。

心气稳定，阴阳相合，

上下相连，内外如一，

此之谓七顺。

Explanation of the 'seven flows'

Power should flow from shoulders to elbows –
The elbows should not run counter to the shoulders;

Power should flow from elbows to hands –
The hands should not run counter to the elbows;

Power should flow from hands to fingers –
The fingers should not run counter to the hands;

Power should flow from lumbar area to hips –
The hips should not run counter to the lower back;

Power should flow from hips to knees –
The knees should not run counter to the hips;

Power should flow from knees to feet –
The feet should not run counter to the knees;

Power should flow from head to body –
The body should not run counter to the head.

When the heart is calm, breathing stable and the *qi* settled, *yin* and *yang* phases can combine, upper and lower can link, internal and external can act as one – this is called the 'seven flows.'

五行说

五行者，金、木、水、火、土之谓也，如人之内有五脏，外有五宫，皆与五行相配合。心属火，脾属土，肝属木，肺属金，肾属水，此五行之隐于内者；目通肝，鼻通肺，舌通心，耳通肾，人中通脾，此五行之著于外者。金生水，水生木，木生火，火生土，土生金，是五行相生之道也；金克木，木克土，土克水，水克火，火克金，此五行相克之道也。

Explanation of the five elemental phases

The five elemental phases are metal, wood, water, fire and earth. They relate to five visceral organs of the human body internally, and to five organs externally. Internally, the heart relates to fire, the spleen to earth, the liver to wood, the lungs to metal, and the kidneys to water. Externally, the eyes connect to the liver, the nose to the lungs, the tongue to the heart, the ears to the Kidneys,[63] and the philtrum[64] to the spleen. The cycle of creation of the five elements is: metal creates water, water creates wood, wood creates fire, fire creates earth, and earth creates metal. The cycle of control of the five elements is: metal subdues wood, wood subdues earth, earth subdues water, water subdues fire, and fire subdues metal.[65]

---

[63] Translator's note: The Kidneys include the adrenal glands, which sit on top of them. It is common to capitalize when using the Chinese meaning of the organs.

[64] Translator's note: The philtrum is the dip in the upper lip, between the lip and the nose.

[65] Translator's note: five elemental phases cycle of creation: metal creates water (metal sweats) → water creates wood (trees need water to grow) → wood creates fire (fire needs fuel) → fire creates earth (all turns to ash when burned) → earth creates metal (minerals are formed in the ground). five elemental phases cycle of control: metal controls wood (axes chop wood) → wood controls earth (roots break up soil) → earth controls water (earth can dam rivers) → water controls fire (water puts out fire) → fire controls metal (fire melts metals).

Translator's note: The explanations of the four tips and the five elemental phases are part of the traditional Chinese world view which is applied to the understanding of the body and in traditional Chinese medicine (TCM). This text is not meant to be mysterious in any way to the Chinese – it is a simple description of well-known physical phenomena. Sometimes things are put into five phase categories for convenience, because of their relationship to something already categorized (the lungs are metal because they create water vapour in the body, the lungs open to the nose, so the nose must be in the metal phase).

Some relevant categories are:					
five elemental phases	metal	water	wood	fire	earth
five techniques	split	drill	drive	cannon	wring
five internal organs	Lungs	Kidneys	Liver	Heart	Spleen
five organs	nose	ears	eyes	tongue	philtrum, or mouth
five tissues	skin	bones	tendons	blood vessels	flesh
five seasons	autumn	winter	spring	summer	transitional, or Indian summer

Continuation of translator's note:

The *yin yang* theory predates the five phases, and is more all-inclusive and flexible. When five phases or four tip categorizations don't work well, *yin yang* theory can override them. But, although these cycles of creation and control may seem arbitrary at times (i.e. a fire can be put out by earth as easily as by water), a more organic way to look at the five phases shows that the categories are not as arbitrary as they may appear. The cycles show that metal stands for phases or functions which are declining (like autumn, *yin* is growing); water stands for phases or functions which are at the maximal state of inaction or rest (like winter, *yin* at the full, about to reactivate); wood stands for phases or functions which are growing (like spring, *yang* is growing); fire stands for phases or functions which are at the maximal state of activity (like summer, *yang* at the full, about to decline); and earth stands for balance or neutrality, so is a buffer between the others (like interseason, *yin* and *yang* in balance).

APPENDIX 239

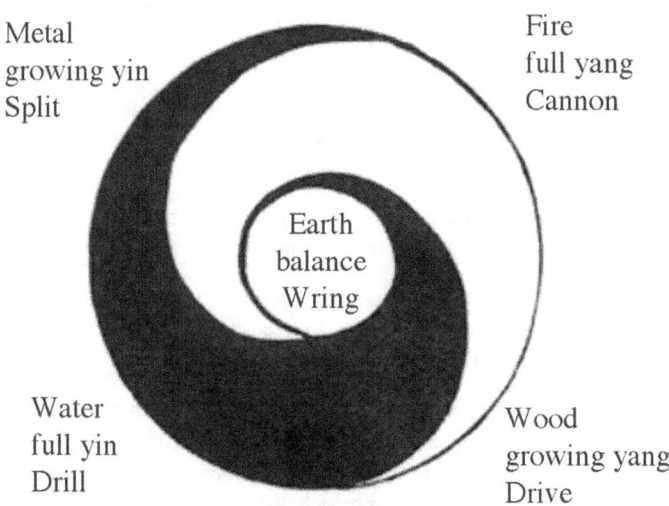

Continuation of translator's note:

Xingyiquan always combines technique with mindset, so this organization of elemental phases can well be used to categorize techniques of defense and attack and the corresponding mindset.

	Mindset	Defense	Attack
Metal	hardheaded	take it, hold your position	focus, controlled attack
Water	flowing, soft	dodge, avoid the force, give in to get your way	sneak around, redirect softly, or get in another way
Wood	alive, aware	absorb and recoil directly	sense, react quickly and get in
Fire	fully committed	charge in to cut off the attack	charge in, no return, don't care what happens
Earth	centered, calm	cover, neutralize, absorb	sense and redirect

Split (metal) uses the full potential of both hands to hold the position by using the back hand to trap and pull down the attack to allow the front hand to apply a clean strike. You don't need to back off to apply it. You can also directly attack with it, controlling the opponent as you go in.

Drill (water) doesn't directly apply itself to the oncoming attack, but slides along and through without force.

Drive (wood) leaves you open as you punch without much assist from the other hand, so you have to react, absorb and be aware of what your opponent is doing to be able to get the punch in.

Cannon (fire) is the technique that will plow through anything if you have enough attitude. You can also charge in with a no-holds barred attack.

Wring (earth) will only work if you are well centered, and can neutralize the opponent enough to redirect the force in all directions (the hands separate with force to the front and back and also twist is opposite directions).

In this way, the five phases can be used to describe more than which technique can be used to defend against which, as they are commonly used (fire controls metal so cannon blocks split, etc.). Cannon isn't the only technique which can counter split, so how useful is this information? With the organic approach, if you want to use cannon, you have to be fully committed, while if you want to use wring you have to settle down and centre yourself. Animal techniques can also be sorted into a five phase category as well as a *yin/yang* category, giving more focus to the mindset.

四梢说

人之血、肉、筋、骨之末端曰梢，盖发为血梢，舌为肉梢，牙为骨梢，爪为筋梢。四梢用力，则可变其常态，能使人生畏惧焉。

1。血梢：怒气填胸，竖发冲冠，血轮速转，敌胆自寒，发毛虽微，摧敌不难。

2。肉梢：舌卷气降，虽山亦撼，肉坚似铁，精神勇敢，一言之威，落魄丧胆。

3。骨梢：有勇在骨，切齿则发，敌肉可食。眦裂目突，惟齿之功，令人恍惚。

4。筋梢：虎威鹰猛，以爪为锋，手攫足踏。气势兼雄，爪之所到，皆可奏功。

Explanation of the four tips[66]

The ends of blood, muscles, tendons and bones are called the four tips. Hair is the visible tip of the blood, the tongue is the visible tip of the muscles, the teeth are the visible tips of the bones, and the claws (nails) are the visible tips of the tendons. When the four tips use their force they can change normal behavior to enable a person to intimidate others.

1. The blood tip (hair): When anger fills the chest it makes the hair stand on end strongly enough to raise a cap, and the blood circulation quickens.[67]

---

[66] Translator's note: The basic connections are standard understandings of TCM, which enable the doctor to diagnose internal problems by examining the tips. How Xingyi puts this understanding to use to psyche oneself up and intimidate others is particular to the martial arts. Intimidation can be useful, so it is wise to be aware of such techniques, but you certainly do not want to practise or even fight in most situations with your hair standing up and your eyes bugging out. This runs counter to most of the other writings, which emphasize calm and centredness.

This makes the gall bladder of the opponent go cold.[68] Although hair itself seems insignificant, you will defeat your enemy with no difficulty.

2. The muscle tip (tongue): When the tongue is rolled the *qi* settles, even if mountains shake.[69] The muscles become hard as iron, and the spirit brave. In one word your impressive strength is shown and your opponent's courage drops and he 'loses his gallbladder.'

3. The bone tip (teeth):[70] When courage is in the bones you look like you could eat your opponent – with bared teeth and glaring eyes. This skill of the teeth can put your opponent in a trance.

4. The tendon tip (claws):[71] The tiger is awe-inspiring and the eagle is fierce. They use their claws as the cutting point of a knife, the hands grab and feet stamp. When you have their lofty mien, then when you grab you will succeed with extreme skill.

---

[67] Translator's note: In TCM, blood includes more than the blood in the blood vessels. It also includes fluid that circulates in the meridians. Someone who has control over blood and meridian circulation can make his or her hair stand on end on purpose to intimidate. The heart regulates the flow of blood, so this ability shows strength of heart.

[68] Translator's note: The gall bladder rules decision making ability, so its being 'cold' or losing it would cause indecision and timidity – the equivalent to 'having no guts.'

[69] Translator's note: See 'prop up' in the Poem of the eight words on page 221 – when the tongue touches the palate it connects internal pathways so that *qi* which has risen and transformed is able to settle down to the *dantian*, thus giving you more power.

[70] Translator's note: The power of the kidneys is manifest in the teeth. The action traditionally ascribed to the kidneys of most importance to Xingyiquan is to store *jing* – the essence that underlies all organic life. The implication is that showing teeth, an aggressive action in any language, would show confidence in your abilities – confidence in your life force's ability to overpower another's.

[71] Translator's note: The power of the liver is manifest in the nails. In TCM the liver rules the tendons and ligaments and maintains harmony in the body by allowing smooth flow of *qi*, blood, and other bodily substances. Also of importance to Xingyiquan, the liver helps harmonize the emotions. When you are calm you have strength. In Xingyiquan, the whole finger or toe, instead of just the nail, is often referred to as the tendon tip, so this calmness would give your hands a solid grip and your stance a solid foundation.

八要说

八要者何，一、内要提。二、三心要并。三、三意要连。四、五行要顺。五、四梢摇齐。六、心要暇。七、三尖要对。八、眼要毒也。

1。内要提者，紧撮谷道提其气，使上聚于丹田。

2。三心要并者，顶心往下，脚心往上，手心往回也。

3。三意要连者，心意、气意、力意三者连而为一，即所谓内三合也。

4。五行要顺者，外五行为五拳，内五行为五脏是也。

5。四梢要齐者，舌要顶，牙要扣，手指脚趾要扣，毛孔要紧也。

6。心要暇者，练时心中不慌不忙之谓也。

7。三尖要对者，鼻尖、手尖、脚尖相对也。

8。眼要毒者，谓目光锐敏而有威也。

Explanation of the eight requirements

The eight requirements are: 1) the internal must be held up; 2) the three centres must join; 3) three minds must be combined; 4) the five elemental phases must flow; 5) the four tips must be kept in order; 6) the heart must be leisurely; 7) the three points must be aligned, and; 8) the eyes must be fierce.

1. 'The internal must be held up' means to tighten the 'grain path' (anal sphincter) to raise the *qi* and cause it to collect in the *dantian*.

2. 'The three centres must join' means power returns down from the centre of the top of the head, power returns up from the centre of the feet, and power returns in from the centres of the hands.

3. 'The three minds must be combined' means that the ability to think (heart and mind), the ability to activate (vitality), and the ability to express (strength, power) must work as one – this is called the three internal unities.

4. 'The five elemental phases must flow' refers to the five fist techniques as the external five elements and the five visceral organs as the internal five elements. [72]

5. 'The four tips must be kept in order'[73] means that the tongue must press on the palate, the teeth must touch together, the fingers and toes must grip, and the (hair) follicles must be tight.

6. 'The heart must be leisurely' means that in practise, you must not worry or be hurried.

7. 'The three points must be aligned' means that the tips of the nose, hands and feet must be aligned.

8. 'The eyes must be fierce' means that the eyes must be keen and show a dignified spirit.

---

[72] Translator's note: The fist techniques and the functions of the visceral organs must flow in harmony with their natural processes, as expressed in the five elemental phases theory. See pages 237-240.

[73] Translator's note: The tongue is the muscle tip, the teeth are the bone tip, the fingers/toes are the tendon tip, and the hair follicles all over the body are the blood tip. See the four tips, pages 241-2.

八字诀

八字者，顶、扣、圆、敏、抱、垂、曲、挺，八字是也。此八字为形意站桩的要点，凡拳式站定时，此八字具备，而每一字又有三种要求：

1。顶：头向上顶，有冲天之雄，头为一身之主，上顶则后三关易通，肾气因之上达泥丸，以养性；手掌向外顶，有推山之功，则气贯周身，力达四肢；舌尖向上顶，有吼狮吞象之容，能导上升之肾气，下行归入丹田，以固命，是谓三顶。

2。扣：两肩要扣，则前胸空阔，气力达肘；手背足背要扣，则气力到手，桩步力厚；牙齿要扣，则筋骨紧缩，是谓三扣。

3。圆：脊背要圆，其力催身，则尾闾中正，精神贯顶；前胸要圆，两肘力全，心窝微收，呼吸通顺；虎口要圆，勇猛外宜，则手有裹抱力，是三圆。

4。敏：心要敏，如怒狸攫鼠，则能随机应变；眼要敏，如饥鹰之捉兔，能予视察机宜；手要敏，如捕羊之饿虎，能先发制人，是谓三敏。

5。抱：丹田要抱，气不外散，击敌必准；心气要抱，遇敌有主，临变不变；两肋要抱，出入不乱，遇敌无险，是谓三抱。

6。垂：气垂，则气降丹田，身稳如山；两肩下垂，则臂长而活，肩催肘前；两肘下垂，则两肱自圆，能固两肋，是谓三垂。

7。曲：两肘（臂）要曲，弓如半月，则力富；两膝要曲，弯如半月，则力厚；手腕要曲，曲如半月，则力凑，皆取其伸缩自如，用劲不断之意，是谓三曲。

8。挺：颈项要挺，则头部正直，精气贯顶；脊、骨、腰要挺，则力达四梢，气鼓全身；膝盖要挺，则气恬神怡，如树生根。

Poem of the eight words

The eight words are 1) propped up; 2) closed; 3) round; 4) alert; 5) enclosed; 6) settled; 7) flexed, and; 8) thrust up. They make up the requirements for Xingyi standing training, and for the set position of each Xingyi posture. Each character has a further three requirements:

1. Propped up: the head must be pushed up with an imposing manner as if hitting the sky. The head is the leader of the body, so if it is raised up then communication through the 'three passes'[74] in the back is easy, and the *qi* of the Kidneys can go up to the *niwan* (brain) to nourish the nature. When the hands push out with the ability to push mountains, then the *qi* will reach to the whole body and force will reach to the four limbs. When the tip of the tongue pushes up you can roar like a lion or swallow an elephant. Then the *qi* rising from the Kidney can go back down to the *dantian*, in order to consolidate the life force. These are the 'three prop ups.'

2. Closed, arced: the shoulders must arc to expand the chest to make room to breathe and allow both strength and *qi* to reach the elbows. The backs of the hands and feet must arc to allow strength and *qi* to reach the hands and make the stance powerful. The teeth must be closed, then the tendons and bones will be taut. These are the 'three closes.'

3. Round: the upper back must be round so that force can spread throughout your whole body, the tailbone will be straight and the spirit can reach the top of the head. The chest must be round to get force to the elbows, slightly close the heart area, and allow breath to flow smoothly. The tiger's mouth must be round to make the hands fierce and brave, then the hands have the strength to hold. These are the 'three rounds.'

4. Alert, reactive: the heart must be alert, like an angry fox grabbing a rat, then it can change to take advantage of any situation. The eyes must be alert like a starving eagle seizing a rabbit, then they can see when opportunity presents. The hands must be alert, like a hungry tiger pouncing on a sheep, then they can move first to control the opponent. These are the 'three alerts.'

---

[74] Translator's note: See the diagram on page 247 for the placement of the three passes. Once the *qi* has come up from the Kidneys through the passes, the tongue touching the palate closes the connection to allow the *qi* to return down to the lower *dantian*.

APPENDIX   247

5. Enclosed, embraced: the *dantian* must be enfolded so that the *qi* does not dissipate, then you can hit with accuracy. The mind must be calm and breathing regular so you can take charge in a fight, and not change in a changing situation. The ribs must be hugged so the hands go in and out in an orderly way and there is no danger in meeting an opponent. These are the 'three embraces.'

6. Settled: the *qi* must be settled down, then the *qi* will sink to the *dantian* and the body will be as stable as a mountain. The shoulders must be set down, then the arms will have reach and agility, and the shoulders will lead the elbows. The elbows must settle, then the arms will be naturally round, and the ribs will be firm. These are the 'three settles.'

7. Flexed: the elbows (arms) must be flexed, bowed like a half moon, then their strength will be abundant. The knees must be flexed, bowed like a half moon, then their strength will be deep. The wrists must be flexed, bowed like a half moon, then their strength will be collected. Then all can go in and out at will, and can use power unstintingly. These are the 'three bents.'

8. Thrust out: the neck must be extended, then the head is straight and the refined *qi* (power from the *dantian*) can reach the top of the head. The spinal column and lumbar area must be thrust upright, then force can reach the four tips, and the *qi* can rouse the whole body. The knees must be thrust into the ground, then the *qi* is calm and the spirit is in harmony, like a tree setting down roots.

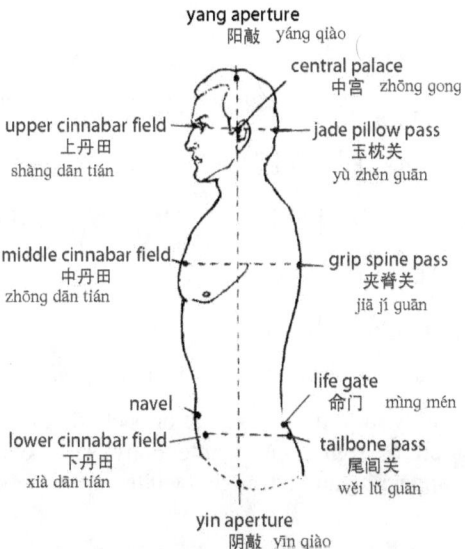

This diagram is translated from The Encyclopedia of Chinese Martial Arts, Zhongguo Wushu Da Cidian (1990) Beijing: People's Sport Publishing House page 378.

九数歌（三体左站桩主要法则）

1。身：前俯后仰，其式不劲，左侧右倚，皆身之病，正而似斜，斜而似正。

2。肩：头宜上顶，肩宜下垂，左肩成拗，右肩自随，身力到手，肩之所为。

3。臂：左臂前伸，右臂在肋，似曲不曲，似直不直，过曲不远，过直少力。

4。手：右手在肋，左手齐胸，后者微塌，前者力伸，两手皆覆，用力宜匀。

5。指：五指各分，其形似钩，虎口圆满，似刚似柔，力须到指，不可强求。

6。股：左股在前，右股后撑，似直不直，似弓不弓，虽有直曲，每见鸡形。

7。足：左足直前，斜侧皆病，右足势斜，前踵对胫，随人距离，足指扣定。

8。舌：舌为肉梢，卷则气降，目张发耸，丹田愈沉，肌容如铁，内坚腑脏。

9。臀：提起臀部，气贯四梢，两腿缭绕，臀部内交，低则势散，故宜稳高。

Poem of 'number nine'

(the main requirements of the left *santishi* standing)

1. Body: If you lean to front or back, this stance will have no power. If you lean left or right your whole body will be off. The stance is straight while appearing angled, angled while appearing straight.[75]

---

[75] Translator's note: This is true on many levels: power triangulates from the ground, angling up from each foot to the *dantian*, but this is in order to drive the force straight

2. Shoulders: Hold the head up and the shoulders down. When the left shoulder turns the right shoulder follows naturally. The reason the shoulders are like this is to allow the whole body's force to reach the hands.
3. Arms: The left arm extends forward and the right arm is at the ribs. They are bent but not collapsed, and straight but not locked. If they are too bent they have no reach, and if they are too straight they have little force.
4. Hands: The right hand is at the ribs and the left hand is at sternum height. The back hand is slightly cocked and the front hand extends its force. The two hands both have a covering power, using force evenly.
5. Fingers: The fingers are spread, taking the shape of hooks. The tiger's mouth is open and full. The fingers are both hard and soft (with power but not rigid). For the force to reach the fingers, you can't use brute force.
6. Thighs: The left thigh is in front, the right braces to the back. Both are bent but pushing towards extension. Although one is straighter and the other more bent, they are always in the chicken stance.[76]
7. Feet: The left foot points straight in front, it is wrong to turn it. The right foot is turned, the front heel aligned with the shin. The size of the stance depends on the player. Grip the ground with the toes to be more stable.
8. Tongue: The tongue is the tip of the muscles, when it is rolled then the *qi* can sink. The eyes will open and the hair stand up, the *dantian* will be full, the muscles will be like iron, and the internal organs will be solid.
9. Buttocks: Lift up the buttocks and the *qi* will reach the four tips, the legs will have power winding around them, and the muscles of the buttocks intersect. If the buttocks are too low then the power of the stance is dissipated, that's why the stance should be up a bit.

---

forward; the hips and stance are straight so that the legs drive straight forward, but the body is angled so that the shoulder leads into the strike; the body can only work with angles because of its structure, and is slightly turned but drives power straight forward; etc.

[76] Translator's note: In the author's style, and so in this book, this stance is not called the chicken stance, but in some styles it is. Li Tianji called this an empty stance or simply *santishi*.

打法歌诀

打法定要先上身，
手脚齐到才为真，
拳如炮形龙折身，
遇敌好似火烧身。

头打起意站中央，
浑身齐到人难当，
脚踩中门守地位，
就是神仙亦难防。

肩打一阴反一阳，
两手只在暗处藏，
左右全凭盖势取，
缩长二字一命亡。

手打起意在胸膛，
其势好似虎扑羊，
沾实用力须展放，
两肘只在肋下藏。

胯打阴阳左右便，
两足交换须自然，
左右进取宜剑劲，
得心应手敌自翻。

膝打要害能致命，
两手空晃绕上中，
妙诀劝君勤习练，
强身胜敌乐无穷。

脚踩正意勿落空，
消息全凭后腿蹬，
蓄意须防被敌觉，
起势好似卷地风。

Poem of fighting methods[77]

If you want your technique to get in you must move your body first. You can only connect if your hands and feet arrive together. Hit like an explosive, your body like a dragon – when you meet your opponent you'll feel like you're on fire.

To hit with your head concentrate on holding your centre. When your whole body arrives at once your opponent will have trouble holding his position. If you plant your foot into the middle (go in the main gate) you take his place – even a spirit would find it hard to defend against you.

To hit with your shoulders absorb then explode back. Keep your hands hidden. Right and left strikes take advantage of this momentum. Within these two words – withdraw and extend – lies a life.

To hit with your hands initiate from the chest. Use your hands like a tiger pouncing on a sheep. To gain contact and maintain force you have to expand and extend, and keep your elbows hidden beside the ribs.

To hit with your hips use left and right to coordinate soft and hard. You have to switch your feet naturally. Then whether you dodge to left or right or enter straight, it is as a sword sliding in. When you get in as you wish, your enemy will topple on his own.

If you hit with your knees you can kill. Use your hands to feint up. This secret should be practised hard. This will strengthen the body, defeat the enemy, and give you great joy.

To hit with your feet, if you concentrate fully you will always get in without missing. That all depends on pushing off from the back leg, Make sure not to telegraph your intent to your opponent, so once you initiate the attack you will charge in like a wind rolling up the ground.

---

[77] Translator's note: I laid out the poem in the Chinese to accentuate its poetic nature. It has a seven beat rhythm that is pretty catchy – obviously developed as a memory aid. The information is intended to clarify and help the student to remember all the important principles of fighting with Xingyi.

七疾说

七疾者，眼要疾，手要疾，脚要疾，意要疾，出势要疾，进取要疾，身法要疾也。习拳者具此七疾，方能完全制胜。所谓纵横往来，目不及瞬，有如生龙活虎，令人不可捉摸者，惟恃此耳。

Explanation of the 'seven quicks'

The 'seven things which must be quick' are the eyes, hands, feet, mind, initiation of the attack, entry, and bodywork. If the player is quick in all these he can certainly win. He will be able to move up and down, side to side, back and forth, quicker than the eye can blink. He will be lively as a dragon or tiger, and no one will be able to keep up to figure out what he is doing.

七星歌

用必七体，头、肩、肘、手、胯膝合脚，相助为友。

七曜着，即：头、肩、肘、手、胯、膝、足七体也，二七一十四个用法（头是双数），为拳中之要领。

Poem of the seven stars

All seven parts of your body should be used: the head, shoulders, elbows, hands, hips, knees and feet, and they can be used together.

These seven combine as two times seven equals fourteen techniques (the head is counted as two) which make up the requirements of the form.

Guo Yunshen speaks on Xingyiquan

1. Theory of three levels:

1. Train essence (jīng 精) to transform energy (qì 气).

2. Train *qi* 气 to transform spirit (shén 神).[78]

3. Train spirit (shén 神) to transform to emptiness (xū 虚). (Train these to transform a person's character and return to the natural state)

2. Three steps of skill:

1. Bone changing (yìgū 易骨); train this to build a foundation, strengthen your body, make your bones as hard as iron, and form a demeanor as awe-inspiring as Mount Tai.

2. Tendon changing (yìjīn 易筋); train this to clear the cell membranes and lengthen the muscles and tendons (it is said that when the muscles and tendons are long they are strong). Then power connects longitudinally and transversely – long without any weak points.

3. Marrow washing (xǐsuǐ 洗髓); train this to cleanse the inside, to lighten the body. When the inside seems empty, the vigorous spirit (shénqì 神气) can move where it is needed, it will be full with no impediment, and the body's movement will be light as a feather.

---

[78] Translator's note: I have variously translated *qi* as energy, activation, and power throughout the book. Traditional Chinese explanations of the body do not worry about nuances between energy and matter – there is no clear-cut distinction. *Qi* is energy, the ability to energize, matter on the verge of turning into energy, and energy on the verge of becoming matter, among other possibilities. Similarly, *jing* and *shen* are both physically and non-physically present in the body and mind. It is possible for *jing* to be the source of life, the essence of life, and a fluid which circulates in the body, and for *shen* to be the vitality of the body and mind, the awareness of life, and the human 'soul.' To the Chinese, the *qi* can be stored in the *dantian*, the *jing* in the kidneys, and the *shen* in the heart with no expectation of finding them there with a microscope. What causes movement is not necessarily separate from the movement itself or from what moves. This is one reason why descriptive passages sometimes seem circular to Western logic. Linguistically, these terms are not hazy in the Chinese language, which does not need to make distinctions which are necessary in English. At the surface level of expression, the Chinese language can use the same word as a verb, noun, or adjective, so naturally the 'thing' being described could be active, matter, or a property.

3. Three kinds of training:

1. Obvious power (míngjìn 明劲); when training this follow the rules absolutely without any changes, the body's movement must be smooth without any awkwardness, the hands and feet must start and hit simultaneously – not at all haphazard. This is what the classics mean when they say you have to practise 'square' to make the centre correct.

2. Hidden power (ànjìn 暗劲); to train this, your vigorous spirit (shénqì 神气) must be expansive and unrestrained. You must move 'round', connected, and lively without any dead spots. This is what the classics mean when they say you have to practise 'round' to make the outside smooth.

3. Transformed power (huàjìn 化劲); the person that trains this moves the whole body, initiates and hits, advances and withdraws without any apparent force, projecting his intent spirit (shényì 神意) instead. Although he uses the power of the mind (shényì 神意), the stances are all regulation like the first two stages – they must not be changed. Although the whole body's movement doesn't use brute force neither does it use no force at all, but uses martial spirit (shén 神), will (yì 意) and technique together. This is what the classics mean when they say 'whatever technique you use, it all comes down to one thing.'

4. Three levels of breathing:

1. Level one breathing while practising a form is: the tongue is rolled up to touch the palate; the mouth is neither open nor closed, and breathing is natural, not intentionally controlled. When the actions of the hands and feet fit regulations they will regulate the breathing. This is the work of training the essence (jīng 精) to transform the *qi*.

2. Level two breathing while practising a form is: the tongue and mouth are the same as level one, but the method of breathing differs. In level one, the movement controls the breathing, in this level the breathing is regulated. In level one the mouth and nose breathing doesn't try too much to connect the external and internal. In this level concentrate on breathing in the *dantian*, so it is called training the *qi* to transform the spirit (shén 神).

3. Level three differs from the previous two. Level one is obvious power; it can be seen from the outside. Level two is hidden power; it has form on the inside. This level has breathing but does not appear to have; this is called embryo breathing (tāixī 胎息). It is neither forgotten nor forced, it is used to

transform the spirit (shén 神). The mind (xīn 心) is completely empty, neither having nor not having, neither being nor not being – the way to the obscure emptiness (that which can't be sensed).

These three levels of breathing enable training in order from beginning to end. That is the theory of *qi* reaching everywhere, it is the way to transform from to 'not having.

Translator's note: Note that master Guo is speaking of deep internal training within, not separate from, forms practice. All training is specific, so using Xingyi to train at deep levels will improve the application of deep power in Xingyi more effectively than would separate training. There is something to be said for separating out the elements and training strength, *qigong*, and meditation, etc., to achieve awareness of each and to obtain specific results more quickly, if that is your aim. For example, strengthening the legs through leg presses will increase their ability to withstand Xingyi stance training. It will not, however, train the legs for exactly the angles, speeds, and directions of power transfer used in Xingyi – Xingyi specific training would still need to be done, and the weight training exercise itself should be carefully selected to take into account the needs of Xingyi. And, in addition, if training of the body core and arms is not simultaneously carried out, the legs will have more strength than the body can transfer to the hands, and the hands will not be able to apply the strength. Injury to the body core, shoulders, elbows and wrists would threaten. As another example, extensive standing *qigong* training would not develop the flow of *qi* in the same way it is used in Xingyi, and may also build up a strong uncontrolled *qi* which could do more harm than good. All training is specific, so any extra training must be carefully planned to apply effectively to the final goal.

Translator's note: Training any martial art involves training cognitive, motor, emotional and spiritual aspects, and the internal styles emphasize training the deep sources of these. Traditional styles such as Xingyi have integrated all the elements needed to fully develop the practitioner, so training the style itself with an awareness of all its aspects will bring this development slowly and sequentially – each element comes when the time is ripe. By the time the practitioner has progressed to emptiness the form is integrated into the body/mind. Note that Guo emphasizes that the form is not lost, instead, when the practitioner has finally reached the stage of 'having' the form, he/she is no longer 'there' to have it.

PRONUNCIATION OF PINYIN, THE CHINESE NATIONAL PHONETIC ALPHABET (WITH INTERNATIONAL PHONETIC ALPHABET EQUIVALENTS)

INITIALS (words can start with these consonants, or have a zero initial)		
PINYIN	IPA	ROUGH PRONUNCIATION GUIDE
p	p^h	Like English p̲et with a considerable puff of air.
b	p	Similar to the *pinyin* "p" but without the puff of air (unvoiced, neither English p̲et nor b̲et).
t	t^h	Like English t̲ag with a considerable puff of air.
d	t	Similar to the *pinyin* "t" but with no puff of air (unvoiced, not d̲og).
k	k^h	Like English k̲ill with a considerable puff of air.
g	k	Similar to the *pinyin* "k" but with no puff of air (unvoiced, not English g̲et).
c	ts^h	Like exaggerating English cat̲s̲.
z	ts	Like the *pinyin* "c" but without the puff of air (unvoiced).
ch	$tʂ^h$	Somewhat similar to English c̲h̲at with a puff of air, but with the tip of the tongue rolled back.
zh	tʂ	Like the *pinyin* "ch" but with no puff of air (unvoiced).
q	$tɕ^h$	Somewhat similar to English c̲h̲at with a puff of air, but with the front of the tongue raised and the tip on the lower teeth.
j	tɕ	Like the *pinyin* "q" but without the puff of air (unvoiced).
m	m	Like English m̲et.
n	n	Like English n̲et.
f	f	Similar to English f̲at, but with the teeth just touching lightly behind the lower lip.
s	s	Similar to English s̲et.

sh	ʂ	Somewhat similar to English <u>sh</u>ow, but with the same tongue placement as the *pinyin* "ch" and "zh."
x	þ	Somewhat similar to English <u>sh</u>ine but with the same tongue placement as the *pinyin* "q" and "j."
h	χ	Raise the back of the tongue and let the breath come through the obstructed passage without vibrating the vocal cords.
l	l	Like English <u>l</u>et.
r	ɹ	Like the *pinyin* "sh" but with voicing.

FINALS

n	n	Like English pi<u>n</u>.
ng	ŋ	Like English si<u>ng</u>.

VOWELS

a	A a ɛ	Usually close to English f<u>a</u>ther (not p<u>a</u>t). Like y<u>e</u>t when written "-ian" or "yan."
e	ɣ e ɛ ə	Usually similar to English p<u>e</u>t, can tend towards a mid vowel.
i	i ɿ ɪ	Usually similar to English b<u>ee</u>. Similar to w<u>e</u>t when written "ui." After c, z, s, ch, zh, sh, and r it is similar to s<u>ir</u>.
o	o u	Usually close to English r<u>o</u>ll. Similar to c<u>ow</u> when written "ao," and <u>owe</u> when in "ou."
u	u y	Usually similar t English o b<u>oo</u>t. After the *pinyin* "x", "q", and "j" and in the vowel groups starting with these consonants, it is pronounced "ü".
ü	y	Similar to French <u>ü</u>. It is written after "n" or "l," because these are the only positions where both "u" and "ü" are possible
y	i	Partially like an English 'y', tending towards i.
w	u	Partially like an English 'w', tending towards u.

TONES IN PINYIN			
NUMBER	PINYIN	NAME	RANGE
1	¯	high level	55
2	´	high rising	35
3	ˇ	dipping	214
4	ˋ	high falling	51
none	° or blank	neutral	in context

With tone sandhi, tones may change according to the preceding or following tone.

The tone marking is put over the main vowel when there are two vowels written together (usually involving the pronunciation of y or w).

ABOUT THE TRANSLATOR

Andrea Falk has practised external and internal Chinese martial arts since 1972. She has studied Chinese art, geography, history, language, linguistics, literature, philosophy, politics, religion, and sociology since then, as well. She received a Bachelor of Arts majoring in Chinese (1977), a Bachelor of Physical Education (1979) and a Master of Physical Education with an emphasis on coaching science (1991) from the University of British Columbia. She trained in wushu full time on scholarship from 1980 to 1983 at the Beijing Physical Culture Institute, earning an advanced studies diploma in wushu under the tutelage of professor Xia
Bohua and instruction from Men Huifeng and others. There she learned the basics of Yang and Chen style Taijiquan, Baguazhang, Xingyiquan, Chaquan, Tongbeiquan, and modern Wushu (Changquan and weapons). She spent two further extended summers at the Institute in 1984 and 1986.

Since 1984 she gradually changed over to learning traditionally, visiting China on extended trips as often as possible. She has trained and/or is training Chen style Taijiquan, Baguazhang, and Taiji Changquan as an inside apprentice of Huan Dahai and elder martial brothers in Shanghai, Xingyiquan and Baguazhang as a close student and friend of Di Guoyong in Beijing, and Baguazhang from friends Li Baohua and Lu Yan. When not in China or traveling to teach, she is usually in Quebec city or at a cabin in the Laurentian hills, Canada.

Andrea has worked teaching and translating books about the Chinese martial arts since 1983. She founded the wushu centre in Montreal in 1984, in Victoria in 1992, and in Quebec city in 2007. She has taught Chen Taijiquan, Baguazhang, and Xingyiquan around the world, but mostly in Canada and England. For years Andrea translated books for her own students, and in 2000 established tgl books and the website www.thewushucentre.ca to bring the best Chinese martial arts books to a wider audience.

trois gros lapins traversent le chemin

ISBN 978-1-989468-20-3

www.ingramcontent.com/pod-product-compliance
Lightning Source LLC
Chambersburg PA
CBHW052047220426
43663CB00012B/2474